mor

Plea

A cl

Dirty politics
Dirty times

Michael Ashcroft

Dirty politics
Dirty times

My fight with Wapping
and New Labour

PUBLISHING

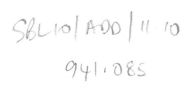

First published in Great Britain 2005

Copyright © Michael Ashcroft 2005

The right of Michael Ashcroft to be identified as the author of this work has been asserted by him in accordance with the Copyright, Designs & Patents Act, 1988.

A catalogue record for this book is available from the British Library.

ISBN 1 904734 11 1

Printed and bound in Great Britain by B•A•S Printers

Published by MAA Publishing Limited

To Eric Ashcroft:
my father, my inspiration

The reasonable man adapts himself to the world: the unreasonable one persists in trying to adapt the world to himself. Therefore all progress depends on the unreasonable man.

George Bernard Shaw, *Man and Superman* (1903)

Contents

Preface

THIS IS not a conventional autobiography. That daunting task will have to wait until the other side of my bus pass. Instead, this is an account of an eye-opening and turbulent period in my life during which I discovered the shadowy side of British politics and the unacceptable face of national newspaper journalism – not as a spectator, but as the prime target.

As the survivor of hundreds of gruelling commercial deals and some of the most vigorously contested boardroom battles of my generation, I thought I had seen it all. Nothing I had witnessed in my business career, however, prepared me for the dirty tricks and the criminality that I encountered from the summer of 1999 onwards. By that point, a year into my tenure as Treasurer of the Conservative Party, most people outside the worlds of business and politics would not have heard of me. In the City, I had acquired a reputation – one that I was not altogether unhappy with – of being a successful, if tough and unconventional, businessman. At Westminster, I was a relative new boy charged by William Hague with turning around the fortunes of the Tory Party's fragile finances.

Unwittingly and reluctantly, I was propelled into the public spotlight as I became the target of concerted attacks aimed at removing me as Treasurer. As the momentum of the assaults on my position increased, I began to see that their underlying purpose was a more sinister, indeed undemocratic, one: to damage the finances and credibility of Her Majesty's Opposition and to destabilise William Hague's position as leader of the Conservative Party. Those trying to undermine my position as Treasurer – and in the process harming my business interests on both sides of the Atlantic – were *The Times*, one of Britain's oldest and most influential newspapers, and the Labour Government, led by Tony

Blair and his cronies. Both were formidable opponents. Among my adversaries, I soon discovered, were some who thought little of using deception, falsehoods and law-breaking in trying to harm my reputation, seemingly indifferent to the impact on my ability to work as an entrepreneur. The old saying about 'not seeing a belt without hitting below it' was tailor-made for them.

Once the campaigns against me had begun in earnest, I had to make a choice: to duck for cover, step down quietly, desert my friends and allow the bully-boys to claim another scalp – or to defend myself, my family, the values I uphold and the political party I have supported all my adult life. In short, I had to decide whether to surrender or to fight and, as has been my instinct over the years, I chose the latter, confident that I held the moral high ground.

When I decided to stand up to *The Times* and New Labour, I had no idea how long, tortuous and costly such a confrontation would be – or how low some of my enemies would stoop to try to destroy me. Indeed, it is only recently that I have become fully aware of the extent of the machinations against me and the indefensible tactics that were employed in the attempts to defeat me. In order to survive, I had to challenge *The Times* and New Labour on many fronts: courtrooms on two continents, Parliament, the media, government offices and departments of state. I had to defend myself in the two countries that I love: Britain, where I was born and largely raised, and Belize, where I spent three years of my childhood and which, three decades later, became my home for a second time.

Eventually I achieved what I set out to do – I won my battles, and my enemies were embarrassed and punished. I forced *The Times* to publish a prominent front-page statement clearing my name. The illegal sources the newspaper had been happy to use in order to blacken my name were exposed. I successfully sued the Government, forcing it to give me an unequivocal apology for its attempts to damage my reputation. Furthermore, I gained access to thousands of documents containing 'confidential' information held on me, and I forced the Government to pay hundreds of thousands of pounds in costs that I had spent fighting an unnecessary legal battle against those who should have known better. *The Times* and New Labour, in contrast, failed to destroy either of their targets: I emerged with a knighthood, a peerage and my good name intact, while the Conservative Party, aided by a firmer financial base, regrouped, reunited and, I trust, will soon rediscover its winning ways.

This book tells the story of my battle against what had once been great and respected institutions. In the years since 1999, those who acted illegally or overstepped the mark have been, or are being, brought to justice. For instance, one overseas government official who broke the law in an attempt to discredit me has been jailed. The process of challenging my rivals has, at times, been wearing and frustrating, but overall it has been fascinating and instructive. My search for openness and the truth has encouraged others to turn on their unscrupulous paymasters. I am grateful for the co-operation that I have received from people on the fringes of the campaign. They had been uneasy about some of the disgraceful behaviour that went on and therefore decided to share some of their inside knowledge of events with me.

I have now been a working peer for five years and it has taken me all that time to piece together the chronology of the various actions against me and to establish who was responsible for them. The gathering of such information has not come easily or cheaply. Fortunately, I have had the means that might not be available to others and the successful results of my endeavours have made the trials and tribulations along the way worthwhile. I believe, too, that my discoveries have raised important questions about the willingness of some of those people in government and in the media to exploit and abuse – and thereby tarnish – the positions they hold.

For years, my detractors have accused me of being 'secretive', 'mysterious' and worse in my personal and business lives when I thought I had little to tell and no reason for telling it. In order to recount my story now, I recognise that I need to reveal a little of my life. There is, however, an important caveat: although I am willing to share intimate details of my life, my wife Susi and my first wife Wendy and our three children have always fiercely guarded their privacy. I have to respect this and I will not betray the trust and the support that they have provided for so long, and for which I am extremely grateful. For that reason, my love for them and my appreciation for the happiness they have brought me will not find expression in these pages.

Just as I feel I need to reveal a little of my early life, it would be odd to treat my battles against *The Times* and New Labour in isolation. I will explain how they coincided with my work as Treasurer of the Conservative Party and how they unavoidably became entangled with my business life. I will outline, too, how I learned from the mistakes of the 2001 election campaign and how I did my bit to try to ensure they were not repeated four years later – during the 2005 campaign.

Knowing where to start my story is the hard bit. I will begin with a brief introduction to Michael Anthony Ashcroft, born 4 March 1946.

1 Trading in Doughnuts

IT WAS in the Queen's Coronation year that I first set eyes on the country that was later to become my adopted homeland. My father, an administrator in the Colonial Service, had been posted to what was then British Honduras – now Belize – following a spell in the African outpost of Nyasaland (now Malawi). The Ashcroft family arrived in late 1953 just as postage stamps from this remote part of the Commonwealth were beginning to display the image of Queen Elizabeth II. When my parents first learned that they were going to British Honduras, they had to study an atlas to discover its precise location in Central America. The country borders Mexico to the north and Guatemala to the west and south, while to the east is the Caribbean Sea. It has a sub-tropical climate, with rainy and dry seasons. Its forests are rich in wildlife – big cats and crocodiles, baboons and monkeys, parrots and hummingbirds.

To a seven-year-old boy, the scenery of this small but beautiful land held less of a fascination than those exotic creatures lurking in the jungle or swimming in the Caribbean. This was just about as different from my birthplace of Chichester, West Sussex, as anything I could have imagined. These were carefree days and I recall them fondly. I attended St Catherine's Academy, a mixed day school. I had an abundance of new friends, the children of local Belizeans and of the expatriate community. Weekends were spent on boat trips to the Northern Cayes, exploring the rainforest close to Belize's disputed border with Guatemala or snorkelling on the 185 miles of coral reef that runs from north to south some six miles off the mainland. This is shorter than the Great Barrier Reef in Australia, but nonetheless qualifies as the longest *living* reef in the world.

Although the Union Jack fluttered proudly in Belize City, where we lived, it would have been hard to find a more ethnically, culturally and linguistically diverse nation. Some pure Amerindian blood remained in the shape of a handful of descendants of the Mayas, whose great civilisation occupied much of Central America for thousands of years. However, this had been seasoned with European – mostly Spanish – genes. Then there were the Creoles, descended from the early British settlers and the African slaves who had been brought from Jamaica. There were also the Lebanese, the Chinese and the North Americans, not forgetting the immigrants from the Indian sub-continent.

Despite the diversity of facial types, skin colours and surnames, the country was largely united by the fact that most of us spoke English and the Queen was, as she remains to this day, our head of state. Much of my personality was formed in these early years, making me cosmopolitan, proud of my essentially British roots and possessed of a passion for Belize that has never faltered.

Today I can return to Britain just over eleven hours after taking off from Belize airport, but my first visit there with my family involved a journey by sea and air that lasted more than a month. My father Frederic, who was always known by the abbreviation of Eric, my mother Lavinia, who preferred to be called Rene because she disliked her Christian name, my sister Patricia, then aged two, and myself had set off from Liverpool in a Fyffes banana boat. This was the traditional way that colonial officers journeyed to their new posts, and we stopped off at Trinidad, Barbados and, finally, the Jamaican capital of Kingston. Once in Kingston, we found there was just one flight a week on British West Indies Airways from Kingston to Belize City via the Cayman Islands. We discovered that the flight had left the day before and so we had a six-day wait for the next one. We spent that time sightseeing, including a visit to the old English pirates' base at Port Royal.

The following week we arrived in British Honduras in the early evening just as it was getting dark. We were met by an official from the local outpost of the Colonial Office, where my father was about to become the principal auditor. Fifteen minutes later, we arrived by car in Belize City. It was my first sight of the city that was to become my home for the next three years. It was a strange mix of colonial-style houses and shanty suburbs.

Our initial home was a first-floor apartment in a large house on the seafront at Marine Parade that was later to become the Mexican Embassy. A couple of months later, we moved into a four-bedroom, two-storey house built on wooden stilts to protect it from hurricane floodwaters. It was situated opposite the American Embassy and was little more than a hundred yards from both my school and the seafront.

British Honduras in the mid-1950s had a population of around 70,000 in a country the size of Wales. It was not for the squeamish: we were liable to find snakes among the washing and lizards above our heads as we slept. It was a country of real character and rich culture which deservedly gained its independence on 21 September 1981. On that date, every town and village in the country held a midnight ceremony at which the new flag of Belize was raised to the strains of the new national anthem.

I HAD been born in digs in Chichester, where my father was stationed, in the year after the end of the Second World War. To be precise, weighing in at a healthy 7lb 7oz, I had been born in my parents' bedroom as my father rushed to summon medical help. When he returned home with a doctor and nurse, my mother had delivered their first child unaided.

My parents had met two years earlier in 1944 at the Winter Gardens Ballroom in Blackpool, the town where my father was convalescing after being wounded on D-Day and where my mother was working as a Red Cross nurse. Both my parents were sturdy Lancastrians and proud of their roots: my father from Bolton, my mother from Burnley. Just weeks after asking my mother for their first dance, my father was given a clean bill of health and was sent back to his regiment.

After my father left the Army, we went to live in Burnley with my mother's uncle and aunt in a two-up, two-down terraced house with an outside lavatory, which could have come straight out of an early episode of *Coronation Street*. My mother's uncle had fought at the Battle of the Somme in the First World War and was only too willing to help a demobbed soldier who was short of money. The shared house was a temporary base for us while my father looked for work. To begin with, he hoped to teach but, with few openings available in education, he decided to explore the possibilities abroad. An opportunity arose when he spotted a newspaper advertisement for overseas Colonial Office staff – in the post-war era, the Colonial Office had dropped its usual requirement of a university education. So my father, who had left school at fourteen, applied and was soon offered a posting to Nyasaland, where we lived from 1947 to 1953. Before leaving for Nyasaland, a final piece of housekeeping was completed when my parents were at last able to marry thanks to the formal ending of my mother's first, loveless marriage.

My parents were very different, yet they complemented each other. My father was regarded by those who knew him as one of life's quiet gentlemen. He was a man of immense integrity who was always generous with his time and advice if a friend was in need. My mother, though affectionate and committed to family life, had a more fiery side. On one occasion, when we were all sitting at the dining table at our home in Belize, my mother lost her temper with my father and threw the dregs of her cup of tea over him. As the sodden tea leaves began to trickle down my father's white shirt, he did not move a muscle, but after a pause he told my mother calmly: 'I always wanted a tea-shirt.' It was typical of her occasional hot-headedness and his placidity. As a couple, they were devoted to each other: both were only children who provided the other with a stability that had been lacking during their own childhoods. My father's father had died when he was thirteen, while my mother had been part of a role reversal that was unusual by any standards. Her grandmother acted as her stand-in mother and looked after her, while her actual mother, who was referred to as her aunt, lived elsewhere. As a child, my mother believed that her grandmother was her natural mother and it was not until she was a teenager that she learned the truth.

My childhood experience encouraged in me a trait that I have never shaken off: an insatiable wanderlust. I have never stopped travelling and I hope I never will. Even when we left Belize in 1956, there was to be one last family adventure in America. We

flew to Guatemala City, where we spent some time before flying on to Mexico City and then travelling by train to New York,
via Dallas, Texas, to visit some relatives who had moved to the
US during the Second World War. From New York, we took the
Queen Elizabeth to Southampton and caught the boat train to
Victoria station in central London. As the Ashcrofts left Belize, it
was impossible to imagine the large part it would play in my later
life.

My father's three years in Belize City were followed by a new
posting to Eastern Nigeria (later to become Biafra), where he, my
mother and my sister Patricia spent five years. Although I was
only ten when my father received this posting, my parents decided that, owing to the poor standard of schools in Eastern Nigeria,
I should go to boarding school in Britain. So, as the rest of the
Ashcroft family set off for Africa, I got down to the one business
that always defeated me: school work.

MY EARLY days as a boarder were neither happy nor easy. I had
been to school only in the sub-tropics, I had an unusual accent
from my years of living in the Caribbean – a difference that was
seized upon mercilessly by my classmates – and I had no affinity,
or feel, for Britain. Moreover, I felt lonely and miserable: my
father, mother and sister had vanished out of my life and it would
be nearly ten months before I saw them again.

My parents had decided that I should go to school in Norwich,
where my maternal grandparents, who lived nearby, could keep a
general eye on me. The farewell – on the London-bound platform
at Diss railway station – was painful. My mother was in floods of
tears, bordering on hysterics. I had thought about the goodbye in
advance and had resolved not to cry. Although I did not shed any
tears, it was difficult to keep a false smile on my face. My mother
later described her feelings of guilt at leaving me. 'I don't think I
ever fully recovered from the pain of that parting,' she wrote. After
her own unusual childhood, she had vowed that her own children
would never feel abandoned and unloved. Yet she had faced a
dilemma and later explained: 'I would find it heartbreaking to

be parted from the son I adored, and yet it was unthinkable that I should stand in the way of Eric's career.' I returned from Diss station to my grandparents' home feeling thoroughly down-hearted and confused.

I suffered because there was no fixed point in my life. I had difficulty adapting to the routine and discipline of school, and the tears that I had held back at the family farewell flowed late at night in my boarding house. The hardest part was that I could not understand why I had been left behind: other children who were boarding could visualise what home was, but I had no notion of 'home' because I had never set eyes on the place where my family were now living. My parents were in Nigeria, a country where I had never been, and every other previous temporary home was history. I was in Norwich with a group of boys and teachers who were strangers to me. I did not receive any phone calls from my parents but they did write regularly, usually every week. I, too, wrote regularly to them, although this was sometimes more out of duty than desire as the school insisted that once a week all board-ers sent a letter to their parents. Virtually every letter I dispatched to my parents informed them that I was saving to buy something – perhaps a record, a book or a bicycle – and it was always gently angled to suggest that they might like to contribute to this worthy cause.

I was aware that my situation was not unique and that many other children were routinely packed off to boarding school at an even younger age. But this did not make my situation less difficult or less emotionally demanding. Some of my fellow boarders prob-ably adapted better than me, others not so well. With my parents both being only children, I had no uncles, aunts or cousins and so there was no big family unit to support me. I was very much on my own. My treats came three times a term when I went to visit my grandparents – my mother's mother and her second husband – for day trips. They were kindly grandparents and I stayed with them during the Christmas and Easter holidays. I knew nothing at that time of the unusual delegation of parental responsibility involving my mother as a child. Then, at the start of the summer holiday, I travelled on my own to Nigeria.

For an eleven-year-old boy alone, the journey was daunting. I caught the train from Norwich to London where I was met by a well-meaning lady from the Corona Society, a wonderful group of current and former colonial officers' wives. The woman's role was to meet me at Liverpool Street station, give me a meal and bed for the night and make sure that I checked in on time for my flight the following morning. Under the watchful eye of airline staff, who were instructed to look out for this 'unaccompanied minor', I flew on a Boeing Stratocruiser, one of the last of the great piston-engine propeller passenger planes, to Rome, Tripoli and Kano in northern Nigeria. Finally a small passenger plane flew me to Enugu, the capital of Eastern Nigeria. The journey by road, rail and air took three, occasionally four days each way, but it was more than worth it: I was overjoyed to be reunited with my family and spent the summer months in the home that I had tried for the best part of a year to imagine – in reality an unspectacular apartment in a government-owned block of flats. With five years between us, my sister and I have never been particularly close, but we have always shared the same sense of humour and I was thrilled to be with her again. Patricia has always been more studious than me – she went on to become a teacher and to marry a teacher – while I always found it hard enough to participate in a lesson and certainly never had any desire to conduct one. My happy times with my parents and my sister as a reunited family were, however, small comfort when it came to saying goodbye again and embarking on the long return journey to Norwich.

Being 'abandoned' – as I saw it then – taught me resilience, independence and determination. I am sure I would be a different person today if I had not had such testing, if then unwished for, experiences. My drive to succeed had its roots in my schooldays. If I had not had these experiences, I would not later have had the overwhelming will to make a success of my life and it would have ended up differently. My schooldays undoubtedly made me self-sufficient. I had to form my own judgements and it stopped me from becoming a procrastinator. My decisions were my own because there was nobody else to take them for me. Yet, at the time, I felt resentment towards my parents. My mother later said that she noticed a change in my behaviour after I started attending boarding school. The boy she had previously described as 'pleasant and cheerful, with an impish smile' became more moody and difficult during the weeks that she saw me in the holidays. Because I did not want to leave my family for the return to school, my mood swings became especially pronounced as each summer holiday neared its end.

The first of two schools that I attended in Britain was King Edward VI Grammar School in Norwich. Usually referred to simply as Norwich School, it was an establishment for boys only, where only a fifth of the pupils were boarders. As a schoolboy, I was restless, almost hyperactive. I was rowdy but my classroom misdemeanours were numerous rather than serious. As far as I know, I was never close to being suspended or expelled, but my disciplinary record was poor. I was constantly in detention, where I had to write repetitive lines promising that my behaviour would improve. I also received the odd caning. Furthermore I had my share of bad luck: one detention was imposed when a friend and I sneaked out of school without permission to watch Norwich City play a home match – only to be spotted by a teacher from the school who was in the crowd supporting his local team.

I could not concentrate properly and my mind constantly wandered. I could sit down for an entire forty-minute lesson and not absorb a single word. My mind was not lazy but it quickly turned to subjects of more interest. Although I had a vivid imagination, I lacked the learning skills to enable me to do well in exams. The only exams I passed were either easy or in subjects that were interesting enough for me to retain information without endless revision. I did well at mathematics because I did not have to try. More by good fortune than academic excellence, I passed an acceptable number of O levels – eight altogether – though with modest grades.

Some newspaper profiles of me have suggested that during my schooldays I was an unhappy 'loner', using the word to imply that I had a character defect. Certainly I could – and indeed still can – be happy in my own company. I have never needed people around me to be content. I can sit and work on my own and I can potter about on my own: activities that most people would prefer to share with others. Yet I also enjoy amusing and interesting company and sharing my time with those I love. At school, I did not lead a solitary existence. I had a small group of good friends and I represented the school at team sports. I was not the best in my year at any sport but I was good enough to play rugby for the school – at second row and wing forward (as flankers were then known) – and I also represented the school swimming team at freestyle. I hated playing cricket, yet today I have a lot of fun watching Test matches.

I did not have traditional schoolboy heroes such as a sporting colossus or a Hollywood film star. My heroes were people who had served their country at a time of crisis. They included Field Marshal Montgomery and Sir Winston Churchill for what they did for Britain during the Second World War. I looked up to both of them for their formidable achievements during a hazardous period of our country's history.

It was at Norwich School that I embarked on my first profit-making exercise. There was a shop opposite the school that sold doughnuts for 3d each, but I discovered another shop some 400 yards further towards the town centre that sold identical doughnuts for a ha'penny less. There were regular whip-rounds among the boys for doughnuts and, after such an event, I was always glad to go on my own to buy them. I had a reputation among my friends at the age of twelve as a bit of a softy – always the person who was willing to go off alone to get the doughnuts. I cheerfully let them remain under this misapprehension because it earned me extra money, even at just a ha'penny profit per doughnut. My early entrepreneurial skills would have yielded an ample enough cash profit over the years had it not been for my schoolboy greed. My profits were never banked: every five doughnuts bought for friends were immediately converted into a free one for me. I considered this to be an acceptable return for providing a rather useful service, one that was prophetically in line with my later business ethics. Although I was not being 100 per cent open about my activities, I was not doing my friends down because in their hunger they were very happy to pay the going rate of 3d per doughnut from the shop next to the school. Yet there were probably people then, as now, who – if they had discovered exactly what I was doing – might have found my practice a little sharp. I looked upon it simply as working to find an edge, the sort of advantage that I would search for time and again in my adult working life.

My early enterprising streak did not go unnoticed. I can remember at least one occasion when my housemaster remarked on my initiative. When all the boys were asked to collect books for charity, I was the only pupil willing to knock on the door of the Bishop of Norwich. I engaged him in conversation and, possibly detecting my unusual accent, the Bishop asked me where my home was. When I replied, 'I used to live in British Honduras,' he said he knew the country and was interested in it – and so I left his palace armed with an impressive collection of old books.

During my final year at Norwich School, I became a day boy. My mother's health had deteriorated in Nigeria and my father had resigned from the Colonial Office so that they could return to England – and we were together again as a family after five years apart. My parents bought a modest three-bedroom bungalow in the village of Cringleford three miles outside Norwich. We later moved to Maidenhead, Berkshire, where my father commuted every day to a new job as bursar of Ashford School for Girls in Middlesex. I therefore switched schools for my A levels and attended the Royal Grammar School in High Wycombe, Buckinghamshire. However, the change of schools and a more settled home life did not improve my concentration or my academic results.

I never had a driving ambition to embark on a particular career but a parable a teacher told me when I was about sixteen made a lasting impression on me. 'If someone goes into your back garden and comes back ten minutes later with half a crown they have found and then another person goes into your back garden and comes back in the same amount of time with half a crown, it can look on the surface as if the two situations are identical,' said the teacher. 'But, in fact, the situations in which the half-crowns were found might be very different. The first man might have been daydreaming in the garden when the sun just happened to glint on the half-crown and he picked it up; while the second man might have been scouring and scanning the entire garden when he found the money. If this is the case, the first man is plain lucky and the second man is also lucky but he has created his own luck by searching even though he did not know what he was looking for.' I took that idea very much to heart. Even if you do not know which direction you are going in, provided you keep searching and probing for the right opportunity – and when it arises grab it – you will make your own luck in life.

By the time I was a student, I knew I would never be the sort of person who sat back and bemoaned his luck or his lot. I was a man on a mission, even though I did not know what the mission was or in which direction it would take me. I was confident that, if I kept searching, something would turn up. As a teenager, I wanted to be rich but I did not know how to go about it. I would dream of discovering a remarkable product that I could patent and which would make my fortune. Yet, in reality, I knew that finding such a money-spinning product was highly unlikely, so I suppose my ambition in life at that point was never stronger than saying to myself: 'I know an opportunity will come. I do not know what it will be or how it will present itself, but I do know that I will make damn sure that I snatch the opportunity when it comes along.' I had also realised that opportunity always looks bigger going away than coming towards you.

I have few enduring memories of my time at the Royal Grammar School, High Wycombe, and the word 'dismal' most accurately sums up my academic achievements. As with my previous school, and however good the teaching, I absorbed little that I was taught. People who know me now sometimes find it hard to imagine that at school I was not fiercely competitive both in the classroom and on the playing field, but competition to me means either to be the best or to be truly outstanding at something. I was never good academically, which I learned to accept, and I was never the best at any sport, which I also accepted. There was, at that point in my life, nothing at which I felt able to excel – and that competitive drive did not come until I was in my late twenties.

My A levels were, at best, disappointing. I passed mathematics but failed physics and chemistry. My results did not surprise me, but they were not what I – or my parents – had wanted. I had been optimistic that I would scrape a pass in physics because it involved quite a lot of mathematics, but the chemistry had required too much concentrated work and simply defeated me. My A levels ended my hopes of studying for a degree in mathematics and psychology at Reading University, a course for which I had been provisionally accepted.

This setback left me with a straightforward choice: to get a job or to enrol on a less prestigious course of higher education. I chose the latter and in September 1965 embarked on a Higher National Diploma (HND) in business studies at Mid-Essex Technical College in Chelmsford. Even though I had messed up my A levels, I still felt confident that I had a creative brain, but it needed to be engaged. If it was not engaged, it was useless. I never succeeded, for instance, in mastering languages because of the work involved in learning them. I did, however, find my business course fascinating and as such enjoyed my studies and learned a great deal. I found accountancy, marketing and the other parts of the course utterly engrossing. It was as if I had discovered a new jigsaw puzzle and I was curious to put all the pieces together as quickly as possible.

It was a time, too, when I discovered new vices: pretty girls, beer and a short-lived twenty-a-day smoking habit. I was a regular at the Railway Tavern, a popular but less than exclusive pub close to the college that always looked as if it desperately needed a lick of paint. However, the student drugs scene never interested me – indeed even as a student I was vehemently and unfashionably anti-drugs. I felt uncomfortable if I was at a party and fellow students openly smoked a joint or if the smell of cannabis pervaded the air. My contemporaries have remembered other traits in my character which were not typical of the average student. I was actively Conservative with a capital C and pro-police at a time in life when it was far trendier to be left-wing and anti-authority. I have no doubt that I was generally more interested in money than the typical student. Early on, I had an ambition to earn – and save – enough money to buy a second-hand Mini, and I achieved this aim within a matter of months. I had a reputation for being good for my word on money matters. If I had to pay a bill, it was always paid before or on the date it was due. Similarly, if I wrote a cheque, it could always be banked immediately and, unlike the cheques of some of my friends, there was no danger it would bounce.

Looking back, I was already more abrasive and larger than life than most of my contemporaries. I suspect my views and values have changed far less over the years than those of my student contemporaries. Even by the time I was in my late teens, I had formed strong, consistent and – at that time – unfashionable beliefs that I still hold to this day. Although I was interested in politics, I avoided the rent-a-mob protesters and the hopelessly earnest. I did, however, play an active role in the college rag scene because practical jokes and fun parties appealed to me. Although I would admit that raising money for good causes was not the prime motive of my involvement in rag week, this was my first flirtation with charity work – another activity that would return to play an important part in my life.

As with my school days, I showed flashes of entrepreneurial flair as a student. I discovered that only one cinema in central London had the rights to screen the live world-title boxing bouts of Muhammad Ali, then known as Cassius Clay (this was of course long before satellite television and 'pay per view'). Even more interestingly, I discovered that demand for seats outstripped the supply and that therefore the tickets fetched considerably more on the black market than their retail price. Always on the look-out for ways to supplement my student grant, I set myself up as a small-time ticket tout. But, as so often happens in business, there were occasional hiccups. On one occasion, a second cinema in London was allowed to open for an Ali fight and the price of seats at the Leicester Square cinema I had bought tumbled as a result. As with the doughnut purchasing at school, there was no vast profit margin from my experiences as a ticket tout. I simply made enough on the sale of a dozen or so tickets to watch the big fight for free. I was a great Ali fan and I loved watching him box. I was not alone, and on one memorable night I found myself sitting behind the comedy duo of Peter Cook and Dudley Moore. My experiences with the second London cinema opening at short notice had taught me a lesson too: there is no such thing as a certain profit from a business proposition and even the best-laid plans can go awry.

Around the same time and with the help of two college friends, I founded my first organised business, Odd Jobs Unlimited, which, though far too small to be a genuine company, exhibited the attitude and enterprise I thought was lacking in most of my contemporaries. We advertised our wares in a local newspaper with the slogan 'You name it, we'll do it'. Those seeking to employ us had to write to the local weekly paper where we picked up letters once a week. Whatever the weather, we gardened, painted or did whatever task our clients required. One of my roles was to work on a local estate cutting the seemingly endless expanse of lawns using a sit-on mower. We were game for anything. Odd Jobs Unlimited achieved its modest aim – enabling us to earn enough for a few pints at the Railway Tavern while we pursued our studies.

During the summer holidays, and when I was living back at my parents' home in Maidenhead, I got a job at El Toucan, a family-run café in the town, making and serving frothy coffees and other hot drinks to a mixture of weary shoppers and local traders. I always tried to be efficient and friendly to the customers because a coffee cost 10d and I knew that, with luck, they would leave me a shilling – which included a generous 2d tip. I also worked as an attendant at our local outdoor swimming pool in Chelmsford. I had the obligatory attendant's whistle around my neck and used to blow it to stop children from running or fighting in and around the pool. The job had one notable perk: it was useful for admiring and, occasionally, dating the local talent. I also managed a pop group called Trident whom I naturally hoped would become the equivalent in fame and wealth to the Beatles. Trident was a four-man rhythm 'n' blues band and my managerial role involved driving the group around in a battered green Transit-style van to their often less than packed gigs. Fame always eluded us, and the band eventually broke up, leaving its members and its manager as impoverished as the day it had been formed.

As a student, I also learned to play bridge, teaching myself the rules and the necessary skills by reading books. I loved the game and quickly reached the point where I was just below county standard. While on holiday and living at my parents' house, I used to play with the ladies – mostly well advanced in years – of Maidenhead Conservative Club. They were always pleased to see a young man take up the game and I was equally delighted that my standard of play was slightly better than theirs. We would play for small amounts of money – 6d a hundred points – and I finished up with a small profit by the end of the holidays.

At this time in my life, I developed a little party trick. I discovered that I could memorise a deck of cards and then, as I turned over the fifty-two cards one by one, predict which one would come next. I occasionally made the odd mistake but not often, and I enjoyed the admiring look on people's faces when they saw what I could do. I started experimenting with similar games to test whether I had a photographic memory in other areas. I found that if someone showed me twenty different objects in succession, I could recite them all in any sequence that was demanded; forwards or backwards starting with any of the objects that I was given. It was my card-counting abilities that were to make me a half-decent bridge player and it was a near-photographic memory that would later give me another edge in my business dealings. Over the years, I have had the ability to retain the smallest details in my head and to think laterally – though I have to concede that age has made these skills less pronounced than they were in my youth.

BY THE time my student days ended, I had long come to accept that I was never going to be an academic genius. However, I had learned to live with my shortcomings – notably my lack of concentration – and found ways of obscuring them.

Recognising that I had weaknesses was one thing, but identifying exactly what they were was more difficult. It was not until I had reached the age of forty-five that the penny dropped. My younger son, Andrew, who was twelve years old at the time, was having problems at school. On the face of it, he seemed to be re-running his father's experience. However, in contrast to the treatment prescribed in my youth, when I was simply told to pull my socks up, Andrew was sent to an educational psychologist who gave him certain tests, including one that I can remember vividly. Andrew was doing some writing when the psychologist went up to the Venetian blinds on the window and ran his hand down them. Andrew looked up because he had been distracted by the sound and, immediately afterwards, had lost his concentration so totally that he could not return to his writing. The psychologist diagnosed Attention Deficit Disorder (ADD), a complaint of which I was entirely ignorant.

So I bought the books in order to read a little on the subject and quickly found that I could not put them down. It was like a great awakening. In reading about the condition as it applied to Andrew, I discovered, for the first time in my life, that I was reading about myself. In every example cited, I saw elements of myself, and every device used to cover the problem was a device to which I had resorted. The scales fell from my eyes and I felt much better for it. ADD is a neuro-development disorder which affects a sufferer's ability to learn and interact with other people. Some of the common indicators are excess fidgeting, lack of concentration, clowning around, excessive talking, short attention span and engaging in high-risk activities. I recognised each of those characteristics in myself: had I ever bothered to fill in an entry for *Who's Who*, I could have listed them under 'Recreations'.

My experience of the problems caused by ADD gave me enormous empathy with Andrew. I began to understand how people with ADD come to be better in certain professions than in others. A disproportionate number of explorers over the years are now believed to have had ADD, their restlessness prompting their ventures into the unknown. Indeed, perhaps my own wanderlust has the same origin. Nowadays, those with ADD often become salesmen relying on the gift of the gab, while more recently I read in an American business survey that the number-one characteristic of successful businessmen is oral persuasiveness. Through Andrew's problems, everything began to fall into place and I realised for the first time that during my schooldays I had suffered from ADD but it had not been understood or treated. Fortunately, with Andrew there was time to help him and everything from his school grades to his attendance improved dramatically.

At my age, it was too late to treat my ADD. To this day, I find it hard to write lengthy business reports. One of the important lessons I learned long ago is not to be afraid of employing others to do what you cannot do yourself. I have always surrounded myself with capable, trusted people upon whom I can rely. Even now, I can go into a lecture and if, after a few sentences, the speaker has lost me I go off into my own little world for the rest of the talk. By the end of it, I will not have heard or absorbed a single word the lecturer said. I take some comfort, at least, from the fact that the time is rarely wasted. I usually put it to good use pondering what I need to do the next day or how to tackle some troublesome issue.

IN THE same way that some academic studies bored me rigid, other subjects have instantly captured my imagination. Encouraged by films and books on the subject, I have always been fascinated by the concept of danger. This, in turn, led to an almost obsessive interest in some of the heroic figures of the Second World War, notably the Cockleshell Heroes, the name given to a small group of Royal Marines who mounted a daring and successful raid on German shipping in the French port of Bordeaux in 1942. I am intrigued by the way people, often apparently quiet and nondescript, come to terms with the possibility, even in rare cases the probability, that they will be killed or wounded in battle. What makes them different – or are we all capable of such bravery in certain circumstances? Why are the bravest so often the most modest? Is it upbringing, training, religion, patriotism, character or values such as honour and duty which makes people prepared to go to extraordinary lengths for their country and their comrades? The biggest inspiration for my interest in courage was undoubtedly my father.

Eric Ashcroft was a tough, independent man and I like to

think that I have inherited those qualities. When his own father died at thirteen, he had to leave school the next year to become the family breadwinner. He had a variety of jobs, including working in the local cotton mill, until war broke out in 1939. He then became one of the first to enlist, joining the South Lancashire Regiment. He was selected for officer training, after which he returned to the regiment. He remained in Britain until the D-Day landings.

At dawn on 6 June 1944, my father found himself on a landing craft crashing through the waves of the English Channel, heading for Sword Beach as part of the British 3rd Infantry Division. I have often wondered what it must have been like for those young men, many of whom, my father among them, were seeing action for the first time. As they reached the beach, they encountered heavy enemy fire. My father's commanding officer, a colonel, was one of the first casualties, shot dead at my father's side by a sniper. My father, too, was struck by shrapnel. Despite wounds to his back and to one of his arms, he refused to be evacuated and carried on fighting until he was eventually ordered from the field of battle. The injuries proved serious enough to end his front-line service.

My father was a modest man but, on the few occasions when I could persuade him to talk about the events of that day, I realised just how brave he and the men he fought with had been. I recall him one day telling me in a quiet, matter-of-fact way that he and other officers had been briefed to expect 75 per cent casualties – fatalities and wounded – on the beach as they landed in Normandy. I have often wondered what it would have been like to have been in my father's shoes that day and whether I, too, could have matched his bravery in my country's hour of need.

My greatest military interest of all has been in the Victoria Cross. Some of the acts of bravery carried out by servicemen who have won VCs simply beggar belief. 'For most conspicuous bravery or some daring or pre-eminent act of valour or self-sacrifice or extreme devotion to duty in the presence of the enemy' – this is how VC citations usually begin, followed by a detailed account of the incident. The exploits of the handful of soldiers, sailors and airmen whose gallantry was such that they won the legendary medal have, for decades, fascinated countless young boys, and I was one of them. The VC is the premier honour for bravery which Britain and other Commonwealth countries can bestow upon their citizens, yet it respects neither rank nor birthright. Despite its great prestige, the medal is a modest Maltese cross, a little over an inch wide, which is cast not from gold or silver, but from base metal with no intrinsic value. The oldest winner of the VC was sixty-one, the youngest just fifteen.

When I was in my early twenties, I became aware that it was possible to buy VCs on the rare occasions that they came up for auction. I started ordering the relevant auction catalogues, but my resources were limited and the prices of the medals were prohibitive. Undeterred, I resolved one day, if my financial circumstances allowed it, to buy a VC. In the meantime, I continued to ask for the catalogues to be sent to me so that I could read more about why individual VCs had been awarded. The more I read about the medals, the more interested I became in them and the more determined I became to own one. It was not until I was forty that I went to an auction and successfully bid for a VC at Sotheby's in July 1986, for one awarded to Leading Seaman Magennis, a diver who, while serving in Malaysia in 1945, fixed a mine to the underside of a Japanese warship which sank as a result of his heroics. Later, too, I satisfied my early schoolboy fascination and bought the medals earned by a serviceman who had won one of them on the Cockleshell Heroes' raid.

The VCs have become my pride and joy. They are part of Britain's history. Over the years, I have helped to collect no fewer than 135 VCs. They are held by a trust which now owns nearly one in ten of all the VCs which have been awarded. Many of these might otherwise now have left the United Kingdom. Some people who know of my interest assume I am an expert in Britain's military history since the introduction of the medal in 1856, though in fact I am not. My knowledge tends to be restricted to the battles and campaigns in which VCs were issued, leaving great gaps in my knowledge of British military history from the mid-nineteenth century until today.

Such rare medals are not cheap and the trust's collection is now worth several million pounds. However, the trust has adhered to a strict rule: it does not 'ambulance chase' or go in search of medals that are not on the market. The only medals in the collection are ones which either the recipients or their families wanted to sell privately, through a dealer or at auction. One of the other sections of medals in the trust's collection is for those won by the SAS, again for the reason that they are often associated with quite staggering acts of bravery. With each of the medals in the collection, there is a small, bound book detailing the exploits for which they were awarded. I do not believe there is another collection of VCs in the United Kingdom – and that includes the Imperial War Museum in London – that is as extensive or as interesting. I am delighted that the trust intends to exhibit the collection in the years to come so that it can be enjoyed by others, and so that the acts of courage and self-sacrifice which earned each medal can be properly remembered and cherished.

To my mind – and I concede that I am somewhat biased – my father was one of the many unsung war heroes of his generation. After he was demobbed – he left the Army with the rank of captain – he set his sights on new and distant goals. He enjoyed his time in the Colonial Office enormously but he gave up a promising career for the sake of my mother's health. Back in England, life was tougher than he had imagined. If he had a character weakness – and this may sound strange to some people – it was that he was too willing to put my mother first. His love for her meant that he was always ready to sacrifice his own interests – most notably his own career.

My father retired at sixty and, after a long and happy retirement, died from leukaemia in 2002 at the age of eighty-four. His regiment sent down the pall-bearers for his funeral and the Last Post was played by a bugler in the church. My father's war medals were on his coffin and I gave the address about his remarkable life. It was a deeply moving day.

Like many children who have lost a parent, I regret not spending more time in my father's company. There were only a few months between the diagnosis of his leukaemia and his death, but they provided time enough for his family to say their farewells. A week or so before he died, my father and I sat together at his home in Goring and had a long, difficult conversation. We discussed how I should look after my mother after he had died. I made my peace with him, telling him that, although he had always been a good father, I had not always been the most thoughtful son.

I am immensely proud of my father and I like to think that he was also proud of me and my achievements. He never had any great goal or ambition for his only son, but he had seen me in my early twenties as a lost and restless soul who seemed directionless. He was not unsupportive, but I think he felt unable to help point me in the right direction. Instead, he watched from afar – but with genuine interest – as I went through my early career stutters and my later business successes. It must have been like watching someone you care for climb up a cliff, lose his grip, fall down, cling on by his fingertips and, finally, pull himself up again.

I miss my father and his distinctive sense of fun. I can still vividly recall that when I was a boy he attended a fancy-dress party in Belize and was wearing a white shirt covered with large and striking scorched-brown burn marks from an iron. He had a sign around his neck which simply read: 'Press on regardless'. It was typical of my father – always doing something slightly differently but with a mischievous sense of humour about it too.

2 Down to Business

MY ACADEMIC studies at Mid-Essex Technical College were as unremarkable as my school years. They had, however, succeeded in pointing me in a career direction – towards the world of business. While I continued to believe in the maxim that 'something will turn up but I don't know what it will be', I increasingly felt that the 'something' would one day involve running a company or venture of my own.

At the age of twenty-one, I was offered – and accepted – my first proper job as a management trainee with Rothmans (then known as Carreras), the cigarette manufacturer. Back in 1967, my starting salary was the grand sum of £925 per annum. I was delighted to discover that I was the only non-graduate of six trainees on the scheme. I felt that I had caught up after failing to get on a university degree course myself. With hindsight, I was perhaps a little too pleased with myself because I soon discovered that my free spirit did not fit well into a company structure.

My two years at Rothmans were undoubtedly the dullest of my life. I learned next to nothing and, from the company's viewpoint, I must have been a waste of time and space. I was working on the financial accounts side, but I was also given day release to study to become a certified accountant. It was a relief to have to spend only four days a week in the office, where I did not consider I was receiving any worthwhile training. I had no job satisfaction and could not see where it was leading, which meant I was easily distracted. I was still managing the pop group and playing bridge and I also enjoyed some motor rallying. Indeed, Rothmans was good enough to pay for me and two other young members of staff to travel to the West Indies to compete in the round-Jamaica 1,000-mile rally. It was great fun and we got off to a good start, only to become lost in the mountains and end up well down the field of competitors.

I passed part two of my certified accountancy course but I did not complete the other two parts of the course, so I therefore failed to qualify. Once again the required application to study for the exams was not there because, as with academic studies, I was not mentally engaged. After two years at Rothmans, where I had been based at the company's office in Basildon, Essex, it became a race as to whether I would resign before I was fired. I just won in what must have been a photo finish, but left without having a new job. I thought I would take a chance and see what opportunities came along.

At this time, I was renting a rather dreary room in Chelmsford. While I pondered my future and waited for the next opportunity to come along, I signed on the dole. The Labour Exchange used to insist that I attend job interviews, mainly in London. The jobs that I went for were largely uninspiring and had no attraction for me whatsoever. I remained on the dole for several months in 1969.

In one of my interviews in London, I was curious to find myself discussing a job that sounded rather interesting. I was told that the finance director of Pritchard Group Services, a large cleaning and business-services company, wanted an assistant at its head office. The successful applicant would not only look after head-office books but would also, as part of the due-diligence team, scrutinise firms which the company was thinking of buying. Due diligence involves studying another company's books to see if they represent a true and accurate picture of its finances and to ensure that it is not trying to inflate its profits to get a better sale price. I am certain that I came across as relaxed at the interview because I initially had little intention of taking the job even if it were offered to me. However, as the interview progressed, I found myself bluffing slightly about my abilities and over-selling myself in order to make a favourable impression. A few days later I was offered and accepted my second – and what was to prove my last – salaried position. My new offices were in Chancery Lane, central London, where I had to take over a set of head-office company books and the consolidation of subsidiary company accounts, two roles that I had never fulfilled before. For the first time in my life

I found myself working on something that I found fascinating. I spent my evenings and weekends learning, virtually from scratch, how to put a set of company books together. I worked backwards, following the book entries of my predecessor, to discover how things should be done.

For a time I commuted to London but after a few months I started dating the secretary to one of the directors at Pritchard. Wendy Mahoney was a young woman with many attractions, not least a comfortable flat in West Hampstead, north London. It was not too long before I left my digs in Chelmsford and moved in with her. We married in April 1972, and over the next six years we had three children: James (born in 1974), Sarah (1976) and Andrew (1978).

Shortly after I joined Pritchard, I was sent to Canada as part of a finance team which had to carry out due diligence on a cleaning firm that the company intended to buy. To start with, I had no idea how to go about my task, but I picked things up as I went along. It must have gone reasonably well, however, because similar trips soon followed to South Africa and Portugal. I was on a vertical learning curve and I was seeing the world at the same time. Within a year of joining Pritchard, my salary had risen to £3,300, more than twice my starting pay with the company. In 1971, I was asked to become chief accountant of one of the company's major subsidiaries. I accepted and this took my salary to nearly £4,000 a year – more than four times my starting salary at Rothmans five years earlier. The following year, however, when I was twenty-six, I became restless to move on.

So in June 1972, two months after getting married, I left Pritchard, which then employed 30,000 people, again with no job to go to but with the idea of starting my own business. There was no row over my departure from the company, but Peter Pritchard, the chairman, had taken against me. There probably were times when I had been too full of myself, although Peter Fox, the principal managing director of one of Pritchard's main subsidiaries, remained a life-long friend until his untimely death in early 2004. Peter was a kindred spirit and the fact that I attended his funeral thirty-two years after leaving the company says a great deal about how close we had become after my departure. Before leaving Pritchard, I told Don Pearce, the chairman of one of the company's main subsidiaries and a main board director: 'The next time I will be back here is to take over the company.' It was said in a light-hearted way with a smile on my face, but it was also a way of demonstrating my determination to succeed on my own.

I was searching for a path which would allow me to be myself. I looked upon money as counters in a game: it measured success. The one skill that I now possessed was the ability to value, to buy and to sell cleaning companies. I had to decide how to put my knowledge to good use. Thus in 1972 Michael A. Ashcroft Associates Ltd was born. In reality, the company was a one-man band although I put my father and my father-in-law Cyril Mahoney down as directors so that it looked more impressive on the note-paper. I did not have a penny of savings and, in fact, on the day I started my business my net wealth was in the red: a small debt on a credit card. The nature of the business I had chosen meant, however, that there was no need to borrow a substantial amount of money.

I worked from a spare bedroom at our new marital home in Maidenhead, Berkshire, a detached three-bedroom house for which we paid £10,950. Using the experience I had gained over the previous two years, I set myself up as a merger broker writing to every cleaning company in Britain. I wrote to literally thousands of firms, having obtained their names and addresses from *Yellow Pages*. I asked them if they wanted to sell their business because, if so, I knew somebody who wanted to buy it. Similarly, if they wanted to buy cleaning companies, I knew of companies that were on the market. I told them that I would take my commission only on successful transactions. I bashed the letters out myself on an old typewriter, although occasionally I employed temporary help to assist me with writing letters and answering the phone.

In 1973, I took on my first full-time employee as well as new rented offices in High Wycombe, Buckinghamshire. Thirty-two years on that employee, Lyn Austen, still works for me and runs a small merger-broking business called Bearwood Corporate Services, which he operates with only a secretary to help him from a small office in Wokingham, Berkshire. It is a characteristic of my business career that people who have stayed with me for a year often stay with me for a decade or more. Several other people have been with me for many years: David Hammond, my business number two, has been with me for twenty-five years; Peter Gaze, my chief financial officer, twenty-two years; Angela Entwistle, my corporate communications director, twenty years; Richard Painter, who oversaw most of my charity work, eighteen years; Lindsey Page, my personal assistant in the US, sixteen years. All my working life I have had a clear division between 'home team' and 'away team'. The home team includes all those working for me, my family, my friends and all those who stick with me through thick and thin. I believe that you move hell and high water for them at all times because loyalty goes both ways. Incidentally, for the purpose of this book, home-team members are referred to by their first names after their initial mention, while away-team members are referred to by their surnames.

My approach to business is straightforward. The key to success is providing services and/or adding value to objects, processes and ideas. I am naturally drawn to businesses which do real things, which provide real services and where competition is fierce. I also, however, like transforming and developing businesses by changing the way they operate. This can take many forms: it might mean making them bigger so that they expand into new markets; it might mean making them more cost effective; often it simply means managing them better.

I would not dream of investing serious money in an area about which I know little. Similarly, I would not contemplate investing money in a country where I cannot compete on equal terms. I am not a natural linguist – one of my few regrets in life – and it is for this reason that in the main I do business only in countries where English is the first language. I would feel disadvantaged dealing with a business rival who knew the local language better than me.

I prefer, too, to invest in relatively straightforward business ventures which have healthy cash flows. In business, cash *is* king. In the early 1970s, I had identified the cleaning industry as an ideal investment for a young businessman of limited financial means. It requires relatively small capital and yet has a stable turn-over. Later, my decision to invest in and build up ADT into the world's largest security company was based on similar principles: burglar alarms require a certain level of capital investment, but security is still very much a service industry in which the bulk of the business comes from leasing and maintaining the alarms on long-term contracts. Car-auction businesses, another of my larger investments over the years, have a higher 'front end' investment in the premises, which presents a barrier to entry for people without much money. However, once that initial hurdle has been over-come, it is cash generative thereafter.

New fads leave me cold. I was never tempted to invest in the dot-com revolution of the mid-1990s for three reasons. First, I have always felt that green fields are for cows (a business started from nothing is known as a 'green field' and I have never liked green-field, or start-up, situations). Secondly, the dot-com revolution was too complicated for me to grasp and, rather than investing time in understanding it, I decided to leave it to others. Thirdly, it involved burning a lot of cash at the outset without any certainty that you were going to get the money – and more – back. I took the view that, if there was something in it, then others should invest their money first and I might come in later. I had hundreds of opportunities to get involved, but I passed them all up. My decision meant I escaped the dot-com crash of the late 1990s which resulted in some businessmen I knew losing millions of pounds.

In 1973, the year after launching my own business, I was a man in a hurry: hard-working, uncompromising and ambitious. It helps when starting or taking over a business to have a goal. My aim, virtually from day one, was to build up the business until it was big enough to be attractive to a large public company. By 1973, there were three of us in the business – myself, Lyn Austen and our secretary. Later that year, I took on two other employ-ees because we were now offering a cleaning-consultancy service. That meant there were now five of us drawing salaries from the cash flow coming into the business.

In 1974, it was time for me to take my first business risk. A cleaning firm, Uni-Kleen, which was owned by a large public company, was up for sale. I believed that, at twenty-eight, I already knew enough about the cleaning industry to take a chance. By now, I could confidently value companies and structure deals and I was determined to buy the loss-making firm for nothing, or for a nominal sum. In the event I bought Uni-Kleen for £1. It was the start of a trend – over the coming decades I would pay a pound or a dollar for a lot of loss-making companies. I calculated that I needed to borrow £15,000 from a bank, and there were sufficient debtors to secure a loan of that size. I went to see the manager of Barclays Bank in Bracknell, Berkshire. His name was Bill Herries and to this day we exchange Christmas cards. Bill knew the business because his branch had been bankers to the public company which owned Uni-Kleen. I persuaded him that I had the know-how and the energy to turn around the business and he agreed to lend me the £15,000 that I needed.

With the company came its 1,000 employees. I kept the name and over the next three years I bought another six cleaning companies. Occasionally I borrowed a little more money but never an exorbitant amount because my existing businesses were always generating cash. I was totally committed to work and had no priorities other than my business. I often worked from the moment I got up to the moment I went to bed, including Saturdays and Sundays. Sixteen-hour days, seven days a week were the norm rather than the exception. I was totally driven because I had finally found something that I could do well, while still learning a great deal at the same time. I felt a bit like a builder who is given the task of constructing a small house even though he has never built one before. It is initially a daunting prospect but eventually he builds it. Then he realises that if he has built a house it is not that difficult to build a mansion. Once that mansion has been built, he knows he is capable of building Buckingham Palace. In other words, as you achieve things your horizons start to open and you realise – whether it is a house or a business – that you can build bigger and better after the completion of each phase.

In 1977, three years after taking over the company, I was

employing 3,000 people. I always knew as I was building the business that I would have to sell it sooner rather than later in order to get the capital to progress to another venture with more potential. I did indeed sell it to a large public company – Reckitt & Coleman, the foods, pharmaceuticals and cleaning-products company. I thought Uni-Kleen would fit well into Reckitt & Coleman's ambitions; fortunately, the board of the company agreed with me and we reached a deal. Uni-Kleen fetched £1.3 million and so, at the age of thirty-one, I was a millionaire at a time when such a label was still rare. Yet, as has been a characteristic of mine over the years when I come to the end of a chapter in my life, I moved on, not knowing what the next chapter would bring. I still kept my original merger-broking business but, other than that, after the sale to Reckitt & Coleman I owned nothing.

The day I sold out I took my senior management team out for a champagne celebration. I felt relief as well as satisfaction because – for the first time in five years – I did not have a business concern. I only had to worry about what to do next, but that could wait until tomorrow. It never once crossed my mind to bank the £1.3 million and live cautiously off the interest for the rest of my days. I had new challenges to embark upon even though I had no idea what they would be. I had found my *métier*. I had discovered what I enjoyed doing and it was something I could do reasonably well. Despite my millionaire status, I was determined to make more money – and quickly. My strategy was simple: to take over struggling companies, reduce expenditure, get rid of the dead wood, build up the business to increase revenues and then sell it when the time was right. Different companies had different problems. My role was to work out why a company was not making money and solve the problem. My first company, Uni-Kleen, for example, was not collecting its debts efficiently and was paying its creditors before it had the income to do so. It was also too inclined to buy expensive new equipment rather than using its perfectly adequate existing resources. I was confident that I could turn its fortunes around by tackling these areas. Provided a business is generating cash, other problems can usually be resolved and eventually the company will grow. If asked for advice, I often tell young entrepreneurs that, if their aim is to own a five-star hotel, they will almost certainly initially have to own several one-, two- and three-star hotels to achieve their goal.

My next major business enterprise was to purchase an interest in Hawley Goodall, a small, struggling tent manufacturer which later became the Hawley Group. Six years after buying the company, I took out a fairly substantial advertisement in the recruitment pages of the *Financial Times* headed simply 'Hawley Group PLC'. I was still in a hurry to expand the company and lead it to success, and the advertisement made it abundantly clear that I was interested only in taking on like-minded, equally driven people. It read:

> In order to keep the Group's and its subsidiaries' (a number of which are quoted) expansion plans moving ahead, there is a requirement for two executives to join the small corporate team based at Farnham Common. Reporting directly to the Group Chairman, the assignments will be far-ranging, including acquisition research, negotiating and subsequent implementation of financial controls and reporting procedures, internal investigations and reorganisations, preparation of circulars to shareholders (including all the necessary liaison with advisers), fund raising, etc.
>
> The pace and requirements will be extremely demanding and, by normal criteria, unreasonable. The commitment required is total and the position will only suit those who are highly ambitious, prepared, if necessary, at a moment's notice to spend 24 hours a day, 7 days a week on projects anywhere in the UK or USA and who feel they could command a salary of up to £45,000 ...

Nobody could accuse me of understating the demanding role that working for me would involve. I suspect, however, that it was the salary rather than the working hours that ensured the advertisement attracted a lively response: £45,000 in 1983 was the equivalent of virtually £100,000 today. I received 750 replies, from which I filled my two vacant positions.

I turned the Hawley Group from near bankruptcy in 1977 into a business-services company which, at its peak less than a decade later, employed more than 100,000 people. Between 1977 and 1986, I invested in a range of companies in the UK including packaging, motor retailing, hi-fi retailing, slot machines and more cleaning firms. I had a substantial investment, too, in home-improvement businesses including double glazing, kitchen, bedroom and bathroom companies. Some of my investments were in public companies quoted on the Stock Exchange; others were in private companies which I owned wholly or in part.

Now that I was doing something that truly engaged me, I discovered that I could be a voracious learner. The bible of stock exchange rules was known in those days as the 'Yellow Book'. I digested it from cover to cover and there was hardly anything in the book, particularly in its application to company takeovers, that I did not understand. I considered that, despite being self-taught, my knowledge of the 'Yellow Book' was on a par with that of any leading City adviser. Similarly, my knowledge of company law matched that of a competent company lawyer and my understanding of accounting standards compared favourably with a senior accountant's.

I played in other areas during the 1980s, sometimes successfully, sometimes less so, and I began taking small share stakes in all sorts of ventures. As I like a bit of fun in life, I thought that owning the Miss World beauty contest would be an amusing perk to keep me going through my long working days. I also believed that if I gained control of Miss World – which I never did – it would be a good brand franchise to promote my other businesses. As a result, I got to know Eric and Julia Morley, who owned and ran Miss World, and they invited me to take a 20 per cent stake in the business. It was fun attending half a dozen or so of the Miss World pageants around the world and I always invited a group of friends and business associates to share in a great evening.

My investment in Pineapple Dance Studios, the central London organisation owned and run by Debbie Moore, was another example of a fun investment. This was the idea of Peter Bain, a board director with Hawley, at a time when the concept of keep-fit and dance studios was catching on. Furthermore, Debbie had become such a well-known name that I considered the venture highly likely to work. So I bought a 20 per cent stake in her business. Lotus Cars had a similar attraction. It was a glamorous brand name which seemed to be going places. I bought a stake in Lotus of about 15 per cent but, when it was later taken over by a Far Eastern company, I lost interest in it. Miss World, Pineapple Dance Studios and Lotus Cars were exciting brand names, but my total investment in all three came to less that £500,000. Inevitably, however, because they were such high-profile names they brought me a disproportionate amount of publicity. They had become a distraction too far and I needed to take the focus away and back to my core business. For a time, I had found that when I went to talk to people about my company the first question would be 'Can you tell us all about your involvement in Miss World?' My fleeting involvement in such ventures *had* been fun but it needed to end and it did – with neither large profits nor heavy losses, and certainly with no regrets. I felt, once again, the urge to move on.

BY 1981, it was time to broaden my horizons. I had bought a house in Fort Lauderdale, Florida, the previous year. Cheap air fares had started to the United States of America and Florida was somewhere in the sun for family holidays. There were also several reasons to develop business interests in the US. I had become restless for a new challenge; Americans spoke English; and, perhaps most importantly of all, the US had the largest business-services companies in the world. I wanted to be there.

I travelled to America with David Hammond, a shrewd and experienced businessman whom I had met by chance because our children attended the same school. David was taken on specifically to help me find the company's first US acquisition: he had good contacts on the other side of the Atlantic and he knew how to do business in the States. David and I set out the criteria for the sort of business that I was looking to buy. We did it by the profile and character of the business rather than what it actually did. We were seeking a small public company in the US service industry. Before leaving for America, we obtained the listings of qualifying companies and went through them meticulously until we alighted on ones which we found interesting. We initially looked into more than 5,000 companies, but a filtering process left us with a dozen or so by the time our plane took off for New York in the summer of 1981.

We had arranged several business meetings and one of the companies that interested us was Electro-Protective Corporation of America (EPCA), which dealt in security and alarms on the eastern seaboard. This was a service business which we had never identified in the UK: Hawley had no links with the security and alarms business. We discovered that the major shareholding was held by one man, Freddie Schnell, and we approached him. He was willing to sell if the price was right and, eventually, we bought his majority stake of 54 per cent for just over $13 million. The following year, in 1982, we bought out the other shareholders so that we owned the whole of EPCA; then we quickly floated 40 per cent of the company on the London Stock Exchange, thereby raising some £6 million.

This was the start of my US operation, which is today centred on Atlanta, Georgia. Among our early acquisitions was an office-cleaning company called Oxford, which was based in Atlanta, and a lawn-care company with more than a million customers called Evergreen, which was based in St Louis, Missouri. In the early 1980s, I made a large number of acquisitions all over America. David travelled to thirty-five states to clinch business deals and I probably visited even more.

I believe in testing the boundaries and doing things differently. During the early 1980s, I looked at the possibility of moving my business interests abroad. In 1984, after considering it carefully with a team of tax experts, I decided that the Hawley Group, then a public company based in London, should transfer from the UK to Bermuda. This move gave us a unique tax advantage at a time when I was determined that my business interests should become more international.

I was, although not deliberately, unconventional in smaller

ways too. At a time when the City of London was entrenched in establishment habits, I was once so busy that for one small takeover deal I sent my driver to represent me at the formal completion ceremony. This is traditionally attended by all the senior figures from both sides – directors, merchant bankers and lawyers – who have been involved in the deal. I had gone to a local pub near our offices in Farnham Common, Buckinghamshire, to ask the landlord to witness my signature on the final contract. Then I had instructed my driver to attend the completion ceremony in the City and do exactly as our lawyers from Allen & Overy asked. I had not intended to cause offence but there was outrage that a driver had been sent to a completion ceremony and my reputation as an outsider grew.

In 1986, I fulfilled my promise of fourteen years earlier when Hawley took over Pritchard, which itself was already internationally established with operations spreading from the US and Britain to Australia and New Zealand. The following year, the Hawley Group bought British Car Auctions, which had already started its expansion on the other side of the Atlantic and owned thirteen auction sites in America. In 1987, we also bought ADT, which was the largest electronic security company in America. At the time, Hawley was the fifth largest security company in America, so it was an audacious move – in business terms a hostile bid. ADT was the equivalent of the five-star hotel that I had always been seeking.

By the middle of the 1980s, I was spending more and more of my time in the United States and I thrived on the American lifestyle. As a consequence, Wendy and I drifted apart, with no acrimony on either side to this day. In 1986 I got married for a second time to Susan 'Susi' Anstey, who had previously been my personal assistant, and we lived in the US. Fortuitously for me, Wendy, who has always been an exemplary mother to our children, also later chose to move to the US which meant I saw more of my two sons and my daughter than I would have done if she had remained in Britain.

In 1988, the Hawley Group was rebranded as ADT. It made sense: while Hawley was a little-known company even in Britain,

ADT was a household name in the United States and beyond. Up to this point, my business career had, by most standards, been successful, but it would be wrong of me to imply that everything I touched turned to gold. Like any businessman, I had failures as well as successes and difficult years as well as highly profitable ones.

I was rarely, if ever, interested in being a passive investor in a company. Instead, I wanted, at the very least, a proper say and, invariably, I was looking for outright control. In the late 1980s, I became interested in two companies which were, and remain, household names – Christie's, the fine-art auctioneers, and the British Airports Authority (BAA), which owns and runs seven UK airports including Heathrow and Gatwick. ADT invested tens of millions of pounds buying a 24 per cent stake in Christie's in 1989 and an 8 per cent share of BAA in 1990.

Both investments, however, had their problems. Christie's enjoyed a strong brand name, but the auctioneering business is highly cyclical and we hit the cycle at the wrong time. With BAA, we realised that with tens of millions of people annually travelling through airports there were new market opportunities. Although we were close to launching a hostile takeover bid for BAA, there were political hurdles which could not be overcome. This was due to the Conservative Government holding a 'golden' – or controlling – share as a condition of the privatisation of the company. It was also a time when some of my other investments on both sides of the Atlantic were less than successful, interest rates were rising and the British and US economies were heading for the doldrums. As chairman and chief executive of ADT, I had to pass on some rare gloomy news to shareholders in the company's annual report for 1990. 'It is disappointing to report the first decline in earnings for over a decade,' I wrote. 'Income before income taxes for 1990 declined 11 per cent to $258 million from $290 million in 1989.'

There was more depressing news to relate to shareholders in my annual report the following year. '1991 was a turbulent year in many ways and ADT was not alone in being affected by the change in business climate,' I declared, noting that ADT had pulled out of its interests in Christie's and BAA. The investment in Christie's made particularly uncomfortable reading. 'The problems which beset ADT during the year meant the original objective of seeking control of Christie's International plc had to be abandoned. At the same time, the fine-art market was also being hit hard by recession and at the end of 1991 the decision was taken to dispose of the entire equity interest that had been built up in Christie's.' In short, ADT took a bath with its investment in Christie's and it cost the company tens of millions of pounds.

A businessman once gave me some good advice. 'You will always make mistakes, but it is possible to go through life making mistakes and they will do your business little or no harm. This is because the trick is to spot the mistake early and deal with it.' Because I am a risk-taker in the business world, I know I will get some decisions wrong, but I work on the basis that the aggregate of all my deals will always leave me ahead. When I have made a mistake, it is a question not of move on and *forget*, but of move on and *learn*.

I have never been in a position where I thought I was going to lose everything. From the time I sold my first business for £1.3 million, I have never put all my eggs in one basket. Similarly, from that day, I have never been highly leveraged, meaning that I have never had a high level of personal borrowings. So from 1977 onwards there was never a chance that I would become personally bankrupt. This does not mean I am cautious. I am more of a thoughtful risk-taker in that I always try to understand the risk that I am taking. If I was able to say in advance that any venture had eight chances of succeeding and two of failure, then the odds are clearly in my favour, but I have to accept that statistically I am going to fail twice in any ten business attempts. The alternative to investing (and occasionally failing) is to do nothing. So I, and other risk-takers in business, are always playing the odds, confident that in the long run our wins will be more frequent and larger than our losses. Any money that I have is always invested but, while some of it is in more risky ventures, other money is in safer securities on which I take a longer-term view and which generally look after themselves.

The 1980s were memorable in many ways. They were the days of bruising takeover battles and colourful businessmen, some of whom ended their careers in the dock. Inevitably, I met some of them at parties and dinners, but their style was never mine and we were never close.

In 1991, I was subjected to my first major legal action: appropriately enough on April Fool's Day. Laidlaw, the giant Canadian waste-management company which had bought a 23 per cent share in ADT, sued us for alleged fraud, for falsifying accounts and for insider dealing. This was all part of the rough and tumble of big-business takeover bids, but critics in Britain seized upon the claims with undisguised relish, forgetting – or overlooking – the fact that in the States corporate litigation is far more routine. In America, when a company goes to war, it goes with all guns blazing. In particular, when it comes to a hostile takeover situation, it is not unusual for one company to make unsubstantiated claims against another. There is a saying in the US that firms 'litigate to negotiate'. It is only if the case reaches court – and most cases are usually dropped or settled along the way – that the allegations are subjected to careful scrutiny and often the more sensational and lurid claims dropped. Journalists in the US know this and therefore do not focus on the more outrageous claims, but British journalists, either because they are motivated by mischief or by an appetite for a good 'story' or because they are unaware of the conventions on the other side of the Atlantic, report the juiciest claims under sensational headlines. My lawyers tell me that, under British law, journalists are permitted to report allegations made in a legal claim under the protection of 'privilege', which means that, even if the allegations prove to be wrong, the newspaper cannot be sued successfully for libel. However, where the response or defence to the claim is not reported with equal prominence, such accounts can be absurdly one-sided. Furthermore, British newspapers usually either fail to report, or record in a brief paragraph or two, the news that a legal action, the outrageous allegations in which they had previously publicised with zeal, has been withdrawn or settled. Such a state of affairs is clearly grossly unfair to the individual or company that has had such allegations levelled against it, but it is a practice that has gone on for years and continues to this day.

All the charges made by Laidlaw were dropped by the end of April as part of an agreement between the two companies. Also as part of the settlement, we had to allow four directors from Laidlaw on to the board of ADT, thereby effectively allowing the fox into the coop. We also accepted the addition of four independent directors, two chosen by Laidlaw and two by ADT. The Security and Exchange Commission (SEC), the US government agency which oversees the securities markets in the US, reinvestigated some of the allegations of impropriety independently. In the event, it took no action and there were no adjustments to our company accounts, which is as close as one ever gets to a clean bill of health. In fact, Laidlaw had problems of its own and sold its share in ADT some years later. Another potential crisis had been tackled head on and averted. I had also learned a valuable lesson – not to be cowed by loud threats and phoney accusations. Laidlaw's legal action – which was barely reported in the American media – had, however, put me in the forefront of the British business press as a controversial figure, particularly as the initial allegations were, for reasons that I have explained, given far greater prominence than the subsequent announcement that my company had been absolved of blame.

More significantly, eight years later the Laidlaw claims came back to haunt me when the Labour Party, helped by *The Times*, tried to blacken my name. Journalists in Britain found from their electronic cutting libraries that one of my companies had been the subject of 'serious' allegations. Once again, most people in Britain were unaware that on the other side of the Atlantic such tactics are common practice in corporate warfare. The uninitiated concluded, however, that there was no smoke without fire, and I was wrongly perceived by some people as having a 'record' for corporate impropriety.

My experiences with Laidlaw led me to review my future and that of ADT. What was more important to me: wealth creation as an entrepreneur or running a big business? Some people have been able to do both but only by preserving a large stake in the company. By this time, I did not have a substantial proportion of ADT. Once businesses get to a certain size you cannot increase your capital at the same rate as when you are building up smaller companies. After careful consideration, I decided I was happier being an entrepreneurial wealth creator in smaller companies and that I needed to redeploy my assets. If my wealth was to grow faster, I had to get my remaining assets out of ADT sooner rather than later.

IN 1996, ADT faced a hostile takeover bid from Western Resources, the Kansas-based energy and security company. I was never keen for ADT to be taken over by this company. Its offer of $3.5 billion was substantially lower than an earlier $5 billion offer from Republic Industries, another US company headed by the dynamic Wayne Huizenga. I had struck the deal with Wayne, whom I had by then known for more than a decade after meeting him at a party in Florida. Wayne's bid, however, had to be aborted when Republic Industries encountered financial difficulties which, in turn, led to its share price falling dramatically.

Resisting the takeover of ADT by Western Resources was not easy. It came at a time when ADT was still struggling and, indeed, in January 1997, the point when Western Resources was pushing hardest to take over the company, ADT had to issue a profit warning to shareholders for the last quarter of 1996. However, resist it we did, with the board advising shareholders in a letter that the bid was inadequate. Having made my own decision about my business future and with the board of ADT keen to get the best possible price for shareholders, I felt I had to seek a suitable buyer for the company. With Western Resources still hovering in the wings – it had bought Laidlaw's 23 per cent share of the company – I had to act quickly. And so began – in my business experience, at least – the deal of deals.

I decided that the most suitable company to take over ADT was Tyco International, a large and rapidly expanding business which was being fêted on Wall Street. Tyco had won many awards, including – ironically as it was to turn out – praise for its corporate transparency. At that time, the chairman and chief executive of Tyco was Dennis Kozlowski, who was being hailed by many as America's premier deal-maker. Kozlowski was the new guy on the block. I liked what he was trying to do with Tyco and I liked his style. I did not know him personally at the time but I rang him, introduced myself and said: 'I think ADT could fit in with what you are trying to do. Shall we meet?'

We met for breakfast in New York at the St Regis Hotel in Manhattan in March 1997. Just the two of us were present and I took to him at once. He came across as a no-nonsense businessman who knew where he was going. Tyco was already in the fire-protection business and had bought a small alarm company in the UK. I knew ADT would suit what Kozlowski was trying to do with Tyco and he had read up on ADT and had come to the same conclusion. By the time we had finished breakfast, we both knew that we could soon be doing business together. Over the next few days, it became clear what the parameters of the deal would be and at what price. He sent a financial team to take a look at ADT, which was relatively straightforward. What took time, however, was the detail of the deal. Kozlowski wanted to structure it so that ADT's off-shore status in Bermuda was preserved in order for Tyco to take advantage of the company's tax status. ADT therefore became the acquiring company in what is called a reverse takeover in which the smaller company takes over the larger one. ADT then changed its name to Tyco, and Kozlowski and Tyco formally took control of ADT on 2 July 1997.

In the sale, ADT fetched more than $6.7 billion, and within months Tyco's stock had virtually doubled. The sums involved and the nature of the deal had really got my adrenalin pumping. I had negotiated the biggest business deal of my life. It is said that a pilot lives for take-offs and landings because they are the extra-special moments. Those sorts of colossal deals are the equivalent of take-offs or landings for a businessman – that is what the game is all about.

I sold hundreds of millions of dollars' worth of my stock over the coming months and years. From the day I did the deal, it was always a question of when not if I would sell. I have never retained a substantial share in a company that I do not control and I needed the capital to diversify into other things. I continued at Tyco as a non-executive director but had no involvement in the day-to-day running of the company. My comparative detachment was a mixed blessing. Five years later and just months after featuring on the cover of *Business Week*, Kozlowski was arrested and led off in handcuffs in front of the TV cameras. He was required to do what is known as the 'perp walk' – the perpetrator walk – where the accused suffers a ritual humiliation once they have been arrested. Kozlowski and Mark Swartz, Tyco's chief financial officer, were eventually accused of stealing tens of millions of dollars from the company in unauthorised remuneration and illegally gaining hundreds of millions in inflated stock profits.

My initial unease had been stirred some months earlier in January 2002 when Josh Berman, a fellow director, and I discovered that Frank Walsh, another Tyco director, had been paid a $20 million finder's fee on a company acquisition. Such a vast fee to a director was impossible to justify, as was the apparent initial intention to keep the payment secret from fellow directors. Later that month, I told Josh, an astute American lawyer and businessman, that I had 'lost trust but not lost confidence' in Kozlowski's ability to run Tyco. Our concerns for the company grew, however, throughout March and early April as Kozlowski became uncharacteristically indecisive. By mid-April, I told Josh that I had now 'lost confidence as well as trust' in Kozlowski's ability to run the company.

Josh and I were convinced that we ought to do something to see whether our joint concerns were justified. We were instrumental in instructing David Boies, a tough, independent lawyer who had been employed by Al Gore to lead the Florida inquiry into allegations of voting irregularities in the 2000 presidential election. David was asked by us to conduct an internal investigation into the way Tyco was being run. By this time, the end of April 2002, Josh and I were so concerned that we encouraged the corporate governance committee, on which we served, to ask Kozlowski to submit detailed information about all his remunerations, stock options, payments to charities, expenses and use of company assets, including property and aircraft.

As we probed, events took a strange turn. On 31 May Kozlowski told the board that the following day he was going to be indicted by the Manhattan District Attorney for alleged sales-tax evasion relating to the personal purchase of some paintings for his art collection. This case against Kozlowski has not come to trial. As it happened, it had nothing to do with the concerns we harboured about excess pay, unauthorised corporate expenses and the like. But of course his announcement came as an overwhelming shock when I still had a stake in the company worth about $250 million.

Kozlowski's indictment meant that, for the first time since I had joined Tyco's board of directors, I was propelled centre stage. Together with Josh, I was one of the principal voices in insisting that Kozlowski, then aged fifty-five and a man who had given twenty-five years of his working life to the company, should resign immediately, which he did on the day that he was indicted. Within hours, shares in Tyco lost 27 per cent of their value. I was then part of a committee which approved John Fort as the interim chief executive and which started searching for a permanent new chief executive and chairman. I was involved in interviewing potential candidates and in choosing Ed Breen, an experienced businessman, for the role. Shortly afterwards, a new, independent director, Jack Krol, was appointed to the board.

Under Tyco's internal rules, the directors come up for re-election every year, usually on the recommendation of the existing eleven-strong board. Given the gravity of the situation, however, I was convinced that this time things needed to be different. I was aware that a chain of events had happened on our watch and – although it would have been easy and legitimate for us remaining board members to distance ourselves from what had happened – I had no doubt of the need for a clean break with the past. I believed that *all* the directors who were on the board during Kozlowski's time as chief executive and chairman should resign. So at the next board meeting I proposed that no director who had served under Kozlowski should be reappointed to the board. I knew in advance that there would be formidable resistance to the move but I calculated that I could win the day. I had been told by both Ed Breen and Jack Krol, the two new board directors, that they would support my proposal. Josh Berman, Jim Pasman, a former director of ADT who had come on to the Tyco board, and John Fort, the interim CEO, had also told me that they would support my initiative. The crucial meeting in November 2002 was a dramatic affair with most directors, including myself, connected by phone rather than physically attending the New York boardroom.

The main problem was that many of the directors felt that by resigning they were somehow admitting that they had acted improperly. They feared that if they stepped down, their reputations would suffer so badly that they might never recover. I, however, did not share this view. I did not believe that resignation in any way implied guilt, neglect or poor practice, but I did believe it offered Tyco the best chance to draw a line in the sand following one of the biggest scandals in corporate history, and it also gave the company the best chance to recover and prosper. I opposed a compromise solution whereby some of the directors would remain on the board for a transitional period. I felt that by continuing on the board, the directors who had served under Kozlowski were putting their own self-interest before the best interests of the company and I made my point forcefully to the board meeting. After a heated debate lasting nearly two hours, it was time to vote on my proposal.

The vote initially ended in a split vote, five to five. This left Ed, as chairman and chief executive, with the eleventh and deciding vote. He said that he believed it was better for the company to have a fresh start, so he sided with my resolution. As the meeting broke up, there was acrimony. Because I was not present in person at the meeting, I was unaware until some time later just how remarkable and unprecedented it had been. However, an acquaintance of mine, a man with twenty years' knowledge and experience of big business in the US, told me months later: 'It was the most tense and dramatic meeting that I have ever witnessed – and I have seen a few.' He added: 'This was a unique meeting. No company of consequence in the US has ever seen its entire board stand down in this way.'

On 11 November, I formally stepped down as a director of Tyco, telling Ed in my resignation letter:

> It would be an understatement to say that recent months have been rather turbulent ... I have been required to make an unanticipated and unwelcome contribution in terms of time and expertise. I do not propose to revisit in this letter my views on the historic shortcomings of the organisation, merely to say that I trust that my actions and the forthright nature of my comments have made a positive contribution to addressing the company's problems during the course of this year.

In his reply accepting my resignation, Ed generously expressed his gratitude for the role that I had played. 'Your resignation speeds the transition that we both believe is in the interests of Tyco and its shareholders,' he wrote.

> On the other hand, the board (and I personally) will miss the wise counsel that you have provided. Your role in retaining outside counsel in April of this year to investigate the conduct of Tyco executives (which you did before there was any public or regulatory pressure to do so) was critical in the protection of the company and its shareholders. You also played a valuable role in securing Kozlowski's resignation several weeks later when a criminal investigation of him for sales tax violations became known ... Since my arrival at Tyco, I have personally benefited from your advice and support. I particularly appreciate you leading the board to agree not to stand for re-election at the next annual meeting. I know it was not easy, and I am grateful for your efforts. Thanks in an important way to your work, Tyco can now be held up as an example of how the board of an embattled company can, by decisive and selfless action, help restore the confidence of shareholders, investors and the capital markets.

Jack Krol, too, sent me a short but gracious handwritten note after the meeting: 'Thank you for the strong leadership you have provided in the past couple of months. Without it, we would still be stumbling around listening to flowery speeches. You came thru [sic] again yesterday by forcing the board to deal with reality and face the issue of people stepping down before the AGM. We will actually look like decisive leaders to the outside world acting in the best interest of shareholders,' he went on. 'I haven't known you very long, but I've concluded in tough spots I want to be on your team and it's actually fun.'

I was interested and gratified to see that David Boies, in his book *Courting Justice*, published in 2004, also considered that the likes of Josh and myself had emerged with credit from a sorry episode. David wrote of his involvement from April 2002 with Tyco and another US company with similar problems:

In each case we were approached by members of the company's board of directors who had become concerned with indications that their top management might be enriching themselves at the expense of the company and its shareholders ...

With the support of the board we moved faster and more aggressively ... than other companies had done. Each of our two clients was also fortunate to secure the services of talented new management teams who moved proactively to restore employee, customer, and investor confidence; to repair the damage prior executives had done; and to support our cooperation with the government and our civil actions against prior executives.

The result was that both companies were restored to profitability ... Tyco's shareholders in particular saw their stock recover to levels above what it sold at before ...

I would, of course, much rather not have witnessed the events that took place at Tyco in the spring and summer of 2002. Given that they happened, however, I can put my hand on my heart and say that I, and some of my fellow directors, could not have done more for Tyco shareholders in difficult circumstances and I am grateful that David Boies and others have publicly recognised our resolve to limit the damage. I should, of course, acknowledge that my determination to handle this difficult situation well was partly inspired by self-interest. I wanted to protect my own not insignificant shareholding in the company – a stake which would have become virtually worthless if Tyco's reputation had crumbled.

The first trial of 'Deal-a-Day Dennis', as Kozlowski had become known, and Mark Swartz finally ended in farce and acrimony in April 2004. The case against the two men ended in a mistrial after six months of evidence and twelve days of jury deliberations during a hearing that cost an estimated $12 million. Judge Michael Obus said he had 'no choice' but to declare a mistrial after two US news groups identified a seventy-nine-year-old woman juror who had been holding out for acquittal. She had received an anonymous threatening letter after she had reportedly made an 'OK' gesture to the defence team.

Kozlowski and Swartz, who both denied acting illegally, had been accused of stealing hundreds of millions in unauthorised payments, bonuses and secret share sales. It was the scale of the alleged fraud that captured the public's and media's imagination, as well as some of the colourful details of the case. Kozlowski could never be accused of being understated, and the money was allegedly used, among other things, to pay for an infamous $6,000 gold shower curtain and a $15,000 umbrella stand at his New York home – a multi-million-dollar apartment on Fifth Avenue also paid for by Tyco. It was also alleged that Kozlowski had spent £1 million of Tyco's money on a birthday party for his second wife, Karen Mayo, which featured an ice sculpture of Michelangelo's David that delivered vodka from its penis. In July 2004, the Tyco scandal took another turn when Mark Belnick, the company's former general counsel, was acquitted on charges of having stolen millions of dollars in the form of unauthorised bonuses and loans, and then failing to disclose the payments from Tyco.

In June 2005, at the end of a retrial which lasted four months, Kozlowski and Swartz were found guilty of grand larceny, conspiracy and fraud. After eleven days of deliberation, the jury of six men and six women found them guilty of twenty-two of the twenty-three charges – they were found not guilty of just one minor charge of falsifying records.

At the time of writing, both men are due to be sentenced later in the summer of 2005 and face the possibility of long jail sentences, although their lawyers said that they would appeal against the guilty verdicts. Whatever happens in the future, Kozlowski's reputation has been severely damaged and he will never again have a prominent management role with a public company. There is no way back. At his best, however, Kozlowski was an exceptional operator – he could spot a good business to buy and he could cut costs – but the jury's verdicts suggest he had a fatal flaw. He wanted the finer things in life – the multi-million-dollar Manhattan apartment and the $20 million yacht – before he could afford them. He became greedy, and that is what led to his downfall.

Shortly before clinching the Tyco deal – during a party at the Grosvenor House Hotel to celebrate my fiftieth birthday – I told my guests that I was going to move out of the fast lane. I felt I had achieved what I had set out to do in my working life. I had built up and run a large company (ADT), which had at one point employed 120,000 people. I had launched friendly and hostile takeovers on both sides of the Atlantic and my companies had in turn been the target of both sorts of bid. I meant what I said at the time, although many who knew me well doubted whether it was true – and they were right. I suppose I should have known that, when it came to it, I would never relish the prospect of watching from the slower and middle lanes as others passed me by. So – as new business and political challenges have come along – I have remained in the fast lane to this day.

Even while my businesses were expanding in the US, I retained some private companies in the UK, including several cleaning companies. In 1998, I decided to gather my British interests into a public property company called Carlisle Holdings, which was listed on the Alternative Investment Market (AIM), the 'junior' London stock market. Later in 1998, I merged this new company with BHI Corporation, which was already listed in the US on

NASDAQ, the North American electronic stock market. BHI held all my business interests in Belize and Central America dating back to 1987. Today Carlisle Holdings employs more than 35,000 people in facilities, staffing and financial services companies spread from Britain to Belize.

Over the years, I have retained the drive to succeed. Inevitably, of course, I have had to learn to delegate. I have ensured that I have a group of talented, trustworthy and hard-working people around me, and I have gradually become more relaxed in allowing colleagues to have a freer rein on how they do things provided they work within mutually agreed boundaries. I am no longer in quite the same rush and I look at things longer term. I am reluctant to say it, but I have mellowed slightly. A friend once told me that his ambition was to die at the age of ninety-two, shot by a jealous husband. I would not go that far, but I share the belief that you live longer and enjoy life more if you have an active brain. My staff tell me that they have never heard me start a sentence with the words 'When I retire ...' What does retirement mean? If it means that I have nothing to do other than read the newspapers, play a round of golf (not that I have ever had the desire or the time to play golf) or lie on a beach, then retirement is not for me. I cannot even begin to imagine how tedious such a life would be. In any case, although I did not know it at the time, when I sold ADT to Tyco in 1997 it was the start of the most active – and controversial – period of my life.

I am often asked what I consider to be the secret of my business success. Why, people ask, have I succeeded where others have failed? I always feel slightly uneasy answering the question, as I do not want to come over as arrogant and there is, anyway, no short answer to the question. Those who know me well, however, say that my attention to detail has been a crucial factor in my business life. They also say that an unconventional mind and an ability to compartmentalise information have brought their benefits. It is vital to know when to buy and sell a business, but nobody can get it right all of the time. I have a reputation as a formidable buyer and seller of companies. I rely largely on instinct and experience to judge when to buy a company and when is the most advantageous time to sell it. Of course, I do not always get the timing right, Christie's being a good example of where I made the wrong call. There are many others.

I also benefit from my flexibility. Colleagues describe me as a workaholic, but it is not a word I would apply to myself. I prefer the word 'lifeaholic'. I strive to live life to the full and I enjoy dealing with a number of things at the same time. Even when I take a short break from work, there will always be part of every day when I am dealing with things that need sorting out. As long as I can do that for an hour or so on the phone every day, I can switch off. I cannot feel relaxed, however, if I am out of contact, thinking there may be problems that I should be dealing with but about which I know nothing.

I am also intensely self-critical. I am not as hard on any employee as I am on myself. After I have completed a deal, I analyse it in depth. Sometimes, if I have made a substantial amount of money on it, people on both sides of the deal might congratulate me, but if I know I could have done better in a single aspect of it, then it gnaws away at me and I feel unsettled. However, if I have been involved in an especially difficult business situation and I have used all my skill and experience to minimise a loss, this gives me an overwhelming sense of satisfaction. If I have lost money, those involved in the deal are unlikely to congratulate me, but that does not matter: I can walk away from it feeling at peace with myself because I know I simply could not have performed any better.

Modern technology means that I do not have to respect time zones. My business success has enabled me to be even more flexible. I am fortunate enough to have a jet, which is capable of flying more than 4,500 miles without refuelling. This gives me the ability to move across the world faster than just about anyone I know. My two motor yachts are fully equipped with the latest business technology. Although I may be staring at a tropical island or at an ice-sheet breaking into the sea, I am never more than a phone call, an e-mail or a fax away from any deal in any part of the world. In times of business crisis, in fact, I tend to go to one of my boats and ponder how to resolve it. I can maximise my time and step from my bedroom into the study where I work. Even if I sleep for seven hours, I have seventeen hours a day in which to work.

I like to get seven hours' sleep a night – although, if necessary, I can manage on far less for long periods. I am not a natural worrier and I have rarely taken a sleeping pill. A fellow businessman said to me a long time ago: 'If you make a list of your problems today and the problems you had twelve months ago, it will be a different list. From the list made twelve months ago, time will have found an answer to those problems, although not necessarily all to your liking. Therefore you must not worry about your problems today because worry is the interest that you pay on the inevitable.' So, to put it another way, even if something terrible happens in your business life, you know that the storm will eventually pass. The skill of the businessman is to minimise the amount of damage to his company during the storm. One thing is certain: you never have the luxury of just fretting. In times of crisis, a businessman needs to show courage and tenacity coupled with innovative and strategic thinking.

SINCE MY childhood days in Belize, the country has retained a special place in my life. One day, in the early 1980s, I was sorting through some of my old papers when I came across a letter from John Waight, an old schoolfriend, dated 1957 – the year after we had left Belize. I decided to trace John and wrote back to him, thereby discovering that he had become a surgeon in Belize.

I received a swift and friendly reply from John, who insisted that I come back for a visit, and so one weekend in 1982, after a business trip to Miami, I flew down to Belize. I checked in at the Fort George Hotel (now the Radisson Fort George) in Belize City, having already arranged to have dinner with John and his wife. We had a delightful evening and reminisced about old times. Then I rang another old schoolfriend, Barry Bowen, who is one of Belize's leading businessmen, owning the local beer company and many other ventures. I got Barry's secretary on the line and she said she was sorry he was not there, but could she take a message. I said: 'Well, he may not remember me. It's someone from his schooldays: Michael Ashcroft.' The secretary, Mags Jones, replied: 'Michael! I never thought I would hear your voice again.' Within two hours, she was round at my hotel with photographs of us as young children – she had been at my school all those years before. So, within hours of arriving back in Belize, I felt that I had returned home. I knew from that moment that Belize was going to play a prominent role in my life thereafter. I did not know how, but I did know that I was just so happy to be back.

Once I started to spend time in Belize, I began to enjoy it more and more. I felt at ease in the country. If home is where the heart is, then Belize is my home. Today I own a colonial-style house on the seafront in Belize City, just a few hundred yards from where I lived as a boy. I like the pace of life and the warmth of the Belizean people. Belize is a convenient two-hour flight from America and, furthermore, I enjoy a sense of belonging to the country. I am a rootless individual, but when I land in Belize I have that feeling of comfort that I am returning home. That sentiment was reinforced when Said Musa, the Prime Minister of Belize, appointed me the Belizean Ambassador to the United Nations in 1998 – an honorary position of which I was fiercely proud. I was able to carry out the role because I had an able deputy, Stuart Leslie, who conducted the routine workload and stepped in for me when necessary; he eventually succeeded me as Ambassador.

My business interests in Belize began in 1987 when I bought the troubled Belize operations of the Royal Bank of Canada for $1, a venture that I soon renamed the Belize Bank. Over the next decade, I built up an extensive business portfolio in Belize with interests in fruit growing, hotels, power, telecommunications and commercial and residential property, to name only a few. As with my interests in Britain and America, I own, or partly own, both public and private companies.

In 1990, I struck a formal deal with the Belize Government. It came about because the Government approached me and asked why businesses were not investing substantial sums in Belize. I told them that I did not think the incentives for foreign-currency holders were sufficient to attract inward investment, which prompted them to ask me what conditions I would require to invest substantially in Belize. In response to this, I prepared a paper for them setting out what I would need and how I was prepared, under the right conditions, to form a public company and to have all my concessions written into law so that they were entirely transparent. At the same time, this would have created Belize's first listed public company.

The Government liked my proposals. With some minor amendments, they were written into law and Belize Holdings Inc (BHI), now Carlisle Holdings, was created. Like all the best deals, it brought benefits to both sides. The Government agreed that my business interests in Belize – under the umbrella of the parent company – would be exempt from certain taxes for thirty years. In return, the substantial amounts of money that I was prepared to invest in Belize helped stimulate the economy and encourage further investment. Not only did I personally invest more money in Belize but, using Belize Bank, I was also able to lend significant amounts of money to local businessmen. When we bought Belize Bank, it had 16 per cent of the market share of banking in the country. Today that stands at 50 per cent. As the Belize Government had hoped, many other foreigners also started to invest in the country's economy.

My unusual deal, however, brought its own problems within a decade of its being signed. As part of a politically motivated campaign, Clare Short, then the International Development Secretary, and her Labour Party allies decided to put pressure on the Belize Government to renege on our agreement, thereby risking the good name and the economic credibility of the very country they claimed they wanted to help. It was to be another unwelcome twist in the lengthy and bitter battle that lay ahead.

3 The Donor

ALTHOUGH I was not particularly interested in politics as a student, my views developed as I grew older. Britain in the 1970s was a nation in turmoil – indeed, at times I feared it was heading for the knacker's yard. A miners' strike had toppled the Conservative Government of Edward Heath and violent protests made some conclude that with a three-day week the country was becoming ungovernable. As an entrepreneur, I saw myself as a natural supporter of the Tories and their values: endeavour, choice and enterprise. Like the Tories, I believed that the state was the servant of the people – not the other way around.

The Royal Borough of Windsor and Maidenhead is where my involvement in Tory politics began. After completing my education in 1975, I had returned to Maidenhead to live. Later I joined the local Young Conservatives with the hope of somehow becoming involved in mainstream politics. I also attended a branch meeting of the Maidenhead Conservative Party, where I was far and away the youngest person present. It would be hard to imagine a more miserable introduction to politics or the party. I went along to a few meetings and found myself among a group of people with whom I appeared to have little or nothing in common, not least in conversation. I did not feel welcome and none of my questions about how to make progress in the party was answered satisfactorily.

Within a matter of weeks, my interest in politics, other than having fun with the Young Conservatives, had fizzled out. I was ill at ease with the snobbery that I felt prevailed in the party. As someone who was not from one of the traditional public schools nor from the professional classes, I was looked upon as an outsider. At a national level, I also had problems with the make-up of the party. Even after the end of the Second World War, we still had, at one point, a Conservative Government in which the majority of the members of the Cabinet had been to Eton. How could this be a meritocracy? How could a political party be truly open if it was based on such blatant privilege and patronage? It contrasted markedly with my own outlook on life: a man should be judged on his ability and talent, not on his genes or where he went to school. So I drifted away from politics and decided it was not for me. It was to be several years before a grocer's daughter rekindled my interest.

I had admired Margaret Thatcher from afar long before I knew her. I thought that if a grammar school girl from Grantham in Lincolnshire could make it to the top in the Conservative Party then there had to be room for a wider variety of people. I also thought, particularly after her admirable defence of the Falklands, that the time had come to give politics another go. Margaret Thatcher *did* allow people at the top to get there through ability, and the meritocracy which prevails in the Conservative Party today is almost entirely due to her and her leadership. Margaret was single-minded and cut through the nonsense. With the Falklands War, for example, she had a direct approach. She knew that the islands belonged to Britain, the Argentinians had invaded them and therefore, unless they withdrew, Britain would send a force to eject them. Another miners' strike saw her equally decisive. Anticipating a second ugly dispute marred by violent picketing, Margaret resolved to increase the nation's coal stocks. She was determined that Britain would be in a position to survive a long dispute and finally curb the power of militant trade unionism, which had grown too strong for the good of the country.

Events in industries that I knew about also propelled me towards her. For years, many public services were overmanned and run in the producers' interests. Some Conservative-controlled councils wanted to cut costs and raise productivity by scrapping restrictive practices and opening local-government services up to private competition – so-called tendering out. This allowed private firms to bid for work such as street cleaning and school maintenance. Although this was common in other countries, the response in Britain was extraordinary. Strikes and sabotage –

refuse trucks were even set on fire – were just a few of the reactions from left-wing extremists. No country could afford to be governed in this way.

By this time in my life, I had made some money. Not only did I applaud Margaret's leadership, but I wanted to help out financially. My first donation to the party in 1981 was £50,000. By the time Margaret stood down as Prime Minister nine years later, I had contributed a total of £1 million and lent another £3 million. This was the start of a close relationship between a party and a donor, a relationship that was to run smoothly and without controversy for eighteen years – until *The Times* and the Labour Party combined to make some mischief for me.

Margaret was the first of five Tory leaders whom I got to know as part of my long and predominantly happy relationship with the Conservative Party. I was first introduced to her in the early 1980s when I was in my mid-thirties. It was impossible not to be impressed by her drive and leadership, together with her vision and commitment to the party and country that she loved. Over the next two decades, I became friends with her and, even more so, with her husband Denis, who, when we were serving on the board of the same public company, had been responsible for introducing me to her. Shortly before Margaret resigned as Prime Minister in November 1990, I had to meet Denis to discuss some affairs relating to our shared business interests. Because he was particularly busy, he asked me to pop round to see him at 10 Downing Street. We were sitting in the Thatchers' lounge going through some papers when Margaret walked into the room. I immediately got up to greet her but she just said: 'Sit down, sit down. Would you boys like a cup of tea?' It was a strange feeling sitting there while the Prime Minister of the day disappeared into the kitchen, boiled the kettle and poured us tea in silence so as not to disturb our meeting.

In 1991, I had arranged to host a dinner party in London for some friends including Denis. The event coincided with news of the allegations that Laidlaw, the Canadian waste-management company, had made against ADT, when it sued my company for alleged fraud, falsification of accounts and insider dealing. This, in turn, meant that a couple of photographers had been hanging around our home in Belgravia, central London, in order to get a picture of me and anyone interesting who chose to visit me. The photographers had observed caterers coming in and out all day and, suspecting that they would wait around until the evening, I felt it was appropriate to ring up Denis and say that, given the controversy, he might prefer not to attend the dinner party. He replied in a matter-of-fact way: 'My boy, I shall be there at the appointed time. And if the bastards are still there, I will stand on your doorstep and wave to them.' If there was one act of loyalty from Denis that I will never forget, it was this: he considered that friends were there to be supported – not abandoned – in their hour of need.

Margaret remains a colossus in British politics and her courage – personal and political – is unmatched by any of her contemporaries. One has only to imagine how Britain would be today without her resolve and leadership to understand why she deserves to be called our greatest peacetime Prime Minister. As a country, Britain could not have carried on in the direction it was heading before she came to power. It took someone with astonishing willpower and principle to change the course of history, and Margaret Thatcher was that person. She offered people hope, opportunity and a chance to run their own lives. I was keen to support her and her beliefs in every way that I could.

My relationship with John Major, who became party leader in 1990, was as distant as my relationship with Denis and Margaret had been close. I could never build up any warmth or enthusiasm for Major, and nor was I impressed by his leadership: I felt that he was weak and indecisive, and he was prone to bitching and moaning about other people, including senior figures in the party. His message about supporting Conservative principles was long on rhetoric and short on substance.

Indeed, with Major as leader and Chris Patten as Chairman, I became so disillusioned with the way that the party was being led that I sent word through an intermediary that I wanted my £3 million loan to be returned. I did not see why my money should be used to support a leadership that was devoid of purpose and direction. This caused a degree of panic because my request for the money arrived at a time when funds were short. In fact, Patten came to see me to try to persuade me to think again. The meeting was over quickly because by that time I had decided I wanted the loan back and nothing would make me change my mind. I explained to him that I was not satisfied with Major's leadership and that if they wanted that sort of money as a loan they would have to look elsewhere. Patten failed to provide any convincing arguments why I should continue with the loan: the best case he could make was that I was a Conservative Party member and supporter. My reply was that it was perfectly possible for me to continue as a Conservative without lending the party millions of pounds. Shortly afterwards, my loan was returned in full – which, I know, caused some inconvenience to the party. I did not, however, consider that to be my problem. I was not turning my back on the party and indeed I had already decided to contribute £1 million to the Conservative Party in the run-up to the 1997 election. I did not give this money to support Major. Rather, I made the donation despite my belief that he was going to lose the election and I wanted to help minimise the damage to the party and do my best to ensure that the Labour Party, under Tony Blair's leadership, enjoyed only a one-term government. As a result of my donation, I received a standard thank-you letter and invitations to the occasional donors' dinner, where, to be fair, Major came across much better than his public image as the 'Grey Man' might have suggested. Overall, however, he lacked the vigour that was needed to lead the party successfully. When, many years later, it was disclosed that he had pursued a lengthy affair with Edwina Currie, the former Tory junior minister, I frankly thought more of him than I had ever done before – perhaps he had more energy than I had given him credit for.

The 1997 general election result was even worse than I had feared. It was a virtual rout, a disaster for the Conservatives and their worst defeat for a century. Brilliant campaigning by Labour had tarred the party with an image of sleaze and incompetence. When Major stepped down as Tory leader, most of the party's leading heavyweights threw their hats into the ring. There was one notable exception – Michael Portillo had been ruled out before the contest started by voters in his own constituency. The much reduced Tory parliamentary party chose the youngest and most inexperienced of five candidates: William Hague, a thirty-six-year-old from Yorkshire who had been Welsh Secretary in Major's Government.

While many welcomed the prospect of a fresh and energetic leader, others could barely contain their bitterness and resentment at being upstaged. I had never met William Hague before he became party leader in June 1997 and only did so after being introduced by some acquaintances of mine whom he had asked for help. One of these 'wise heads' was Cecil Parkinson, a former Chairman under Margaret Thatcher, whom William persuaded to take up his old role. It was a smart decision: Cecil was clearly not vying for William's job yet he had a wealth of political experience to count upon. His appointment bought time for William to come to his own conclusions about the composition of his Shadow Cabinet. I had first met Cecil in the wake of his resignation as Trade and Industry Secretary in 1983 after details emerged about his private life. We had been introduced by a mutual friend and we hit it off immediately. Cecil is shrewd, articulate and wonderful company, and we have shared some tremendous laughs together over the years.

Another veteran from Margaret Thatcher's days was her party Treasurer, Lord Harris of Peckham, who urged William to appoint his good friend Sir Graham Kirkham as Treasurer. William did so and Graham accepted. At the same time, Cecil asked me, on William's behalf, if I would become the Deputy Treasurer. I was keen to do my bit for the party and so I, too, accepted. As the new treasury team, Graham and I did not exactly get off to a flying start. Because of all his other commitments, Graham was finding it difficult to devote the considerable amount of time his new role demanded. The party was incurring losses; its overheads were bloated; donations were few and far between; and morale was low. Financially, at least, the party was in desperate trouble. William and Cecil were concerned about the lack of progress in turning around the party's financial affairs and in June 1998 they came to the conclusion that I should take over as Treasurer from Graham. At the time, the next election was three or four years away but there was no doubt about the scale of the challenge that lay ahead. If the party had been a private company, its investors would have had to bail it out. Instead, it was left to me to try to dig the party out of the hole in which it found itself. Incidentally, I was pleased later when Graham deservedly received a peerage.

From the day we met, William and I have enjoyed a certain mutual chemistry. Over the years that followed, I have developed immense respect for his abilities and nothing has happened since he stood down as leader to diminish my early assessment of him. As party leader, William had a brilliantly analytical mind, was focused under pressure and always remained calm in a crisis. It was one of the greatest disappointments of my political life that the electorate did not share my belief that William would have made an exceptional Prime Minister. He is a man who would have been a credit to this country in high office and, hopefully, he still will be one day.

I always suspected that it would be extremely difficult for the Conservative Party to win the 2001 election. It would have taken an even greater swing than the record 10 per cent towards the Labour Party in 1997 for us to regain office. My assessment when I took over as Treasurer was that we would need two general elections to regain power. However, I did think that, under William's leadership, we had a realistic chance of reducing the Labour majority substantially. I hoped that this would mean that William would remain as leader and that he would lead the party to victory in the next election.

ONE OF the most appealing traits of American life is the tendency of many wealthy individuals to see it as a part of their civic duty to support charities. There are always causes and campaigns that governments ignore, and many of the best ideas to have emerged from the US have their roots in charities and the freedom to innovate that they provide. In the 1980s, when I started working and living in America, I became a convert to the practice of donating money to worthy and innovative causes.

When Pc Keith Blakelock was murdered in the Broadwater Farm riots of 1985, I was sickened beyond belief. Here was an unarmed police officer – a forty-year-old father of three – simply carrying out his duty in London and yet he was set upon by a vicious mob and hacked to death. I was outraged and wanted to do something. The day after reading about Pc Blakelock's death, I rang Sir Kenneth Newman, the Metropolitan Police Commissioner, and told him that I would like to make an anonymous reward for information leading to Pc Blakelock's killer. Ken said that he did not want to spend my money unnecessarily because officers were closing in on their suspect. Indeed, an arrest and charges soon followed. Our discussion turned to the system by which the police offered rewards for information that might lead to arrests and convictions. It was a broad, imprecise area, and so Ken invited me to lunch at New Scotland Yard for a fuller debate on the subject.

During my travels in the US, I had become aware of Crimestoppers, an initiative started in 1976 in Albuquerque, New Mexico. It enabled members of the public to help prevent and solve crimes by providing information via a special telephone number, and sometimes receiving cash rewards for their efforts. I discussed this initiative with Ken over our lunch and asked if he thought it could work in the UK. Ken, in turn, told me that by coincidence he had been thinking along the same lines and had sent two officers to the US to look into the scheme. His enthusiasm led me to introduce Crimestoppers to the UK. In October 1987, I brought in an experienced executive, Richard Painter, to help set up the project. Thanks to his efforts and the dedication of others it has been an overwhelming success.

Community Action Trust (CAT) was launched as a pilot scheme in the Metropolitan Police area. At the launch party in Westminster, I was joined by Douglas Hurd, who was Home Secretary at the time, and Sir Peter Imbert (now Lord Imbert), who by then had taken over from Ken as Commissioner of the Metropolitan Police. Fortunately for us, Peter shared Ken's enthusiasm for the project and it was a joy to work with him.

Initially, CAT concentrated on preventing crimes against the person. Denis Thatcher was a co-founding trustee and was passionate about the scheme from day one. Anonymity was, and is, the key to its success: callers are not required to identify themselves; their calls cannot be traced; and individuals know that they will never be forced to appear as witnesses in a trial. Crimestoppers seeks to break down the wall of silence that surrounds most crime and which criminals exploit to avoid arrest. The principle of anonymity ensured that those who had information to share – but felt they risked retribution if they went to the police – were suddenly willing to pass it on. I became chairman of the trustees of CAT at its inception, a role I still have to this day. The number, too, remains as it has always been: 0800 555 111.

The Crimestoppers Trust, as CAT was renamed in 1995, required a three-way partnership between the business community, the police and the media. Businesses had to put up the money to finance the scheme, the police had to be prepared to act on the information from the public and the media were needed to highlight the charity's work. Once Crimestoppers had proved it could be successful in the London area, we had to get the rest of the forces throughout the country on board. Some joined willingly, while others dragged their heels.

Denis Thatcher's bugbear was crime and the effect it was having on the average, law-abiding citizen. He loved the fact that Crimestoppers gave the man in the street the means to fight back. He rarely missed the opening of a new force initiative and even agreed to attend the Strathclyde launch in Glasgow, despite the fact that the city was hardly the natural centre of support for the Tory Party and fans of his beloved Margaret were few and far between. Denis, however, was Denis: at one point during the launch reception he turned to Richard Painter and said in a loud voice: 'Hey, this place is full of lefties.' At the launch in Avon and Somerset, he agreed to be filmed and photographed riding on a police motorcycle, which inevitably brought huge media coverage at national and local level.

Region by region, Crimestoppers spread throughout the UK over a four-year period, and Denis was always an enthusiastic trouper for the cause. On one occasion, he appeared at the launch of a campaign called SNAP – Say No And Phone – at the Ministry of Sound, a London nightclub. The campaign was aimed at young people and encouraged them not only to turn down offers of drugs but also to report dealers to the police. Some T-shirts had been specially prepared for the launch and Denis was given one with the Ministry of Sound logo on the front and a picture of him superimposed on it with just one word underneath: 'Den'. I suspect that Denis had rarely, if ever, been called 'Den' during his adult life, but he accepted the T-shirt – and his newly abbreviated name – with good grace and humour.

Since its inception in the UK, Crimestoppers has received more than 753,000 calls leading to more than 67,400 arrests, together with the recovery of property worth more than £88.1 million and drugs worth almost £118 million. The charity is busier than ever and now receives an average of 6,500 calls a month which lead to almost 575 arrests. Each week there is an average of sixty-one arrests for drug offences and one for murder or attempted murder. It is fascinating that independent research has shown that two-thirds of the offenders identified through Crimestoppers were either unknown to the police or not suspected of involvement in the crime in question. If information leads to the suspected offender being charged, the caller is entitled to a reward, which is paid anonymously. In practice, only 4 per cent of callers seek a reward – or, to put it another way, more than nineteen out of twenty people contacting Crimestoppers with useful information are motivated by reasons other than personal financial benefit.

Rewards for information are relatively small, ranging in most cases up to a maximum of £1,000 which might be given for a murder or a serious sexual assault down to £50 for a petty burglary. Those who help Crimestoppers include convicted criminals, who see its Freefone number on posters in prisons up and down the country. The confidential nature of the Crimestoppers operations prevents me from disclosing the identity of the big-name criminals who have been brought to justice largely or partly due to the charity's work. However, one notorious serial rapist, who had no previous convictions, was caught solely because a neighbour rang our Freefone number with her suspicions and revealed where the man, who was unknown to the police, could be arrested. DNA tests proved her suspicions to be accurate and he is now behind bars. Over the years, I have contributed nearly £5 million towards supporting Crimestoppers. I am proud of its achievements. It helps empower the community and harnesses the support of the public in the fight against crime. It remains the only national charity in the UK that helps to *solve* crime.

Even now individual crimes occasionally appal me so much that I feel I cannot simply sit back and do nothing. Over the years, I have underwritten several substantial rewards through Crimestoppers that to this day have remained anonymous. I do not intend to break that anonymity now. My role in one high-profile case did, however, become public knowledge. I was profoundly shocked by the murder of Jill Dando, the television presenter, in April 1999. I did not know Jill but I was horrified that an innocent person could be shot outside her home in the middle of the day. Through the police I put up an anonymous reward of £50,000 for information leading to her killer's conviction. My role would not have been known to this day had William Hague not mentioned it in a letter to Tony Blair in which he defended my role in public life. His letter was later made available to newspapers and so my role in the case became widely known.

There is no crime that disgusts me more than the abuse of a child. I became shocked by how easy it had become for paedophiles to use the internet to target unsuspecting girls and boys. A recent NOP survey reported that three in every four children between the ages of seven and sixteen now have access to the internet. In 2003, I gave £200,000 for a new initiative between Crimestoppers and the Metropolitan Police. Safer Surfing was launched in October of that year and its aim is to make children aware of the dangers posed by internet chatrooms. As with Crimestoppers, I hope the Safer Surfing initiative will eventually become nationwide.

Just as I do not like to invest substantial amounts of money in businesses that I do not control, I rarely donate large sums to charities or good causes in which I have no involvement. I favour a hands-on approach and insist on driving a project forward rather than giving money to a charity and risk watching the money either being frittered away or remaining stagnant in a bank account. Similarly, I do not give significant amounts of money to charities if I have little or no interest in the causes that they are working to help. Law and order, however, is a subject close to my heart and so, too, is education.

DESPITE – OR perhaps even because of – my own academic failings as a schoolboy, I am a staunch believer in the value of a sound education. All too often it is the poorly educated, the illiterate and those who have dropped out of school who drift into crime. I am convinced, however, that schools and colleges need to gear their teaching more effectively to the realities of a student's future working life. I have therefore devoted time and money to this end.

Mid-Essex Technical College, the scene of my HND course in business studies when I was in my late teens, has returned to play a part in my life again only relatively recently. Since my student days, the college has been incorporated with Anglia Polytechnic University (APU). In 1999, I was invited back to APU to meet the college's management over lunch. I arrived early on a warm, sunny day in order to wander around Chelmsford and revisit all my old haunts – everywhere from the house where I lived to the pub, the Railway Tavern, where I drank. I was rather surprised and amused to discover that I was an alumnus of a university without ever having taken a degree. I liked what I saw and I eventually made a substantial commitment to APU totalling more than £5 million. This support enabled APU to construct the Ashcroft International Business School, which was officially opened by the Earl of Wessex in May 2003.

It is one of the largest business schools in the country with 3,000 pupils and 80 full-time staff. I hope the school will succeed in encouraging enterprise and excellence, and will inspire a new generation of entrepreneurs. As part of my continuing support, since 2001 I have paid for three Belizean students aged from seventeen to twenty-one to enrol at the business school each year. These young men and women, many of whom live in remote rural villages and have never left Belize, are being academically and socially challenged and, without exception, have adapted well to their new lives. APU has been equally generous to me. In 1999, the university held a ceremony at which it awarded me an honorary doctorate in recognition of my international achievements in business. In November 2001, I was invested as Chancellor of APU, in succession to Lord Prior, the former Conservative Cabinet minister.

APU may have been my biggest venture in the world of education, but it was not my first. Years earlier, I had helped pay for a new college to be set up on a derelict site in Putney, south-west London. I had come up with the idea of funding a college in 1989. At the time, industry was complaining about the quality of students leaving school. Kenneth Baker, the then Secretary of State for Education and Science, was an astute politician and he threw the ball back into industry's court. He asked businessmen to invest in secondary education and help fund the sort of colleges that they wanted to see as well as help run them. I had a meeting with Ken and told him that I wanted to build a college which was imaginative and forward thinking. The objective of the new college was to recruit youngsters of secondary-school age who had a special aptitude for technology. We had a leaflet drop in south-west London in December 1990 and got an overwhelming response. As this was ten months before the college opened it was still a building site with half-built rooms. It required a great leap of faith on the part of the students and their parents to believe that we were actually going to be ready for the following September.

The college broke with the conventions of the time. We created the school around a longer-than-normal working day. We realised that we were in a London suburb where most parents were working and we were concerned that youngsters should have the opportunity to stay at school for the duration of the normal working day. We therefore kept the school open from 7.30 a.m. to 5.30 p.m. every weekday and offered breakfast for those who arrived early before school commenced at 8.30 a.m. This meant that we were not only providing an education for the children but also supporting hard-working parents. We also operated a five-term rather than a three-term year. Our aim was essentially to have five terms of eight weeks each, with a two-week break in between most terms and a four-week break over the summer. Research had indicated that both pupils and teachers got tired towards the end of a sixteen- or seventeen-week term and this was a way of refreshing them once they started to flag. Of course, it created some problems, particularly when families had other children at schools with three terms, but overall it worked well and the academic results began to speak for themselves. We paid our teachers slightly more than the going rate, partly because they had to work forty weeks a year rather than the standard thirty-eight, but also because we wanted to attract bright, energetic and highly motivated staff.

ADT College, named after my former company, was founded in September 1991 and it was one of fifteen city technology colleges built and opened between 1989 and 1995. The college cost £13 million to build. ADT contributed £2.75 million to its construction and I have continued my support for it ever since.

Today ADT College provides a free education for more than 1,000 children aged from eleven to eighteen. I wanted the college to be run like a business, with a Director of Finance and Administration handling much of the administrative side so that the Principal could concentrate on what he or she does best – helping the children to receive a good education. Children of all abilities and a wide range of ethnic backgrounds come from all over southwest London and, now that the college is up and running, it is mainly funded by the Department for Education and Skills. I have been chairman of the trustees of ADT College since its inception. I am thrilled with the way the college has turned out. It is hugely oversubscribed every year and has regularly been the best-performing state school in the area. The college's most recent Ofsted report is full of praise for the way that it is run. 'This is a highly effective and successful college with excellent leadership,' it concludes.

I have also been heavily involved in charity work in Belize and I have given around £3 million to charitable projects there. Most of that money has been used to set up the Information, Technology and Teaching Programme for the Children of Belize. I was concerned that youngsters in secondary schools did not have access to computers. Once again, I got Richard Painter to help set up the project, which he did between 1992 and 1996. We installed computer laboratories, with all the necessary support equipment, in thirteen high schools throughout the country. This was not always as straightforward as it seemed. One of the schools chosen for a laboratory had no electricity: children were literally taught by candlelight if there was insufficient daylight. We said, nevertheless, that we were happy to supply the equipment if the Government provided the electricity. So, today, the students at the school have both electricity and computers. Teachers in Belize were, of course, not familiar with computers, so we paid for staff from ADT College in London to travel to Belize to teach them the new skills so they could pass them on to their pupils. In short, we used one of our schools in Britain to help another in Belize.

As in Britain, I have been keen to support education pro-jects in Belize. I have paid for basic library books at schools in the poorer areas of the country and provided the training for the teachers using the new facilities. It has meant that thousands of children have had access to hundreds of books – non-fiction and fiction – to help them with their schooling. There were countless other projects too, including the Michael A. Ashcroft Stadium in the town of Independence. It is one of the best sports stadiums in Belize and is used for soccer and other sports. I provided funding for hospital incubators in Belize City, the construction of the Be-lize Arts Centre in Belize City and a basketball court in the town of Ladyville. In addition, I have helped fund an orphanage and a drug-abuse centre, both in Belize City, and the local version of Crimestoppers.

I have also supported other projects in the Caribbean out-side Belize. In 1993, I set up the Ashcroft School in the Turks and Caicos Islands, where I have some small business interests. It is an independent, fee-paying infants and primary school which takes children from the age of two to twelve. I am the chairman of the trustees and it is a mixed-ability school with high levels of attainment, on the island of Providenciales. It began when I had bought some land for property development, which included a school that did not have a particularly good reputation. We decided to transform and upgrade the school. I have since given nearly £500,000 to the school, some of which has been used to build two new blocks of classrooms and a computer laboratory and recruit new teaching staff to come over from England.

My charity work brought me into contact with many wonderful people. One of them was Diana, Princess of Wales, and I got to know her well. She was attractive, energetic and fun. I enjoyed her company and we shared what some people might look upon as a rather childish sense of humour. If my fondness for her was reciprocated, it was because I was unconventional and said what I thought in contrast to the yes-men who, perhaps inevitably, surrounded her.

I first met her at a charity function in the late 1980s. I still squirm in embarrassment at the memory. My mouth must have been operating faster than my brain – some would say not for the first or last time. As we were preparing to go in to dinner, there was a group of half-a-dozen men listening to her talk about the unfair criticism that the Prince of Wales received from the media. She said that if Prince Charles tried to do something he was criticised, if he failed to do something he was criticised, and he was therefore in an impossible position. 'Who, at the end of the day, would want his job?' she asked. To which I replied in what were virtually my first words to her: 'I certainly wouldn't, ma'am, with the possible exception of between midnight and 6 a.m.' The Princess blushed a delicious shade of pink and giggled sweetly. I suppose I had felt intuitively that someone surrounded by pomp and formality all her life might appreciate a risqué comment that others might find offensive. As we walked in to dinner, the other men in the group flashed me glances as if to say: 'I think you got away with that one.'

I went on to attend many charity events with the Princess over the years and we enjoyed a warm friendship. I was honorary president of the London City Ballet at a time when Princess Diana was the patron. On one occasion, ADT arranged a joint initiative at a greyhound track with the London City Ballet. We were sitting next to each other in the grandstand at Wembley dog track in north-west London and the Princess had been laughing and joking all evening. After one race, she was required to go down on to the track to present the trophy to the owner of the greyhound that had won the ADT Stakes. The Princess handed the prize to the owner and was standing behind the winning greyhound with me next to her. I said to her under my breath: 'Ma'am, it's a tradition at this point that you lift the tail of the winning greyhound.' She reached forward with one hand and, when it was more than halfway to the dog's tail, I whispered again: 'I am only joking, ma'am.' At this point, her outstretched hand slipped back smartly to its original position. We made our way back to the grandstand via the stairway and, once we could no longer be seen by the crowd, Diana sat down on one of the steps and burst into hysterical laughter. 'You won't believe what he nearly made me do,' she told her senior aides, pointing at me. Shortly afterwards, her royal chaperones spoke sternly to my wife and urged her to 'control' me.

I was devastated to learn of the Princess's death in August 1997 in a car crash in Paris. I was in Belize at the time and someone in my London office rang me up to break the news. I found it almost impossible to grasp what had happened and to comprehend why the life of such a vibrant young woman should have been cut short. I had last seen her a few months earlier when she had been in tremendous form and looking to the future. As I began to take in the enormity of the event, I felt sad and, later, angry that she had died in such an unnecessary way. I will always admire the Princess's positive attitude to her work, her disregard for pointless conventions and her desire to test the boundaries. I flew to Britain to attend her funeral at Westminster Abbey. The evening before, I had urgent business matters to deal with, but, after working long into the night, my thoughts naturally turned to the Princess. I took a walk – it was by then 3 a.m. – down the Mall towards Buckingham Palace where hundreds of people were camping overnight in order to gain the best vantage point from which to see the funeral procession. Many of the mourners had lit candles, and it was a mood of tranquil grief that I have never come across before and I suspect that I never will again. I found the funeral service itself, particularly Sir Elton John's rendition of 'Candle in the Wind', powerfully moving. It was a reminder that when life itself is so fragile, we need to use every moment to the full.

4 Rough Waters

LONG BEFORE I started giving large amounts of money to the Conservative Party on a regular basis, a small section of the media had come to the conclusion that I could not have been so successful in business without being, at best, sharp and, at worst, corrupt. Some thought I was simply too brash – it is true that at one time I did drive a Rolls-Royce. I am sure that some of my critics thought that it was only a matter of time before details of my supposedly dubious past emerged.

I have to admit that, unlike other businessmen of my generation, I chose not to court the media. I preferred to concentrate my time and energies on growing my companies and maximising my profits rather than spending long, boozy lunches with business journalists in order to encourage favourable publicity. As my companies got larger, however, my name started appearing more frequently in the business pages of national newspapers. There was the occasional mischievous pop at me in a business diary column, probably inspired by a rival or a City source who had taken exception to my unconventional way of doing things. Throughout the 1990s, my name also appeared with increasing regularity in *Private Eye*, the satirical magazine. For some inexplicable reason, Michael Gillard, a regular contributor to the magazine under the byline Slicker, relished the prospect of making trouble for me.

Trying to deal with scurrilous stories in *Private Eye* had defeated wiser men than me over the years. If you sue the magazine, you are liable to be ridiculed or branded a bad sport. If you do nothing, you allow inaccurate stories to go uncorrected and, sometimes, even to gather momentum. With hindsight, I was probably too laid back in my approach to *Private Eye*. I allowed myself to be persuaded by my legal advisers that the magazine had a limited circulation, that readers did not treat its accusations seriously and that to get lawyers involved would have encouraged even more mischievous articles about me.

After I had been appointed party Treasurer in June 1998 and after being nominated for a peerage by William Hague in early 1999, the stakes became higher. I had switched from being a private individual to being a public figure for the first time in my life. Before taking on the job of Treasurer, I had understood and accepted that I could expect greater media scrutiny than I had experienced before. Nobody, however, could have imagined the scale and the persistence of the attack that lay ahead.

Establishing exactly where my story begins is difficult. There is a sense in which it starts independently in at least four places: the middle of the North Sea; Atlanta, Georgia; the 'village' of Westminster; and the offices of *The Times* in Wapping, east London. Whether things would have played out quite so dramatically if any of the four had been missing, I can only guess. What I can say with certainty, however, is that during late 1998 and early 1999 fate dealt me a tricky hand.

MY STAR sign is Pisces. I am not a great believer in the value of horoscopes but, if there is something to them, then the planets must have been totally in the wrong place on 25 April 1998. At 3.21 a.m. British summer time, the MV *Rema*, a Belize-registered freighter heading from Berwick-upon-Tweed in Northumberland for Terneuzen in the Netherlands, slid silently below the surface of the North Sea. The ship, which had been built in the Netherlands in 1976, took with her a cargo of thousands of tonnes of stone chippings and her four-strong British crew, who perished without trace.

There was no obvious reason for the disaster. The weather was generally good, with south-westerly winds blowing between force three and force four. There was no appreciable moonlight but visibility was good and the seas were calm. Yet, without warning and twenty-two miles out to sea from Whitby, the *Rema* plunged bow first to the seabed. The vessel sank so quickly that none of the crew was able to send a call for help or get into a life-raft. A search-and-rescue operation was launched but without success, and it was assumed the ship had sunk and the crew had drowned. The location of the ship was identified the next day on the seabed. The loss of life was a tragedy, but the sinking initially received little coverage in the national newspapers.

It was not until nearly a year later that one newspaper – the *Sunday Express* – began to show a significant interest in the story. By this time, I was Treasurer of the Conservative Party. The *Sunday Express* had discovered that – in the woolly language that journalists favour – I was 'linked' to the *Rema*. I found it bizarre that I was suddenly coming under personal scrutiny. I did not own the ship – indeed I had never heard of it. I did not employ the crew and knew nothing about their work. I did, however, own 70 per cent of a company called Belize Holdings Inc (BHI), which, in turn, had bought a 50 per cent share in Belize International Services (BIS) that, in turn, had a contract to run the shipping register in Belize. It was for this reason alone that the *Rema* was to play a significant part in my life.

The shipping register to which I was 'linked' is called the International Merchant Marine Registry of Belize (IMMARBE). BIS was responsible for registering merchant vessels for IMMARBE in return for an initial fee and, after that, an annual fee. Given the size and nature of my international business interests, it is hardly surprising that I had no involvement in the day-to-day running of BIS. The company had, in any case, assigned the job of running the register to Morgan & Morgan, a law firm. In business terms, I had a 'passive' interest – one, incidentally, that I later sold. My company BHI had supported efforts to improve BIS's safety standards, a process which even critics of the register acknowledge was under way at the time the *Rema* sank. BIS wanted to tackle criticisms – in some cases they may even have been justified – that Belize and other countries had a 'flag of convenience'.

The sinking of the *Rema* had occurred outside British territorial waters, but IMMARBE nevertheless asked the British-based Marine Accident Investigation Branch (MAIB) to conduct an inquiry into the incident on its behalf. This meant that not only would the investigation be thorough, but it would be impossible for critics to claim that IMMARBE was seeking to cover up the cause of the accident. On 16 June 1998, the investigation began and it was later upgraded to an inspector's inquiry, which is even more thorough.

If the *Sunday Express* had chosen to take an objective, albeit belated, look at the sinking of the *Rema*, I would have had no complaints. My grievance arose when the newspaper, then edited by Rosie Boycott – an ultra-liberal who as editor of the *Independent on Sunday* had campaigned for the legalisation of cannabis – implied that I had blood on my hands. The *Sunday Express* had come to the remarkable conclusion that I must have been personally responsible for the loss of life. Not only that, but the newspaper wanted to make out that I had a track record as being careless – even totally irresponsible – with human lives.

So, fully eleven months after the sinking of the *Rema*, the first highly prominent and totally negative articles about me – three in the same issue – were published in the news and comment pages of a national newspaper. By any standards, the *Sunday Express*'s articles of 28 March 1999 represented an all-out assault on me. There was a short front-page article headlined 'Top Tory and ships of shame'. The 'full story', as the paper billed it on page 1, appeared on pages 10 and 11 under the headline 'The Tory tycoon, a flag of convenience and the freighter lost with all hands'. There were four journalists bylined on the article, including my old tormentor Michael Gillard. It was unusual for Gillard to be linked publicly to a story about me because he preferred the anonymity of his platform in *Private Eye*.

It was, however, the newspaper's comment page that went ludicrously over the top. The *Sunday Express* carried a leader article under the headline 'Shipping cash shames Tories' which ran to four paragraphs:

The Conservative Party sometimes seems to lurch from one public relations fiasco to the next with barely a pause for breath in between. The news that their treasurer Michael Ashcroft – the man who has given so much money to them that he is said effectively to own the party – profits from the licensing of unseaworthy and dangerous ships which are killing hundreds of people is disastrous for party bosses at Smith Square.

The cheap licensing of unsafe vessels is an international issue for the simple reason that ships do not stay at home. They need not even 'live' in the country where they are registered. A shipping disaster can endanger the lives and environment of people around the world.

The flag Mr Ashcroft profits by, from Belize in central America, has an appalling safety record.

Tory party bosses cannot defend a situation where they are being funded by a man who earns money from a practice which takes these risks. They ought not to accept this funding as long as he profits from a flag of convenience described by the International Transport Workers' Federation as one of the 'shabbiest, shoddiest and most unscrupulous' in the world.

This was not comment, of course – it was a direct attack. Quite apart from the ridiculous suggestion that I effectively owned the Conservative Party, the article was as inaccurate as it was libellous. I found the *Sunday Express*'s claims deeply offensive and distressing. It was utter nonsense that the Belize register was licensing unseaworthy and dangerous ships that were killing hundreds of people. The facts were a matter of public record and easily available. I discovered that between 1989 and 1999, fewer than twenty people had died in accidents on Belize-registered ships and that included the four crew who perished on the *Rema*. This meant that an average of less than two people were dying in accidents each year – a record which compared favourably with any register in the world. Working at sea can be hazardous, particularly for those in fishing vessels. This means that, even with the most stringent safety measures, people occasionally die carrying out their work.

The allegations by the *Sunday Express* were so serious and unacceptable that I could not allow them to go uncorrected. I

initially decided, however, to seek a low-key solution to my grievance rather than instruct libel lawyers. I was hopeful that we could
remedy the inaccuracies without the need for costly and lengthy
legal action. I wrote a courteous, private letter to Boycott pointing out the offensiveness of the claim that I profited from the
'licensing of unseaworthy and dangerous ships which are killing
hundreds of people'. I said I found that statement 'particularly
hurtful and outrageous. Any death at sea is tragic, but it is quite
untrue to suggest that ships registered in Belize have suffered a
greater proportion of fatalities than those registered elsewhere. It
is also irresponsible of you to suggest that casualties are necessarily
the fault of those who merely manage the register.' I then pointed
out the true figures for the Belize register before telling Boycott
that I was seeking a retraction and apology or 'I will reluctantly
instruct my solicitors to take the necessary action'. I felt that,
given the nature of the newspaper's grossly defamatory article, I
could hardly have been more restrained and I expected the newspaper to climb down immediately.

Not a bit of it. The response I received was from the *Express's*
legal department rather than from Boycott herself. The lawyers
tried to defend the paper's indefensible comments, but this was
my first significant legal skirmish with a national newspaper and I
was not going to back down. So I too instructed my lawyers and,
four weeks to the day after publishing its original article, the newspaper admitted the error of its ways and published an apology on
25 April 1999 – appropriately the first anniversary of the *Rema's*
sinking – under the headline 'Michael Ashcroft'. It concluded:
'We are happy to set the record straight, withdraw the allegation
and apologise for any embarrassment caused.' As with the majority of newspaper apologies, the prominence – or lack it – meant
that the statement did not redress the damage caused by the original article. This is not accidental. Newspapers depend on the
trust of their readers and they feel that conspicuous apologies tarnish the product. It is only because they are largely self-regulated
– by the Press Complaints Commission – that they can get away
with this. I chose, however, to accept the apology rather than
to seek the damages to which I was undoubtedly entitled. With

hindsight – and to deter others – I should perhaps have pressed the case to a more crushing conclusion.

The articles in the *Sunday Express* enabled the Labour Party to make political capital out of the controversy. They also encouraged other journalists and politicians who opposed me to look more deeply into my business interests, especially my role in the shipping register.

John Prescott, the Deputy Prime Minister and a former merchant seaman, is never slow to seize the chance to land a blow on an opponent – metaphorically on this occasion. In a speech to the United Nations in New York on 22 April 1999, he said: 'All my life as a seafarer and a politician, I have campaigned against the abuses of flags of convenience, which have cost thousands of seafarers' lives.' Although he did not identify me by name, he said that Belize had the worst record in Europe, America and Canada for ships being detained as unseaworthy after inspection by port officials. I would concede than in the early days of the register, which was set up in 1993, some ships were on the register that ought not to have been, but it was not me – or my company – that was running it. As so often, Prescott was simply making a cheap jibe for political gain. Furthermore, Prescott flouted the convention that if a politician is going to criticise another country in the United Nations he should warn that nation in advance.

I was hopeful that the apology in the *Sunday Express* would encourage other newspapers to act responsibly and treat my tenuous involvement with the Belize shipping register with caution. In reality, I had more hope of winning the National Lottery without buying a ticket. At the height of the campaign against me by *The Times*, for example, other newspapers decided to jump on the bandwagon, trawling through old cuttings and shipping records in an attempt to embarrass me. Some of the stories on my interest in the shipping register were ludicrous as the left-wing media sought to heap guilt by association upon me. 'Cocaine seized on ships in Tory chief's list' was the headline to a story in the *Observer* on 18 July 1999. The paper had 'discovered' – I use the word loosely – that back in 1994 United States customs had seized two ships sailing under the Belize flag. On one ship was 209lb of cocaine hidden under animal manure and on another was 4,300lb of the same drug hidden in the hold.

So not only was I meant to be personally responsible for the safety requirements of all ships flying the Belizean flag, but now a newspaper was suggesting that I was personally responsible for the legality of every pound of cargo that they carried. It was a discreditable piece of journalism unworthy of the newspaper's fine traditions. Only the sixteenth and final paragraph of the article told the true story: 'There is no suggestion that Ashcroft knew of the purpose to which ships on the register were being put.' Of course, by this time the damage had been done. The story was a classic case of a newspaper putting two and two together and making at least seventeen. Shipping registers are not tasked with monitoring smuggling activities – this is the job of national and international law enforcement agencies.

The unfair and inaccurate stories relating to the sinking of the *Rema* brought me, William Hague and the Conservative Party months of embarrassment. Yet the tragedy was to have a further serious implication for me. During the first year of my tenure as party Treasurer, William Hague had privately told me that he was going to nominate me as a working peer. This was, he said, in recognition of my work and support for the Conservative Party. He particularly wanted to acknowledge publicly his gratitude for my work as Treasurer which, although time-consuming and pressurised, is of course unpaid. When William told me of his intentions, I was enormously flattered: I especially welcomed the opportunity of a seat in the House of Lords because it would enable me, in due course, to participate in a debate on any issue of the day and to have the sort of voice that was impossible in my more conciliatory role as party Treasurer.

Under the unwritten conventions of the British constitution, the leader of the Opposition is permitted by the Prime Minister of the day to nominate a small number of people for a working peerage. At the time, each nominee was, in turn, considered by the Honours Scrutiny Committee, a small all-party body. The committee consisted of Lord Hurd of Westwell, the former Tory Foreign Secretary; Baroness Dean of Thornton-le-Fylde, the former trade union leader; and Lord Thomson of Monifieth, of the Liberal Democrats. The aim of the committee was to ensure that all nominees were fit and proper people to hold a seat in the Upper House. This process was, by tradition, highly secretive but, provided there were no objections, the Prime Minister then approved the nominations made by the Opposition leader and recommended the appointment to the Sovereign. If, however, a nominee was turned down, he or she was not formally given the reason or reasons and, furthermore, had no right of appeal.

The official report into the sinking of the *Rema* was not due to be published until early 2000, but I discovered that the possibility that I would be criticised was being cited by the Honours Scrutiny Committee as the principal – but from my point of view unanswerable – reason why it had been unable to approve my peerage recommendation from William Hague. I learned that the other three reasons given in May 1999 were that I was a tax exile, that I was the Belizean Ambassador to the United Nations and that I had allegedly underwritten the finances of the Conservative Party. Yet again, it seemed that the planets were firmly in the wrong place for me.

ON 24 April 1998 – by chance the very day before the *Rema* sank – a British freelance television reporter called Toby Follett, who was then twenty-eight years old, had arrived in Atlanta, Georgia. Follett was there to make a low-budget television documentary for Channel 4 about international crime and the way in which the drugs business used expensive works of art to launder money.

In 1992, the United States Department of Justice – in the shape of its Drug Enforcement Administration (DEA) – had launched an operation through its Atlanta division. Called Operation Dinero, it targeted various aspects of drug trafficking and money laundering in Central and South America. DEA investigators set up a number of front businesses, including a bank in Anguilla, British West Indies. These businesses offered a range of under-the-counter money-laundering services to drug-trafficking groups, including loans, cashiers' cheques, wire transfers and peso exchanges, as well as the facility to establish holding companies and shell corporations. Taken in by the subterfuge, the Cali mafia – the Colombian gangsters widely regarded as running the world's biggest illegal-drugs organisation – engaged the bank to sell paintings by Picasso, Rubens and Reynolds with a combined value of $15 million. They had been bought with 'dirty' money, and the ultimate objective – the essence of money laundering – was to end up with some 'clean' money. Over a period of three years, Operation Dinero resulted in eighty-eight arrests in the United States, Spain, Italy and Canada and the seizure of nine tonnes of cocaine, together with the impounding of more than $50 million in cash and other property.

Follett was interested in Operation Dinero and, no doubt sensing the opportunity of some favourable public relations, the DEA seconded a junior Atlanta-based analyst called Jonathan Randel to assist in the agency's dealings with Follett's television crew. Randel had joined the DEA in May 1992 as an intelligence analyst, a job title that was later changed to 'intelligence research specialist'. Randel, who it appeared was keen to seek a career path outside the DEA, struck up a friendship with Follett during the filming and shared with him his secret ambition to break into the movie business. He also told Follett that he had access to some confidential, and potentially interesting, databases on numerous prominent people. One of these was called NADDIS: the Narcotics and Dangerous Drugs Information System.

NADDIS is a confidential DEA computer database on which are stored hundreds of millions of items of information relating to up to five million people. The vast majority of these people are law-abiding citizens who, for various reasons ranging from the places to which they have travelled to the people they have met, have come to the DEA's attention. The purpose of the database is to collate and cross-reference ostensibly unconnected information in order to try to identify links and establish leads to possible suspects. The DEA is acutely aware of the potential damage if data from the system should fall into the wrong hands, and access to it is strictly controlled, supposedly on a need-to-know basis. Those working for the DEA understand that if sensitive information on agents, informants and the like were to be misappropriated it could do untold damage to secret operations and even lead to loss of life.

In theory, the guidelines to those drawing up the NADDIS register, which was started in 1974, say that it should not be cluttered 'with information of no practical value'. However, most individuals, companies and organisations on the index are not suspected of involvement in criminal activity. This means that the NADDIS system has become an enormous repository of often insignificant and inaccurate information.

In Randel, Follett had found a new and valuable 'contact' who was prepared to exploit his privileged position in the DEA to divulge confidential information. In late 1998, after Follett had returned to Britain, he asked Randel to run checks on a number of well-known British figures including Mark Thatcher, the businessman son of the former Prime Minister, and Tim (Lord) Bell, the senior advertising and public relations consultant. Another of the names that he ran through was mine and – bingo – it showed up. My name appeared on several occasions in various NADDIS files while, presumably, the other names did not.

Given the nature of my lifestyle and the Central American location of many of my businesses, I now know that it is not surprising that my name was contained within NADDIS. When I initially learned this fact, however – courtesy of *The Times* in the summer of 1999 – I was somewhat surprised. NADDIS sounded so official and daunting that I was at first concerned that I was somehow – and mistakenly of course – under some sort of investigation. I was to discover several months later, however, that the 'exclusive' club boasting a NADDIS number included Sir Denis Thatcher, Crimestoppers and the London City Ballet. They and millions like them had been added to the register in the same way that I had been – innocently and unknowingly because of their tenuous connection with someone already on the database: in the case of Denis, Crimestoppers and the ballet company because of their links to me. I eventually realised that having a DEA record and a NADDIS number were not something about which I should get too excited.

Excitement, however, was exactly the reaction of Follett when he was told by Randel that my name appeared on NADDIS files. To Follett, it was as if all his Christmases had come at once. Indeed, he plainly got so excited that any concerns he should have had about Randel compromising his position and breaking the law passed him by. Between 9 February 1999 and the end of June of the same year, Randel queried the name 'Ashcroft' no fewer than seventy-four times in the NADDIS system. During that period, he also accessed countless files on some of my associates, as well as other files he suspected might be related to me and my companies.

Randel was taking a big gamble with his 'freelance' research. At the time, he was working on the West African desk of the DEA. His analytical work should have been restricted to checks on people and businesses with links to West Africa – I had none unless you count my visits to Eastern Nigeria in the late 1950s as a schoolboy visiting my parents. Randel had no reason or justification for searching files that related to me. Besides he should have known – or would have been able to find out – that there was no official investigation into me or my companies and that I had never been suspected by the DEA of committing any offence. Randel should also have realised that, every time he searched for a name or a topic in the DEA's database, it left a 'fingerprint' on the computer system that could be traced back to him. He was playing for high stakes: if he was discovered abusing the system, he would lose his job and could even face criminal prosecution. Furthermore, if Randel had genuine concerns about any aspect of my business or personal affairs, he could, and indeed should, have reported it to his superiors – something he never did.

Randel, however, seemed oblivious to both the carelessness and the illegality of his actions. He happily sent copies of the relevant references to Follett who, in turn, used them to try to encourage Fulcrum Productions, a large independent television production company, to persuade Channel 4 to commission a documentary. Follett was emphatic that 'Ashcroft and the drugs trade' would make entertaining viewing, and Channel 4 expressed enough initial interest for them to give him some modest funding so that he could return to America to conduct further research.

On 28 April 1999, a year after his first meeting with Follett and three days after the *Sunday Express* was apologising to me over its article on the *Rema*, Randel flew from Atlanta to Los Angeles international airport, a distance of 2,000 miles across four time zones. There he met Follett, who had flown in from London. The two men stayed in a hotel in Los Angeles before hiring a car and driving together to Phoenix, Arizona, a distance of 560 miles each way. It was here that they began investigating a convicted American drugs trafficker, Thomas Ricke, who had been instrumental in the importation of ten tonnes of marijuana into the United States and had subsequently laundered nearly $700,000 of the proceeds through Belize. This is where they imagined that I came into the story, although in fact they crucially chose to misinterpret or ignore one vital element of the evidence that 'linked' me to Ricke, who was jailed in 1992 for money laundering.

An associate of Ricke's had deposited $25,000 for him with the Belize Bank, which I controlled through one of my companies, but he had deposited far more with Barclays. Follett and Randel ought to have paused for thought at this stage. Why, if I was meant to be the Mr Big of the money-laundering world in Belize, had just a small amount of the supposedly illicit earnings been deposited at the Belize Bank? In any case, how could I, with no day-to-day involvement in bank transactions, be expected to be suspicious of such a routine deposit? Were the shareholders or directors of Barclays also suspected of helping to launder money for Ricke? I trust not, because I am sure they were as innocent of any wrongdoing as I was.

Follett returned to Britain armed with his results about Thomas Ricke and some up-to-date information from his DEA mole, while Randel – no doubt still dreaming airily of his glamorous future in the movie business – flew back to Atlanta to continue, for the time being at least, his more mundane day-job. Follett was now confident that Channel 4 would commission the documentary. However, when production executives studied the new 'evidence', they were not convinced that it amounted to enough for a documentary. Instead, programme makers told Follett that they would 'think about it'.

IT WAS in Westminster that another strand to my troubles had started to work loose. I faced opposition, as might be expected, from the Labour Party but also, more surprisingly perhaps, from within my own party. In late 1998, Robert Gascoyne-Cecil, then Viscount Cranborne and now the Marquess of Salisbury, had struck a secret deal with Tony Blair on the issue of hereditary peers. Despite being leader of the Conservative peers in the House of Lords, Cranborne had – quite extraordinarily – failed to seek approval for the agreement from William Hague, or even to inform him about it. When this act of betrayal was discovered by William, it quite rightly and inevitably led to Cranborne's dismissal in December 1998 as party leader in the Lords.

At the time, Cranborne admitted that he had 'behaved quite outrageously' by exceeding his authority and going behind his leader's back. Despite the admission that he was in the wrong, it had not stopped him seething with indignation and resentment against William ever since. I have always been fascinated by the Cecil family, who throughout history have brought professionalism to duplicity. They have been wonderful political schemers – and Cranborne was soon to show that he splendidly upheld the great family tradition. My only substantive conversation with him before his sacking was in his room at the House of Lords a year or so earlier. He asked me whether I would make a donation to the start-up fund of Business for Sterling, a project which he supported. I asked him what sort of contribution he was looking for and he replied: 'Seventy-five thousand pounds.' Shortly after our conversation, I made a £75,000 donation to the project. In the months and years after Cranborne was sacked, he would display a strange way of thanking me for my generosity.

At about this time, Cranborne's daughter Georgie was stepping out with George Bridges, an ambitious young Tory and Old Etonian who had been a policy adviser and speech writer to John Major when he was Prime Minister. Perhaps inevitably, given their personal and political links, Cranborne and Bridges became extremely friendly. Bridges, however, was also well connected with political journalists at *The Times*: indeed, so well connected that he was employed as a leader writer on the paper. Bridges was, in private at least, openly hostile to my links with the party in general and with William in particular. The Cranborne–Bridges alliance quickly appreciated that *The Times* could be a useful vehicle for their personal venom against William and me.

WHEN I was appointed party Treasurer in 1998, the editor of *The Times* was Peter Stothard, who, while at Oxford, had edited *Cherwell*, the student newspaper. After an unusual career that included spells at the BBC and Shell, he was appointed editor of *The Times* in 1992 at the age of forty-one. By 1999 and seven years into the job, he was still waiting to make his mark. He was little recognised outside the national newspaper world of Fleet Street (that name persists although the titles left EC4 for cheaper commercial sites long ago). As editor, Stothard had failed his proprietor on two fronts. Despite massive new resources being put into producing and promoting *The Times* – and despite a costly price war with its main rival – he had not significantly closed the gap between sales of his newspaper and those of the *Daily Telegraph*. In 1993, a year after Stothard became editor, the cover price of *The Times* was reduced to just 10p and millions of pounds were spent on promoting and subsidising the paper. Even with these advantages, sales of *The Times* still fell far short of the *Daily Telegraph*'s and the whole price-war episode had been a wildly expensive failure.

Editorially, too, the paper was not making the sort of waves that someone as demanding as Rupert Murdoch expects from his editors. Front-page exclusives and newspaper awards were scarce and, more importantly, the newspaper under Stothard's editorship had never claimed a big-name scalp. Stothard could only look on in awe as the accolades were heaped on his rival broadsheet editor Alan Rusbridger, whose paper the *Guardian* had succeeded in bringing down Jonathan Aitken, the Minister for Defence Procurement. After the newspaper had revealed Aitken's shadowy dealings with Saudi arms dealers, the minister sued the *Guardian* in April 1995, promising to use 'the sword of truth' to win his legal action. Two years later his libel trial collapsed when he was exposed as a liar. This left the paper to carry its famous front-page headline 'He lied and lied and lied'. Within two years, Aitken was jailed for perjury, and his downfall – at the hands of the *Guardian* – was complete.

By the spring of 1999, Stothard was searching for a scoop that would get the chattering classes – particularly Westminster – discussing him and his newspaper as much as they had Rusbridger and the *Guardian*. An editor working for News International has a life expectancy which is shorter than that of most pets. Stothard was edging towards ten years in the post. He needed either to stave off the inevitable or to end his editorship on a high. He had set his sights on an early target in the form of Greg Dyke, who wanted to succeed John Birt as Director General of the BBC. *The Times* campaigned against the appointment of Dyke, a successful millionaire businessman as well as an experienced television executive, for six months from January to June.

A leader article in *The Times* on 4 June 1999 read: 'Editorial responsibility requires clear independence of party. For defenders of Mr Dyke to point out the benefits of rich men partaking in civic life is to misunderstand the special nature of editorship ... It is wrong that Mr Dyke should have been encouraged to seek the job, wrong that he should have advanced so far towards it and wrong that the Leader of the Opposition should have been required to intervene. But these wrongs are within the governors' power to right.' Three weeks later, Greg Dyke was appointed Director General of the BBC and *The Times*'s campaign had ended in abject failure.

Throughout most of the twentieth century, *The Times* had supported the Conservative Party. Rupert Murdoch, the owner of the newspaper and three other national titles, had made it clear, however, during the middle and late 1990s that he did not want his newspapers to support the Tory leadership slavishly and without good reason. Prime Minister John Major, who represented a gentler strain of Toryism than that championed by his redoubtable predecessor, had started to disappoint his one-time admirers. He had lost his grip on the party and pro- and anti-EU extremists, who seemed to have forgotten that the Labour Party might still be a threat, fought with each other. Allegations of financial sleaze compounded the misery, and by the general election of 1997 Murdoch had encouraged his editors to distance themselves from a government whose days seemed numbered. Instead, editors were free, within limits, to make up their own minds which party – and leader – their newspaper supported. In the build-up to the election, *The Times* was clearly unimpressed by Major's leadership and was Euro-sceptic. On election day itself, however, it fell short of giving its all-out backing to the Labour Party and rather sat on the fence.

Stothard saw himself as a mover and shaker in the world of politics, particularly Tory politics. He despised William Hague in the same way, albeit to a lesser degree, that he had been contemptuous of John Major. He wanted Michael Portillo to lead the party and he considered William, like Major, unworthy to sit at its high table. Furthermore, he was no friend of William politically. He considered himself to be a Tory grandee, a member of the elite group which looked down on those who had not attended the right schools and universities, and who were not, therefore, good enough for a place at the high table. Stothard feared a swing back to Thatcherism under William's leadership, although he was momentarily reassured that the party was moving in the right direction when the two of them met for lunch.

The Times carried articles based on the way that Stothard – rather then William himself – wanted the Conservative Party to move. For example, on 26 April 1999, Philip Webster, the paper's influential political editor, wrote a story headlined 'Hague unruffled by split with Old Guard'. The story began: 'William Hague delivered a "like it or lump it" message to his Tory critics last night as he prepared to take the break with his party's Thatcherite past a stage further.' It was a 'break' with the past that Stothard clearly wanted but that never actually materialised. Eventually, he seems to have concluded that William should be replaced as leader after he sacked his modernising deputy leader, Peter Lilley, in June 1999 following his disastrous 'dump Thatcherism' speech earlier in the year. Stothard became keen to run stories knocking William, while some of his political staff wanted to go even further and print stories actively supporting the Labour Party.

Stothard's decision to move *The Times* to the left was, of course, welcomed by the Labour Party, which was not slow to forge alliances with key senior staff on the newspaper. There were several interesting links between Blair's Government and *The Times*. Philip Webster, the paper's political editor, had been among the first of its journalists to be won over by New Labour. Andrew Hood, a special adviser at the Foreign and Commonwealth Office, was an old and trusted schoolfriend of Tom Baldwin, then the deputy political editor of *The Times*. Baldwin had taken a demotion from his job as political editor of the *Sunday Telegraph*, where he was regarded as a talented maverick, to join *The Times*. Alastair Campbell, Blair's Machiavellian press secretary who was to become a key figure in the campaign against me, also had a close working relationship with Baldwin. Within a short time, the Labour Party and *The Times* had formed a mutually beneficial alliance that would have seemed unthinkable just a few years earlier.

IN THE spring and early summer of 1999, *The Times* was looking for William Hague's Achilles heel: step forward Michael Anthony Ashcroft. Here was a man whose appointment as party Treasurer had gone virtually unnoticed but whose minimal press coverage, particularly in *Private Eye*, portrayed him as brash, arrogant and a tax exile. He had deep-rooted associations with a Central American country that few had heard of and over which some suggested he exerted an unhealthy influence. He was, for instance, even Belize's Ambassador to the United Nations. Could this be right?

That spring, my business interests too had, for the first time in years, attracted publicity in the business pages of the British broadsheets, especially *The Times*. Through my company, the Carlisle Group, I had made a £200 million-plus takeover bid for a troubled company, Corporate Services Group (CSG). With hindsight, it was perhaps unwise at that time to put myself back in the City spotlight, but then again I have always found it difficult to resist what I think to be a good business proposition.

At the time, CSG, a training and employment group, was in

difficulties. It had been forced to issue two profit warnings and there was a boardroom battle in the wake of a shareholders' revolt. City journalists felt uneasy about my bid, claiming that it was 'too complicated' – I intended to merge two of my companies in order to make the necessary offer for the company. *The Times* was less than fulsome in its support of the bid. Paul Durman, one of its business reporters, quoted one anonymous critic as saying: 'If this is a white knight, they must be colour blind.' An investor, who was also anonymous, was reported as exclaiming: 'Don't ask me to explain the bid. It's difficult to establish the value of a bid from a vehicle that has yet to be created.'

The paper's business diary on the same day – 2 April 1999 – commented: 'It's hard not to have a sneaking admiration for Michael Ashcroft's utter disregard for his reputation as "the controversial tycoon". If he had any concern at all for losing that tag, he would not be plunging so wholeheartedly into the mess at Corporate Services Group ... Mr Ashcroft has pitched in a mind-bogglingly complex takeover proposal from a company that has yet to be formed ... Mr Ashcroft clearly thinks he can make a killing from CSG, but, to spice things up, has chosen to thumb his nose at almost the entire City while he does so. With so many players involved, this one is set to run and run.' I can imagine that a financial or business journalist might find such a deal complicated, but I would expect a money manager, who is paid to understand the value of securities, to have grasped it fairly quickly. I deeply resented the suggestion that a complex deal had to be 'dodgy' when this was a perfectly legitimate tactic and a long-standing method over the years by which I had managed to obtain an edge over a business rival. Just because a bid might seem complex to some does not make it unethical: it is a fact of life that – unlike public takeovers – many private deals conducted by venture capitalists are complicated. This is often because the number of people involved is small – but they know what they are doing.

The following day – 3 April – Durman profiled me for the business pages under the headline 'Brace yourself for the return of the deal junkie'. His article began: 'The City does not like Michael Ashcroft and Mr Ashcroft views the City with barely disguised disdain. But after years of self-imposed exile, Belize's most famous ambassador is back with a bang, pitching a £200 million plus takeover bid into a situation that already had all the makings of a financial soap opera.' The article dragged up some of my more controversial business deals and concluded: 'Even if he fails to snatch CSG from under the noses of the institutions, it will surely not be long before he steals the limelight elsewhere on the corporate stage.'

Although this was several weeks before the decision by Stothard to mount a campaign to discredit me, I suspect my attempts to take over CSG caused my name to appear on the radar of political and newspaper observers.

THE 'GET Ashcroft' campaign – as I chose to call it – was launched by *The Times* in early June 1999, fully a year after I had become Treasurer of the Conservative Party. The first story against me was based on some leaked information, which I was later told originated largely from two men: Viscount Cranborne, the former Conservative leader in the House of Lords, and George Bridges, the former policy adviser to John Major turned leader writer. The 'information' was that the Conservative Party was becoming increasingly dependent on my donations. Not only did Cranborne want revenge on William, it seems, but he had also come to despise everything that I represented. The feelings, incidentally, were reciprocated: Cranborne represents everything that I find unpalatable about a tiny section of the Old Guard of the party – boorish arrogance, an insistence on being exclusive rather than inclusive, and valuing blood and one's public school above intelligence, ability and achievement. These were the very characteristics that brought down Barings Bank. Incidentally, at the start of the campaign Cranborne had promised Bridges that he would be able to produce a damaging memo or letter that had been sent to John Major. It was meant to have suggested that I was 'dodgy' and 'untrustworthy' and questioned whether the party should continue receiving donations from me. This 'document' was never, at any point, produced by Cranborne and I have to doubt therefore whether it ever existed, especially as Major continued to accept donations from me.

The campaign was inaugurated with a prominent story across the entire top of the front page. It was headlined 'Massive donations make Tories "the plaything of one man"'. Beneath the main headline was a smaller one that read: 'Billionaire tax exile is giving party up to £360,000 a month, reports Tom Baldwin'. The story began:

> William Hague has been told by senior Tories that the massive level of support given to the party by its treasurer, Michael Ashcroft, threatens to turn it into the 'plaything of just one man'.
>
> Two authoritative sources within the party have told *The Times* that the billionaire businessman and tax exile has been backing the party with up to £360,000 a month. Over a period of a year, the support from either Mr Ashcroft personally, or his trusts and companies, is believed to be approaching £4 million.
>
> Funding on such a scale would mean that the treasurer is meeting about a third of the Tories' annual costs – an unprecedented proportion for any political party.

The story was as flawed as it was hyped. The newspaper had taken elements of the truth and exaggerated them to the point where they became inaccurate and misleading. I was donating £83,333 a month to the Conservative Party, not £360,000; I was providing fractionally under £1 million per year, not £4 million; and I was meeting about 10 per cent, not a third, of the party's annual costs of approximately £10 million a year. There could not have been 'two authoritative sources' because the information was wrong. Nobody with a respect for the truth or with genuine knowledge of the inner workings of the Conservative Party could have believed there was any risk of it becoming the 'plaything of one man'. Similarly, nobody at this time had raised concerns about the level of my funding with either William or me. Instead, senior party officials – both elected and unelected

– were overwhelmingly grateful that, with the party in such a desperate predicament, they had found someone prepared not only to take on the role of Treasurer but also to help the party out financially. Furthermore, for the whole time I was party Treasurer, I never once tried to influence or become involved in the policy-making process. I do not think there is anyone who could articulate my views on any controversial policy or area. I was always careful not to reveal my thoughts on such subjects because as part of my role in raising money for the party I had, for example, to persuade both the passionately pro-Europe and the passionately anti-Europe to write out cheques.

It was only deep in *The Times*'s article that the denials of its claims could be found. They came from Michael Ancram, then the Conservative Party chairman, and a senior but unnamed Tory Party official. Michael described the £4 million a year figure as a 'total fabrication', while the official said the figure of £360,000 a month was 'exaggerated'. In the previous year when, for the first time in its history the Conservative Party chose to publish a list of all donors who had given more than £5,000, it had been widely acknowledged by the party that I was the largest donor, giving a total of around £1 million. This meant that the party could hardly have been accused of being secretive or uncooperative. *The Times*'s story suggested the party had been lying about its information – a serious and false allegation.

On page 21 of the same 5 June 1999 issue, Tom Baldwin and Paul Durman wrote a longer background piece on the subject of my donations to the party. It read more like a profile of me. A lengthy list of anonymous figures was quoted to paint an unattractive picture of me as a bullish, money-grabbing, anti-establishment figure. 'He's driven. He just wants more and more money. There is no such thing as enough,' said one supposedly 'admiring financier'.

All hopes that the issue of 5 June had been a bizarre, one-off attack on me evaporated when the paper's next edition went on sale after the weekend. There was a front-page story on Monday, 7 June headlined 'Tory concern' that stated: 'Senior Tories will raise concerns this week about the extent to which the party is funded by Michael Ashcroft, its treasurer. MPs will prompt a debate at the weekly meeting of the 1922 executive, the party's ruling body.' On page 2 was a longer article headlined 'Financier's role is unhealthy, say Tory MPs'. The article, however, did not quote a single Tory MP or senior Tory official by name about his or her apparent concerns. Instead, it regurgitated most of the claims that had been made on Saturday and threw in a few more sniping, anonymous quotes for good measure. 'It's a pretty unhealthy position because if he wants to call the shots, there's nothing to stop him. It wouldn't matter if he was the Archangel Gabriel, it still wouldn't be a good thing,' one anonymous official was quoted as saying.

By the following day, Tuesday, 8 June, the thrust of the paper's attack had switched from the news pages to the comment pages. If I had any doubts that this was going to be a concerted campaign, this dispelled them. *The Times* carried a leader article headlined 'One Man Band: The Tories cannot afford to rely on their treasurer'. It read:

> The last two years have not been easy times for William Hague. His poll ratings are in the doldrums and his party is in dire financial straits. Donors are fewer and less generous just at the time when their money is most needed. In this hour of need, the Conservatives appear to be relying on the munificence of one man, Michael Ashcroft, its billionaire party treasurer.
>
> Mr Ashcroft, who spends most of his time in Florida, has apparently been backing the party with assistance of up to £360,000 a month. Such a seemingly high level of support from a treasurer has led some Conservatives to wonder if their party is not so much financed as 'kept'. There is talk of the Tories becoming 'the plaything of one man'. Last year Mr Hague pledged that 'we are not going to have in the future any of the kind of controversies that have dogged us in the past over funding'. The Tory leader may soon be chewing those words.
>
> The Conservative Party's financial plight is enough to

make any bank manager wince. With Labour dominating the political landscape, only the most committed Conservatives are making large donations to party coffers. Many Tories are deterred by the party's new, laudable practice of publishing the names of all those who have provided more than £5,000. As a result, the party accounts last year reported that donations had 'decreased significantly', while its deficit stood at a numbing £11 million. Staring into this financial abyss, Mr Hague might be forgiven for accepting Mr Ashcroft and his millions. Yet if the Tory leader's political antennae had been twitching, he would surely have paused.

The article went on:

Mr Ashcroft may hold a British passport, but he can spend only 90 days a year in this country. Also a naturalised citizen of Belize, he has turned this tiny Central American nation into his own Monopoly board, owning its biggest bank, significant stakes in its utilities, fruit industry and media and holding the position of Belize's High Representative at the United Nations. In an age when party funding is a highly charged political issue, Mr Hague should have seen the potential hazards of appointing the most entrepreneurial of tax exiles as the Conservative Party treasurer. He should have realised that, by cashing Mr Ashcroft's cheques, the Tory promise not to accept 'any foreign money' would be seen as very ambiguous.

These objections either did not occur to Mr Hague or did not disturb him. Perhaps he felt that he had no choice. Taking what seems to have been a very loose definition of the word 'foreign', he has gratefully accepted Mr Ashcroft's support. The party chairman strongly disputes reports that Mr Ashcroft exerts transatlantic influence on party policy. But to a party desperate to put behind it the accusations of influence-for-sale, impressions matter.

One thing that the Tory leader can do is to re-

double his efforts to broaden the party's fiscal [sic] base
so that it does not rely so much on Mr Ashcroft. It must
be hoped that the treasurer would support such moves.
The European election provides the party with an opportunity to identify its strongest supporters. Success might
even bring some more large donors and, it must be hoped,
Mr Ashcroft would support that too. Only thus can Mr
Hague ensure that his party is not the rich man's plaything that critics fear that it appears to be.

It was deeply irritating to see the nonsense about the level of my
donations continuing even though the newspaper had been told
that its allegations were inaccurate. The suggestion from *The Times*
was still that I was funding the Conservative Party to the tune of
£4 million or more a year, which was utter nonsense.

The onslaught by *The Times* continued and on Wednesday, 9
June 1999 it carried a lengthy story on the fact that I had bought
a house in London. In fact, the property had been bought by my
wife, Susi. Under normal circumstances such a non-event might
have made, at most, two paragraphs in a political or business
diary. *The Times* deemed it worthy of a spread across two-thirds
of a news page with the headline 'Ashcroft in £1.6 million move
to Westminster'. The story – again I use the word loosely – read:
'Michael Ashcroft, the Florida-based billionaire and Tory benefac-
tor, has bought a "spectacular" home within yards of Conservative
headquarters to help him to oversee the party's activities. The Tory
treasurer, who is thought to be keeping the party in business with
monthly cheques of up to £360,000, plans to use the £1.6 million
house as a base during his trips to London.' The paper then went
on, once again, to repeat the same old claims about my financial
support for the party that it had made earlier in the week. Finally, it quoted yet another anonymous source – a senior aide to
John Major – as saying: 'We were certainly aware that there were
anxieties expressed about Ashcroft by our treasurer's department.
Since then a number of people have said to me that they will have
nothing to do with the party if Ashcroft is involved in it.'

Even by the low standards of *The Times*, a thoroughly

legitimate and above-board house purchase was a tenuous reason for having a snipe at me. The newspaper, however, seemed to be having doubts about the accuracy of what it believed was the level of my financial support for the party, saying 'it is thought' that I was keeping the party in business with cheques of up to £360,000 a month. But who thought this and why? Both the party and my aides had already made it abundantly clear that the figures were wrong, yet still the newspaper persisted in using inaccurate information.

The Times was getting so desperate for some 'dirt' on me that it paid thousands of pounds to dispatch one of its reporters, Damian Whitworth, to Belize. After days of digging around in Belize City, he wrote two reports which appeared on pages 1 and 10 of the paper on Friday, 11 June. These suggested that Whitworth had not been sent to report on me and my companies in a balanced and objective way. He had tried to portray everything that related to me in a poor light.

The page 1 story was headlined 'Ashcroft made ambassador after helping Belize party to victory'. The report began: 'Michael Ashcroft, the Conservative Party treasurer, was made Belizean Ambassador to the United Nations after he helped to bankroll the election victory of the party he favours in his adopted country.' On page 10 another story from Belize written by Whitworth ran under the headline: 'Small country where Ashcroft is a big noise'. The article began: 'Michael Ashcroft, the Conservative Party treasurer who has had links to Belize since he lived here as a boy, dominates the business landscape of the country to which he returned to make money in later life.' On the same page was a report from James Bone in New York headlined 'UN post offers a grand title and tax breaks'. The article stated: 'The diplomatic post that Michael Ashcroft holds as permanent representative of Belize at the United Nations headquarters in New York gives him far-reaching immunity from American law and the threat of lawsuits.'

For once, there was little wrong with the general accuracy of the stories, but it was the way they were written to which I took exception. They were trying to present widely known facts as if I had done something wrong or underhand. It was true that I did have diplomatic immunity but that was because I was a diplomat for my adopted country. I had no greater or lesser immunity that any other diplomat, and I certainly never abused it – I even paid my parking fines. The snide insinuation from *The Times*, however, was that I had sought diplomatic immunity because I was doing, or planned to do, something illegal. Similarly, in Belize, as in Britain, I had substantial business interests, but this was my job and I had never made any secret of the fact that I was ambitious and driven in my attempt to make my ventures large, successful and profitable.

There was no let-up in *The Times*'s coverage the next day – Saturday, 12 June. There was a picture of me on page 1 with a short article headlined 'They seek him everywhere'. The whole of page 19 was devoted to me: a main story from Belize about my business and charity work, a smaller story about my business interests elsewhere in the Caribbean, and, most interestingly of all – certainly from my point of view – a short piece headlined 'Delay over peerages'. It read: 'The controversy over Michael Ashcroft's massive financial backing for the Tory Party has forced the Government to delay publication of a new list of peers. Although the Conservative Party treasurer's name was nominated by William Hague for a life peerage, it is understood that he was blocked at the last minute by the Political Honours Scrutiny Committee. The decision was taken so late that the announcement of the new list of peers – planned for May 29 – was postponed with a day's notice. Several new peers had to cancel celebration parties. The full working peers' list, which is separate from today's Queen's Birthday Honours, is now expected to be unveiled next Saturday.' I and the others who had been nominated had, of course, been told of the delay, but I was decidedly unimpressed that such confidential information was being shared with *The Times* and its readers.

By now the paper had reporters delving into me, my companies and my roles all over the world, yet most of the material they were 'discovering' about me was readily available on the internet or was otherwise public knowledge. The team of reporters had not uncovered anything newsworthy and their stories made no serious allegations against me or my companies. Nevertheless, *The Times* was presenting each article as if it contained major revelations – and they were 'revelations' which inevitably made me appear sinister.

Thus began a pattern of activity that was to dog me during the summer of 1999. I will not provide the full list of the negative articles that *The Times* carried about me, but I need to quote from some to give an indication of the scale of the onslaught. In total, there were tens of thousands of words published about me in stories which appeared day after day, many of them on the front page beneath sensational and misleading headlines. If there was good or positive news the story was either ignored or reduced to a paragraph or two. For instance, when it was made public that William Hague was backing me despite the paper's campaign against me, *The Times* carried a single-paragraph story buried on page 2 on Monday, 14 June. The entire article read: 'William Hague threw his full support behind Michael Ashcroft despite the controversy surrounding the Tory Party treasurer. His aides went out of their way to praise Mr Ashcroft after it emerged that Mr Hague had attended a fundraising dinner at his home, along with eight wealthy businessmen, on Thursday.'

After *The Times*'s initial attack on me, Tim (Lord) Bell, who had masterminded the Tory Party advertising campaign under Margaret Thatcher, thought it would be a good idea if Stothard and I got together. I was prepared to meet Stothard in case there was anything he wanted to put to me on an off-the-record basis – after all, I had nothing to hide. So Tim arranged a breakfast for the three of us at the River Room of the Savoy Hotel in central London on Thursday, 17 June. It was a genial enough encounter – the first time that I had met Stothard – and I felt we had enjoyed a pleasant breakfast. I had explained firmly but politely to him that the amount of money *The Times* had reported I was giving the Conservative Party was untrue. I even helpfully tried to suggest to Stothard how his false figure of £360,000 a month may have come about: during my early period as Treasurer the party had lost roughly this amount in a single month and someone may have assumed – quite wrongly – that somebody would have had to make up that loss and that that somebody must have been me. As I left the breakfast table, I hoped this would be the end of the matter, but I also suspected that Stothard was not a man I could trust.

I felt I had judged Stothard's lack of integrity correctly when he made inquiries after the meeting about whether he could consider what I had said over breakfast to be on the record, though it was quite clear that all the parties had agreed that we had talked off the record. I was not happy to rely on him to report our wide-ranging meeting fairly and accurately: I felt instinctively that he would be highly selective about which words he chose to report and which he chose to ignore. So I repeated that what I had said was undoubtedly off the record, a response that Stothard was evidently unhappy with.

I had learned, shortly before my breakfast with Stothard, that – because of the concerns of the Honours Scrutiny Committee – my name was not on the newly published list of peers. I suspected, too, that this fact would be leaked by New Labour – almost certainly to *The Times* – and that it would report it in as sneering and as negative a way as possible. Within two days of our breakfast, my prediction had come true: *The Times* gleefully reported the story on Saturday, 19 June under the headline 'Party sidelines Hague candidate for red benches'. Although I was extremely disappointed not to be on the list, I was not surprised given the publicity surrounding the newspaper's campaign against me. I resolved to be patient and to remove the obstacles that stood in my way.

That weekend Amanda Platell, William Hague's loyal and talented press secretary, of whom I am enormously fond, was keen that the Conservative Party should not be seen to be on the defensive. She suggested that I give one or two newspaper interviews to journalists who would be willing to allow me a fair hearing. I chose to grant the first political interviews of my life to two journalists who could be trusted to be fair – Joe Murphy, then the political editor of the *Sunday Telegraph*, and Simon Walters, the political editor of the *Mail on Sunday*.

I told Joe that the claims made by *The Times* about the

amounts of money I had been giving to the Conservative Party were completely untrue. I had, in fact, given £2 million to the party over the previous two years. 'You cannot appoint a treasurer who is perceived to be wealthy, but who doesn't lead the way,' I explained. 'The very fact that I put in a sum means I can ask others to do the same.' Incidentally, when the Conservative Party eventually published its annual accounts for the year in question, they showed unequivocally that the figures I had given relating to the level of my donations were correct and *The Times*'s were wrong. Needless to say, the newspaper failed to publish an apology or a retraction – or even to publish the correct amounts.

I said to Simon that I had not given up hope of becoming a member of the House of Lords. 'I think every Treasurer of the party has gone to the Lords and I hope I don't set a precedent by being the first who doesn't.' It is a quote that has often been used in profiles of me over the years, but I meant what I said.

I was told that Stothard was less than pleased that – having refused to be quoted directly in his paper – I had then chosen to give interviews to two rival national newspapers. The stories to which *The Times* devoted significant amounts of space became ever more bland. Two journalists – Tom Baldwin and Paul Durman (whom the incompetent broadsheet had bylined Paul *Durnam*) – wrote a lengthy story on Thursday, 24 June headlined 'Ashcroft moves office to cash-for-questions house'. *The Times* revelled in reporting that my Carlisle Group had moved its UK address to 19 Catherine Place, close to Buckingham Palace. The building had formerly been occupied by Ian Greer, the political lobbyist at the centre of the 'cash for questions' scandal that destroyed the career of Neil Hamilton, the former Conservative Trade Minister. Rationally such a non-event – my company moving from one London office to another – warranted, at the most, a paragraph in a business diary. Stothard, however, had long ceased to be rational. By now, I knew that I was in for a long and difficult summer.

5 Raising the Stakes

DURING JULY 1999, *The Times* started to print increasingly grave allegations about me. On Tuesday, 13 July it carried a story across the whole of its front page headlined '"Shadow" over Tory treasurer: Leaked Foreign Office memos pose questions about Ashcroft's integrity'. The newspaper had obtained Foreign Office documents from three years earlier. I was far less concerned by what the 1996 documents said – essentially the idle and mischievous scribblings of a little-known diplomat – than by the breach of confidentiality that allowed them to come into the possession of *The Times*. Those who were determined to cause the Conservative Party in general and me in particular damage and embarrassment now stretched well beyond the paper.

The memos were written after I had met some Foreign Office officials to discuss my proposals to set up a bank in the Turks and Caicos Islands. It was a straightforward business proposal: I had experience of banking in Belize and wanted to expand those profitable interests elsewhere in the Caribbean. Charles Drace-Francis, a Scottish diplomat with responsibility for the region, was reported by *The Times* as having written a letter in October 1996 in which he speculated that I was pushing the request because 'he now has about $1 billion in cash and would obviously like to have his own bank to put it in – but cannot use the Belize bank'. The letter, which was sent to Patrick Moody who then headed the economic relations unit at the Foreign Office, continued:

Incidentally, I noticed, –
a) Mr Ashcroft looked rather hungover,
b) his crumpled shirt was missing a button at the sleeve which he affected not to notice at first,
c) we went to a rather 'lower' dive than usual.

Later he added: 'I found it slightly odd for a man with $1 billion burning a hole in his pocket to look so worried.'

I felt irritated that someone who had gone out of his way to 'befriend' me should be writing such snide things about me behind my back. The reference to my crumpled shirt and missing button was unofficial diplomatic code: a reference to someone's 'laundry' is meant to suggest that he or she may be involved in money laundering. I felt that Drace-Francis was nothing more than a snob: his basis for regarding me with suspicion appeared to be simply that I had made a great deal of money. Furthermore, even his less serious claims were untrue. As a moderate drinker, I did not have a hangover – I have not had one since my student days. I have also, unfortunately, never had a billion dollars in cash in my life. Incidentally, when Drace-Francis was interviewed in August 1999, as part of an official leak inquiry, he confirmed that his allusion to 'laundry' was a play on words and was meant to refer to my alleged money-laundering activities.

The *Times* article of 13 July marked another unwelcome milestone. The newspaper started tagging all of its major stories about me 'The Ashcroft Affair'. This was utterly preposterous. The 'affair' was one entirely of the paper's making, yet the initial – and continued – use of the tag wrongly suggested to readers that there was a continuing scandal involving me.

A second document was also leaked to the paper: a Foreign Office telegram from Gordon Baker, the then British High Commissioner in Belize, to Drace-Francis. The telegram, written in April 1997, said that Baker was no nearer knowing the truth of the 'rumours about some of Ashcroft's business dealings. But those rumours do cast a shadow over his reputation which ought not to be ignored.' To this day, I have no idea to what these unidentified rumours and unsubstantiated tittle-tattle refer. I doubt if Baker does either.

The Times the following day was unrelenting. It was now clear that on virtually a daily basis the newspaper was going to devote pages of newsprint and thousands of words to anti-Ashcroft stor-ies until I resigned or was removed as party Treasurer. Its issue of Wednesday, 14 July devoted its 'splash' – the main page 1 story – and pages 4 and 5 to articles about me: the thrust of the front-page story was that I had resisted an attempt to clean up the Belize economy despite an official report that the country was open to the laundering of South American drugs money. I have never resisted any attempt to clean up the economy of Belize. The way the newspaper worded its article suggested that the country was fundamentally corrupt, which was untrue: the official report had been concerned about the extent of regulation that would be required in the future. The simple truth was that, to the best of my knowledge, there had never been at that time any corruption of any substance in Belize. *The Times* also carried a cartoon by Peter Brookes portraying me as William Hague's puppet-master and him collapsing on the floor in a heap. The message was abundantly clear: I was going to bring the leader of the Opposition down unless William acted first to get rid of me.

A leader article in the paper's comment section on the same day was headlined 'Hague and his money: Ashcroft and the Tories must soon be parted'. The article was the most stinging criticism yet of my role. It read:

> It is not hard to see why senior Tories were so reluctant to be drawn yesterday on the subject of their buccaneering paymaster, Michael Ashcroft. The Conservative Party desperately needs the billionaire's money: it desperately does not need the questioning which must inevitably follow from our reports of yesterday and today.
>
> William Hague entered office with a strategy to break with the 'sleaze' associated with the Major government. He quickly apologised for the Tories' errors, gave his activists greater say in the party organisation and formed an Ethics and Integrity Committee to patrol his party's morals. It can be argued that without Mr Ashcroft's millions, especially in the immediate months after electoral destruction, he might barely have had a functioning party at all. Yet, with his continuing dependence on Mr Ashcroft as party treasurer, he risks all the rewards that a successful strategy might bring.

As we have reported in recent weeks, there is deep Conservative concern that a single man should have such power over their party. The more that becomes known about Mr Ashcroft, the more worrying the identity of that powerful man becomes. Mr Ashcroft has undoubted financial skills: some of his critics show clear animus against him. And yet his foreign residence, overseas tax status and the stream of revelations about his political and business methods in the Caribbean do not make comfortable reading for Conservatives ...

The leader continued:

The Tories' professional campaigners, even as they spend Mr Ashcroft's money, know that they can never attack the Labour Party for taking questionable donations while their treasurer is in the post. Cashing Mr Ashcroft's cheques was surely in breach of the spirit, if not the letter, of the Tory leader's promise not to accept 'any foreign money' ...

Mr Hague has an awkward choice. His party can continue to take massive sums of money from a man who, according to the British diplomats whom we reported yesterday, has a 'shadow over his reputation that ought not to be ignored'. He can put the kindliest possible construction on our report today that Mr Ashcroft appeared to threaten the governor of Belize's Central Bank that he would withdraw his considerable business interests from the country if financial regulations were tightened up ...

Yet, only last year, Mr Hague pledged that 'we are not going to have in the future any of the kind of controversies that have dogged us in the past over funding'. If Mr Hague were to win the next election, Mr Ashcroft would be running the finances of the party in charge of Britain's economy. Yesterday the party chairman, Michael Ancram, dismissed the latest revelations as part of a 'political campaign' against the Tory treasurer. That is nonsense. Mr Hague can either continue with this stalling tactic and continue to keep his treasurer. Or he can turn away from the *Realpolitik* of Belize and face the reality of British politics.

By now *The Times* was no longer making any secret of its objective: to get me removed as Treasurer. The leader article effectively challenged William to sack me on the spot. It was Michael Ancram who had, in a private conversation with me, correctly assessed the motivation of *The Times*: every word of the article had been slanted to suit the newspaper's twisted political agenda. It would be tedious to challenge and correct the article sentence by sentence. In any case, how can anyone defend himself from such a woolly charge that he had a 'shadow over his reputation'? The giveaway, however, was that even *The Times* acknowledged that the US report had only said that money laundering was 'a potential threat to Belize', thereby confirming that at the time in question it was not a problem.

As the campaign against me by *The Times* intensified, some senior colleagues in the Conservative Party were getting increasingly agitated. The Opposition always hopes that newspapers, particularly the broadsheets, will be full of stories which put the Government on the back foot. This was not the case for much of the early summer of 1999. Although William Hague and Michael Ancram, the party Chairman, were models of understanding, there was a very small number of others in the party who were not so patient nor so considerate about my plight. I came under growing pressure to 'do something'. I, in turn, explained to the party that I had to wait until the newspaper clearly overstepped the mark. I initially told party officials that it was impossible for me to sue for defamation because I had not actually been accused of anything clear and specific enough. Any libel lawyer will tell his or her client to beware of suing on a general comment or an opinion or a subtle or ambiguous insinuation because the debate becomes so subjective and the outcome uncertain. The libel lawyer's bible, *Gatley on Libel and Slander*, puts it this way: 'The only person who can contemplate with equanimity bringing an action for libel or slander is one with ample means, whose reputation is unblemished, whose past contains no skeletons, and whose complaint is of a damaging and clear public misstatement of a specific fact.' Indeed, if the misstatement is not clear enough, it may either be held to be comment or it may give rise to a prolonged trial which, in turn, tends to be complex and expensive.

I employed lawyers to scrutinise every word written about me in *The Times*. For many years, I had used Keith Godfrey of Allen & Overy, the London firm of solicitors. Keith, who had a brilliantly sharp mind, had acted for me in virtually every transaction of my business life in Britain since the mid-1970s and I trusted him totally. However, on this occasion Allen & Overy could not represent me because the firm was acting for News International, the owner of *The Times*, on other matters. Because of this conflict of interest, I turned to David Hooper, an experienced and well-connected solicitor who worked for the City law firm Biddle. I also employed two experts in the field of defamation – James Price QC and Mark Warby, who is now also a silk. David, James and Mark knew that, as soon *The Times* moved from reporting tiresome innuendo to making a clear and specific factual allegation that directly attacked my integrity and damaged my reputation, I wanted to serve a writ on the paper. I was prepared to bide my time because I knew that, when I did sue for defamation, I intended to go all the way to court – and I wanted to be sure that I was going to win. While it was irksome to see potential targets go by, I knew that if I held my nerve a better opportunity to sue would come along. It was like a lion stalking its prey: it has to be prepared to allow some opportunities go by in order to have the best chance of catching its target.

After taking legal advice, I thought long and hard about suing *The Times* for defamation over its articles of 14 July. By suggesting that I had 'ferociously resisted' attempts to clean up the Belize economy, the newspaper was undoubtedly inviting its readers to make the inference that I and my companies preferred a regime that facilitated money laundering and drug running. Such a suggestion was preposterous. My company was a prominent member of the Belize Offshore Practitioners Association (BOPA). The organisation had vigorously supported all moves that enabled the early detection of financial crime and money laundering. BOPA had, in fact, drafted new legislation to assist in the national fight against these illegal practices and had supported a move by the Government of Belize towards accession to the Vienna Convention of 1988 against illicit traffic in narcotic drugs.

I had also briefly considered making a complaint to the Press Complaints Commission (PCC), the newspaper watchdog. This has certain advantages: it is a relatively quick, straightforward and low-cost process and newspapers can be forced to print corrections. However, the PCC had no power to award damages, it was often reluctant to find against newspapers and, all in all, I was not convinced that this route was the wisest. Complaining to the PCC was simply not appropriate given the scale of the newspaper's assault on me. In addition, the PCC will not consider a complaint if it is the subject of legal action. I decided that at the right time my response needed to be through the courts with an action for defamation aimed at ending the campaign by *The Times* once and for all. I was assured by my lawyers that I would win in a legal action against the newspaper over its 14 July articles, but I decided to be patient and wait for another attack on my name that was even more blatantly defamatory. I was confident I would not have to wait long.

I was fortunate, in some ways, that this relentless attack by *The Times* had not taken place in the early months of my period as Treasurer. By the summer of 1999, I was a year into the job and I like to think that I had established my credentials as an effective fundraiser, controller of costs and reorganiser. This meant that the party was keen to keep me, not to ditch me. If I had been a new or ineffective Treasurer, I suspect the party would not have been so loyal to me. I was also, of course, continuing to support the party financially.

On several occasions during the onslaught, I considered my position and debated whether, for the sake of the party, I ought to tender my resignation as Treasurer. Instinctively, however, I felt that the greater the pressure, the more I should resist. I had taken the view that it was *The Times's* objective to force me to step down. I knew I had the moral high ground: I had done nothing illegal, nothing to be ashamed of and nothing that made me inclined to fall on my sword. All in all, the more I thought about it, the more determined I became that my enemies at the newspaper should not get me.

On Wednesday, 14 July 1999 – in the wake of the latest on-slaught from *The Times* – I did, however, think the time had come to make a public statement to defend my professional integrity and to deny the ridiculous and offensive suggestion that I had attempted to thwart efforts to clean up Belize's economy. My statement was virtually lost amid yet another front-page splash in *The Times* the next day, and further stories on pages 4 and 5 were devoted to attacking me and my business interests in Belize. My statement sought to explain the real reason that I had become involved in the debate on the future of Belize's economy: having struck a firm deal with Belize's government in 1990 – one that was due to last for thirty years – I feared that politicians were about to renege on it.

The statement ran to just four short paragraphs, yet when *The Times* carried it on page 5, it acted outrageously, cutting it sub-stantially and changing the order of the sentences to make it read strangely. The opening lines, which were largely removed by the paper, read: 'I am appalled at the persistent campaign being waged against me by *The Times* and the distortions they have published. The reports in the last two days have been comprised of often incorrect, largely unconnected, insignificant incidents and details out of which they have sought to insinuate wrongdoing on my part. I condemn this process of smear. I can firmly state that the conclusions they seek to draw from it are without foundation.' The statement went on: 'My concern, as chairman of my company, with a duty to its shareholders, was that the basis on which I, and others, had invested in Belize was retrospectively to be changed. It was to this that I was reacting firmly as would the chairman of any company in similar circumstances. I and my company have always supported the need for Belize to operate a well-regulated offshore financial services sector. I deeply resent any insinuation to the contrary. I regret the attempt of political opponents and *The Times* to damage my reputation and standing. I also deplore the publication of these wholly unwarranted attacks on me.'

On 15 July, for the second time in as many days, *The Times* carried a lengthy leader on me. It was headlined 'Bunkered down: Ashcroft's statement does not address the questions'. The article devoted considerable space to yet another Stothard-inspired rant:

Parties under pressure have a tendency to retreat to the bunker. It was from behind positions which were, in every sense, defensive that the Major Government sought to avoid open engagement with many of its troubles. Well-founded investigations were rubbished, serious allegations shirked. The names of Ian Greer and Tim Smith must be etched, in frustration, on the bunker wall. William Hague promised to conduct his leadership in an altogether more open fashion and showed early signs of his commitment to candour. But the Tory party's reaction to the growing concern about the business background of its treasurer, Michael Ashcroft, has so far disappointed.

The party is back in the bunker, declining to test its case in the open, shirking examination of the questions. Last night sniper fire came back from the bunker. A statement by Mr Ashcroft was aimed at its investigators: he condemned *The Times* for our journalistic campaign – the treasurer tried to shoot the messenger. But Mr Ashcroft's statement is very far from the open engagement with troubling questions which the situation demands.

The reports we have published this week have caused well-founded disquiet among senior Conservatives. A past member of the party's board of finance, John Strafford, has expressed public concern, and the former prime ministerial aide, Sir Timothy Kitson, has asked for the matter to be referred to the party's Ethics and Integrity Committee. The worries stretch from right to left across the Tory family. And they will only be deepened by our reports today about the peculiar financial arrangements between Mr Ashcroft and Belize's electricity company.

Those reports had tried to suggest that there was a scandal over a perfectly legitimate payment to one of my companies from the Belize Government in a deal relating to the partial privatisation of Belize Electricity. The leader next purported to answer my statement:

> Rather than addressing these concerns in a proper spirit of openness, the Tories have sought to close matters down. Mr Ashcroft's statement alleges that our reports have been 'often incorrect, largely unconnected and insignificant'. He provides no detailed explanation of which reports are incorrect and which insignificant.
>
> Is it insignificant that a man who holds the purse strings of a potential British Government should have been reported threatening Britain's interests to advance his own? Is it without significance that such a man would resist regulations intended to tackle crime because his own financial interest, albeit legitimate, might suffer? Is it of no significance that companies connected with Mr Ashcroft should enjoy peculiar tax benefits as a consequence of his political influence in Belize?
>
> These incidents may be unconnected in Mr Ashcroft's mind but they connect very clearly in the minds of many Tories. They form a pattern of behaviour which has provoked genuine disquiet. And which demands detailed explanation.
>
> Conservative attempts to question how troubling information about Mr Ashcroft came to light is intended to divert attention from the real issue, his fitness to hold the office he enjoys. Rather than questioning the provenance of these revelations, throwing sand in questing eyes, the Tories should address themselves to answering the concerns raised. It is time to come out of the bunker.

On Friday, 16 July, there was yet another prominent front-page story and yet another spread on me on pages 4 and 5. The front-page story was headlined 'British diplomat tells Tories to launch Ashcroft inquiry'. The newspaper had based its story on a letter it had been sent by David Mackilligin, the former British High Commissioner in Belize for four years until 1994. The article stated that Mackilligin wanted William Hague to launch an inquiry into my activities and said that I could not escape responsibility for making Belize 'a tempting target for drug runners'. It was a strange intervention, but then Mackilligin is a strange man. Andrew Mitchell, a Conservative MP, recalled visiting him when he was Britain's commercial and aid counsellor in Indonesia. Not long into their meeting, Mackilligin swept a pile of papers violently to the floor before leaping on to his desk where he began shouting: 'I hate this country! I hate it! I fucking hate it!' Mackilligin then moved on to the coffee table where he stood doing an impersonation of a chimpanzee before telling Andrew: 'There. Now you've seen a mad diplomat.' However, *The Times* was never that choosy about who provided information about me: it would probably have accepted it from a real chimpanzee provided the information was potentially damaging. Andrew is now shadow minister for international development and deservedly in the Shadow Cabinet.

I later discovered another interesting twist to Mackilligin's letter, which was much longer than the correspondence that usually appears on the letters page. His original letter had been heavily edited and this had changed the meaning of it. I knew this because Mackilligin had spoken with a journalist from another newspaper – the *Mail on Sunday* – and had complained about the editing. Indeed, he was so angry that he faxed a journalist on the *Mail on Sunday* a copy of his original letter, pointing out the differences between it and the published text. *The Times* later said it had been forced to cut the letter for 'reasons of space'. The cuts had conveniently, from Stothard's point of view, included virtually every word that Mackilligin had written in support of me and my dealings with the Foreign and Commonwealth Office (FCO). The parts of the letter that were cut included his statement that, as regards my business interests in Belize, I had been treated by the FCO in the same way as any other British businessman. Even more significantly, Mackilligin said in another unpublished sentence that I had never tried to wield any 'improper influence' and that if I had done he was confident he would have heard abut it on the efficient 'FCO grapevine'.

By now, *The Times* was effectively operating a Belize office from the Radisson Fort George Hotel, close to my home in Belize. Dominic Kennedy, one of the paper's reporters, had been sent to dig for 'dirt' on me. He was trawling around a long list of political and business contacts in the country, many of whom either refused to talk to him or reported straight back to me what Kennedy had been questioning them about. By now, too, I realised that I had to prepare myself for a lengthy and costly battle against *The Times*, and that, as is my nature, I might have to go on the offensive sooner rather than later.

I was not the only one who was unhappy with the amount of negative attention that I and the nation of Belize were receiving. I was fortunate at this stage that, partly out of self-preservation and partly out of loyalty towards me, a number of influential organisations and individuals came to my defence. The Government of Belize, most of all, was angry at the way *The Times* was seeking to portray the country as a small nation dominated by corruption and eager to profit from money laundering. On 19 July 1999, the Government of Belize wrote an open letter to British newspapers in general and *The Times* in particular giving unequivocal support to the role that I had played in the country. It read:

> Britain and Belize are separated by 4,000 miles of Atlantic Ocean, but in many ways we are very close. Her Majesty the Queen is our Head of State, we speak English, and we are governed by the rule of law. The ties between our two countries are many, various and strong.
>
> It is particularly distressing, therefore, that British newspapers should appear intent on inflicting damage to the good reputation of our small but proud nation.
>
> We have reason to be grateful to Ambassador H.E. Michael Ashcroft, for his commitment to our country has in recent years become an investment boost to our developing country. He has invested in Belize, and others have

followed his example.

This does not mean, as has been suggested, that he exerts an unhealthy control over our country. His appointment as our Ambassador to the United Nations reflects our confidence in his ability to represent us effectively. He has no role in the formulation of policy.

Michael Ashcroft is a very successful businessman, who has earned a reputation in Belize for being tough. But he is also fair, and, in our experience, entirely trustworthy and reliable.

We consider as baseless and preposterous recent allegations of improper influence and pressure, of money laundering and of drug trafficking.

The statement went further:

The Government of Belize or our Central Bank have never been asked any questions about Michael Ashcroft by the United States Drug Enforcement Agency [sic]. Indeed, only last week, we contacted the US Embassy in Belize which categorically repeated that there is no information even suggesting that Michael Ashcroft is under investigation or on some watch list. Additionally the structure of our banking system is inimical to money laundering, and Michael Ashcroft's companies have been amongst the most active supporters of financial regulation and control.

There are already indications of the damage which our country might sustain as a result of the current rag-bag of unsubstantiated allegations in the British press which seems to be totally insensitive and unmindful of the possible negative effect on investor confidence.

We have no wish to become embroiled in the political affairs of Britain, but the time has now come when the British press should either produce evidence to substantiate its allegations or cease this campaign of smear and whispering, which not only stains the reputation of

Michael Ashcroft but puts at risk the economy and liveli-hood of the Belizean people.

The Government of Belize was not alone in springing to my defence. Keith Arnold, the Governor of the Central Bank of Belize, had written an open handwritten letter three days earlier – on 16 July – putting the record straight. 'As Governor of the Central Bank of Belize since January 1992, I can confirm that the Drug Enforcement Agency has never sought assistance from the Central Bank of Belize on any money-laundering matter relating to Mr Michael Ashcroft or any of his business interests in Belize.'

On the same day that the Government of Belize issued its supporting statement, the US State Department's Western Hemisphere Affairs department drew up a press release that was intended as guidance for journalists. Headed 'Belize: Concerns about Michael Ashcroft', it read:

> Context: Articles in London newspapers have accused Michael Ashcroft, a citizen of both the UK and Belize, of shady financial dealings. The articles implied the USG [United States Government] was concerned about Ashcroft's possible involvement in money-laundering and that the USG had raised these concerns with the Government of the UK. Ashcroft is extremely wealthy and has tremendous influence in the financial sector in Belize. He is also active in politics in the UK, and the allegations may be part of a politically-motivated smear campaign to discredit him in the UK. However, the USG has no information linking him directly to money laundering. Nor have we ever raised specific concerns about Ashcroft with either the Belizean or British Governments.
>
> Q: What concerns about Michael Ashcroft has the US Government raised with the Government of the UK?
>
> A: Embassy London has not made any approach to the British Government about Michael Ashcroft. We know of no United States Government approach to the British Government about Mr Ashcroft.

Not surprisingly perhaps, given *The Times*'s motives, these statements were given no coverage. Indeed, on 16 July, just as Keith Arnold, the Governor of the Central Bank of Belize, was penning his letter of support, events had taken an interesting turn in the newspaper's offices in London E1.

AS THE days and weeks passed in the summer of 1999, it was clear that the campaign against me was failing to gain critical mass. Peter Stothard, Tom Baldwin and others were troubled: the scalp they wanted was eluding them and their campaign needed new material and new life. John Bryant, the paper's deputy editor, who is well grounded in news, had been saying for weeks: 'Where's the silver bullet? We need the silver bullet.' At this time, *The Times* operated two separate fiefdoms. The comment and opinion pages were under the sole discretion and direction of Stothard, while the news pages were left under the supervision of Bryant. Each fiefdom left the other well alone and the system worked well until the newspaper began running story after story about me. Then Stothard started encroaching on Bryant's 'patch', resulting in, first, a collision and, eventually, a disaster.

Toby Follett had been disappointed by the response of Channel 4. Without telling either Fulcrum or Channel 4, he went in search of a new market. He approached the *Independent* with a view to selling his story, claiming that he was able to support it with confidential documents. Follett had placed some stories with the paper in the past but on this occasion the *Independent* was not interested in buying his 'scoop'. Rather helpfully, it pointed out that *The Times* had been running a campaign against me – one that seemed to have passed Follett by.

So on the morning of Friday, 16 July 1999 Follett rang *The Times* and was put through to the editor's office, where John Bryant took his call. Follett explained that he had been working on a Channel 4 documentary about me and, having seen the stories *The Times* had been running, was concerned that the newspaper was about to steal his thunder. He said that he had a 'briefcase full of documents' and was prepared to pool his investigative work with that of *The Times*. Bryant was interested by what Follett had to say and invited him to the newspaper's offices at 3 p.m. that afternoon.

When Follett arrived at the main reception of News International at 3 p.m., he was taken to see Bryant, the former *Daily Mail* executive who had first come to public attention many years earlier when he helped Zola Budd, the South African middle-distance runner. Stothard was still at lunch, so Bryant and Follett had a long discussion during which the deputy editor concluded that his visitor was a complete flake. Bryant was preparing politely to show Follett the door when Stothard returned from lunch and ushered Follett into his office across from Bryant's. The deputy editor followed the two men into the room.

Follett then produced some of the Drug Enforcement Administration (DEA) documents containing my name. He spread them out on the table in Stothard's office, but made it clear he was not prepared to leave them with the newspaper. At some stage during the meeting, Bryant excused himself, saying he needed to visit the lavatory. He took his own papers with him, but at the same time managed to scoop up some of Follett's documents. As he passed the secretaries outside, he handed them Follett's documents and whispered, 'Quick. I want you to get the best possible copies of these. I'm going to the loo. On the way back, I'll pick up the originals from you.' This was done, and when Bryant returned to Stothard's office, so did Follett's papers, just as surreptitiously as they had left in the first place.

Follett was to have a busier afternoon than he had expected at the offices of *The Times*. An overexcited Stothard had called in Tom Baldwin and Alastair Brett, the paper's legal manager, to join the meeting. As Follett talked of his contact, Jonathan Randel, and the position he held in the DEA, a mood of triumph overtook Stothard, Baldwin and Brett. At last, it seemed, they had the 'silver bullet'. Bryant was less persuaded and sought out Andrew Pierce, a senior reporter, putting him on notice that there were some documents that needed to be checked out. By the time Bryant returned to the meeting, Stothard had taken the decision to run a story in the next day's paper. Bryant's immediate reaction was 'No': he felt this was a difficult story which needed to be properly checked out and corroborated. Was it all a hoax? Even if it was not a hoax, what did it all mean? More time was needed, Bryant warned. 'Ashcroft's a litigious man. He'll sue,' he said. Stothard would hear none of it. He went out of the meeting and asked Pierce to call Jonathan Randel. By now, other reporters had sensed that something was up and a palpable sense of excitement started to grow in the newsroom. Pierce started by ringing international directory inquiries to get the number for the DEA in Atlanta. The next call was considered so vital that, as Pierce made it from his desk, Stothard sat anxiously behind him, eager to witness the call at first hand. Pierce then rang the DEA number and asked whether Jonathan Randel worked there. 'Of course,' came the reply. Pierce checked Randel's job title and asked to be put through to him. Randel answered the phone and confirmed that he knew Follett. Furthermore, he confirmed to Pierce that he knew of me. 'Has Ashcroft been interviewed by the DEA?' Pierce asked. Randel replied, 'He has not been questioned personally, but his name, his bank and his businesses have been tied to our inquiries.' Randel lied when he said that I had been 'tied' to the inquiries, but this rushed four-minute conversation – together with the documents that the journalists had seen – was enough 'proof' for *The Times*. By the time Follett left the newspaper's office, he had made it clear that he was after two things – his name attached to one or more of the future stories (which newspapers are often reluctant to agree to when dealing with freelancers they do not know) and money (although he had apparently agreed to divide any earnings with Randel). When Follett eventually departed late that afternoon, he took with him all his documents – unaware that some had been copied and that these duplicates would remain in Wapping.

I will provide my detailed comments later on the substance – or rather the lack of it – of the NADDIS documents. The copies of the chaotic and haphazard records listed, among other things, my 'links' to the case of Thomas Ricke, the American jailed in 1992 for laundering money gained from organised crime. There were other hastily written records of possible 'links' I had to three other drugs investigations but, crucially, nothing to suggest that I had been, or was currently, at the centre of a DEA investigation. Follett also had a second set of documents which he had obtained during his earlier 'fact-finding' trip to America, but these likewise provided no evidence that I or any of my businesses had done anything wrong.

Perhaps the desperation of *The Times*'s journalists for a big story initially clouded their judgement. Once they had hurriedly digested the contents of the DEA reports on me, however, senior journalists at *The Times* must have known, as reasonably intelligent people, that they effectively had a gun but no bullets. From that moment onwards, therefore, their aim was to show the gun and not let their readers know that there were no bullets. Such little journalistic integrity as they had shown up to that point now evaporated. The paper no longer made any pretence of carrying news stories: it was simply trying to smear me.

Instead of carefully checking out the story and asking experts to analyse the importance and relevance of the NADDIS records, *The Times* scrambled together a story for its issue the next day. Most days the paper was off-stone at 8 p.m., but on Fridays the deadlines were earlier and the paper went off-stone at around 7 p.m. This meant that just four hours after Follett had walked into the building with his DEA documents, and against the advice of the experienced executive in charge of news, Stothard took a breathtaking risk with my reputation – not to mention that of his newspaper – by publishing a story the next day. 'Drugs agency has Ashcroft on its files' was the front-page splash in *The Times* of Saturday, 17 July. The story read:

> The US Drug Enforcement Administration has a series of files in which Michael Ashcroft, the Conservative Party treasurer, is named after several years of investigations into cocaine smuggling and money laundering in Belize.
>
> Official DEA documents seen by *The Times* in its London offices yesterday make numerous mentions of Mr Ashcroft and his extensive business interests in Belize and the Caribbean.
>
> Mr Ashcroft had come under scrutiny as part of four

separate investigations dating back to the late 1980s to the early 1990s. 'He has not been questioned personally but his name, his bank and his businesses have been tied to our inquiries,' a senior DEA source told *The Times* last night.

This so-called senior DEA source was, of course, Jonathan Randel. The article continued:

There is no suggestion that the DEA, a federal body with sweeping powers to stem the flow of drugs pouring into America, will lay charges against Mr Ashcroft, who spends most of his time in Florida. Mr Ashcroft was not spoken to by the DEA in the course of its inquiries.

The Tory party treasurer's name appears for a number of reasons, including his ownership of the Bank of Belize and the role played by his firms in regulating the country's lucrative offshore shipping and financial services industries. At least one of the investigations has a European dimension.

Until the day before publication, when I was approached by *The Times*, I had no idea that my name was recorded on DEA files. I had to respond to the paper without seeing the details of my record, but I was determined to give a vigorous response. The paper, for once, used my statement prominently in the story:

If such a file exists, and I have no evidence that it does, obviously it contains no facts that would sustain a charge as there has been no such charge, and the DEA has never even made any attempt to contact me.

I make this categorical statement: I have never been involved in drug-trafficking or money-laundering. My business affairs are entirely proper and no amount of smear, rumour or innuendo will alter that fact.

I am a tough and determined man and I have made many enemies over the years. I also have many aggressive competitors, and I am involved in politics which has always attracted dirty tricks and smear tactics. Now I can add *The Times* to my list of enemies. However, being an enemy doesn't make you right, simply hostile.

I set up Crimestoppers in 1987. I am Chairman of the Trustees. I have given this organisation millions of pounds and over the last 12 years it has been responsible for 29,000 arrests. Given these facts – as opposed to rumours – I clearly do not condone wrong-doing.

I regarded the story as a despicable piece of journalism. It was simply a smear tactic using the DEA references to cause me maximum embarrassment and damage. Yet there was not a single allegation against me and I had never even been questioned, let alone charged, by the DEA or any policing authority. *The Times* had hurried into print when only a cursory check with the DEA would have revealed that millions of people around the world have a DEA reference – and even a NADDIS number – solely because of the nature of their job or the people they have travelled with or met either professionally or socially.

The paper, yet again, used the story as its front-page lead story and had more background – much of it repeating claims and innuendoes of recent weeks – on pages 4 and 5. I sensed, however, that *The Times* was getting increasingly desperate and that I might not have to wait long before the paper overstepped the mark even more outrageously than it had done already.

I TOO, however, had spent a busy few days deciding my strategy against the newspaper. My battle with *The Times* was reaching crunch-point and I felt that it was important for me at this stage to be seen as confident of my position, which was exactly what I was. So that weekend I gave interviews to three media organisations – two newspapers and a radio station – that I was convinced would give me a fair hearing.

My first interview was with Andrew Alderson, the chief reporter of the *Sunday Telegraph*, whom I agreed to meet on the recommendation of a friend. I revealed details of my funding to the Conservative Party, which at that point totalled more than £3 million. The aim of the disclosures was to show just how inaccurate the initial stories in *The Times* had been. It was, however, another story which the journalist picked up independently – but which I eventually confirmed off the record to be true – that caused the biggest stir. The *Sunday Telegraph* revealed in a front-page story of 18 July that I had been promised a peerage by a government minister if I defected to the Labour Party. The minister told me that I could 'get an honour quicker with us than the Tories' given that Labour was in power. Even now I do not intend to identify the minister because it was clearly intended as a private conversation and I do not want to break his, or her, trust. I have no doubt, however, that the approach – which I quickly dismissed – was serious.

I also gave an interview that weekend to Jeff Randall, then the editor of *Sunday Business*. I acknowledged to Jeff, who is someone I have known and respected for many years, that the controversy over my interests in Belize was damaging my party. 'This is not good for the Conservative party, I accept that. But everyone takes a buffeting in politics and I guess I have been overdue [one],' I said, adding: 'I'm one of life's buccaneers and I'll take on a very aggressive challenge.'

Finally, and perhaps most significantly that weekend, I gave an interview to Andrew Neil, the broadcaster, publisher and writer, for his popular BBC Radio 5 Live show called *Breakfast with Andrew Neil*. It was my first interview for radio or television about the problems that I had faced as Treasurer of the Conservative Party. Andrew has a reputation as a tough questioner, but he is also fair. He prefaced our interview by briefly summarising *The Times*'s campaign against me. 'And now Michael Ashcroft is fighting back. He's given interviews to both the *Sunday Business* newspaper and the *Sunday Telegraph*, and he's given a broadcast interview – but only one: it's to this programme.'

I told Andrew that I had no intention of stepping down as Treasurer of the party and that at no time had I offered my resignation to William Hague. I also tendered my first explanation for how I thought I had ended up on Drug Enforcement Administration files. Andrew said: 'But it is, surely, of concern to yourself and to everybody else that you are making numerous appearances in Drug Enforcement Agency [sic] files?' I replied: 'The only thing I can answer to that is that the suggestion is outrageous. But there again, I do operate in the Central American area, and therefore I would expect that someone who is one of the largest movers and shakers is always of interest. But I did speak yesterday to the American Ambassador who was there for five years until last year [in fact George Bruno was in post 1994–7]. And he confirmed to me that as far as he was concerned the American authorities had no worries or concerns about me at all.'

I was open with Andrew about my financial assistance to the Conservative Party. I confirmed that £3 million was a reasonable estimate of my total donations at that point. Andrew then asked: 'In addition to the £3 million that you've talked about in donations to the Tory Party from yourself, have you paid off previous debts due to the Conservatives and are you helping to secure the existing debt?' I replied: 'No. I've never guaranteed any overdraft of the Conservative Party and, no, I haven't paid off any debts other than the part which came through the contributions that I've just mentioned to you.'

Giving any interview, but particularly one to a radio or television programme, is always a gamble because you do not know what is going to be thrown at you. As I have indicated, I am a private rather than a secretive man, but I believe that given the unusual circumstances it was the right thing to do. Tim Franks, Radio 5's political correspondent, clearly thought I had emerged from my grilling well because he was asked by Andrew Neil for his live reaction to my decision to speak to two Sunday newspapers and Radio 5 Live. The political correspondent replied: 'It's almost slightly surprising that he hasn't spoken until now, because it's been the whole perception of the man in the shadows, this perception of sleaze, that word you keep using in your interview, "controversy", that's surrounded him. And in a sense it makes absolute sense for him to come out now and to deny all this because at the moment, up until this point, we just had these stories running in the newspapers and there'd been nothing really concrete to counter it. So I think tactically it's absolutely the right thing for him to have done. And clearly he has absolutely no intention of offering his resignation.'

EVEN AS my interview was being aired on the morning of Sunday, 18 July, Toby Follett was preparing to revisit *The Times*'s east London offices. He had a busy few days ahead of him as the newspaper worked day and night to prepare its latest stories against me. Indeed, Follett went to the offices of *The Times* for three consecutive days until Tuesday, 20 July, and had a series of meetings with senior representatives from the newspaper.

Over the weekend, I had asked David Hooper, my solicitor, to write to the editor of *The Times* urging him to publish the DEA reports on me in full. David wrote to Peter Stothard on 18 July saying that Andrew Pierce, the paper's assistant editor, had indicated that *The Times* intended to publish extracts from the report over the coming week. 'If Mr Pierce is right, it clearly exposes your paper's intention to use the report selectively in an attempt to damage and smear our client's reputation rather than to inform the public by the publication of accurate and truthful information. If the latter had been the case you would have published full details yesterday,' David wrote. 'Your approach seems to belong to the realm of the witchhunt rather than proper reporting. Smear and innuendo appear to be being used to mask a lack of hard information. Publishing carefully selected quotations of the DEA report would be in clear breach of your obligations under the Press Code. Considerations of fairness and the right of reply seem to have been jettisoned some time ago. If there is any justification for publishing the DEA report it should be published in its entirety.'

Predictably enough, Stothard refused to publish the reports in full. Over the weekend, however, the news was dominated, not by my minimal references in DEA documents, but by a tragedy: the death of John F. Kennedy Jr in a plane crash off the eastern coast of America. For once, even *The Times* had to concede that this was of more interest to its readers than yet further smears about the Treasurer of the Conservative Party. For a couple of days, articles about me received reduced prominence, but the newspaper continued to print negative stories.

On Monday, 19 July, *The Times* carried a front-page story headlined 'Portillo raises doubts about Ashcroft links'. The article, written by Tom Baldwin and Roland Watson, read:

> Senior Tories led by Michael Portillo, the former Cabinet minister, have questioned William Hague's judgement in appointing Michael Ashcroft as Tory party treasurer. Mr Portillo has told friends he had always feared that suspicions over the sources of Mr Ashcroft's wealth might embarrass the party.
>
> It is also understood that John Major, when he was Tory leader, was told by advisers to 'keep his distance' from the controversial billionaire.
>
> At the same time, another former Cabinet minister gave warning that unless Mr Hague could mount a concerted fight to clear Mr Ashcroft's name, he would have to reconcile himself to losing his treasurer. Although Mr Portillo emphasised he had no specific evidence against Mr Ashcroft, he said privately that the rumours surrounding the businessman's activities should have been enough to prevent him from being appointed to such a senior post in the party.
>
> The former Defence Secretary told friends that the Tories had to do more to counter their reputation for sleaze, saying the issue could keep the party out of power in the way industrial unrest in the 1970s did for Labour. *The Times* has disclosed that the Drug Enforcement Administration in America had files naming Mr Ashcroft and his Belize businesses in connection with investigations into money-laundering and drug-trafficking. DEA sources said there were no plans to charge the Tory treasurer with any offence.

In an interview with BBC radio, Mr Ashcroft said:

'What I have managed to piece together is that there was something that terminated in 1992 and in which it was more a general look at Belize than me.' He said it was outrageous to suggest that he had personally been involved in money-laundering or drug-trafficking.

He also made it clear that he had no intention of resigning as Tory party treasurer and said he had not even spoken to Mr Hague last week. He said: 'I am one of life's buccaneers and I'll take on a very aggressive challenge.'

I was initially slightly surprised by the comments that had been attributed to Michael Portillo. However, he assured me later that they had been taken out of context and apologised if the misunderstanding had caused me any embarrassment. Since I was all too aware myself of the sloppy standards of the newspaper's reporting, I was happy to accept Michael's explanation. For all his complexities, I believe he is a decent man.

On the same day, *The Times* also devoted page 4 to me with the disgraceful headline 'Ashcroft admits US drugs inquiry' – it was clearly designed to imply that I was actively under suspicion of being involved in skulduggery – rather than a more truthful and representative headline indicating that I denied any involvement in drugs trafficking or money laundering. A more appropriate and accurate headline would have been along the lines of 'Ashcroft denies any role in drugs trade'.

That Monday morning of 19 July, even as the newspaper kept up its frenzied attacks on me and with Follett still midway through his debriefing, there were those on *The Times* who had serious reservations about the wisdom of its stories about me. John Bryant, the newspaper's experienced and wily deputy editor, called all those involved in the stories about me – with the exception of Stothard – together for a meeting. He said there should be no more 'stuff about Ashcroft' in the paper until the 'silver bullet' had been produced, as he was not satisfied from what he had seen that there was anything in the DEA material that met the required standard of evidence. The meeting broke up with a general sense of relief, but one of those present, Tom Baldwin, went behind

Bryant's back to Stothard and persuaded the editor to overrule the deputy editor's diktat.

The newspaper's reporting continued to go from bad to worse. *The Times* used Randel's documents to stage an assault against me in its edition of Wednesday, 21 July. On this occasion, I was photographed on the front page leaving Tory Central Office after a routine visit. The accompanying story was headlined 'Tories strive to defend embattled treasurer' and was a pathetic attempt to try to persuade readers that my days as Treasurer were drawing to a close. Perhaps the paper felt that if it made this claim that I was about to be sacked as Treasurer often enough it would somehow come true. The article began: 'The Tories have launched a concerted effort to bolster the position of Michael Ashcroft, the party treasurer, amid a growing belief at Westminster that his days are numbered.' The phrase 'growing belief' – without any attribution – is another tired old journalistic trick: unidentified and supposedly numerous people were lumped together as if they held a common opinion. Who were these Westminster sources? Members of the Labour Party? Journalists on *The Times*? Whoever they were – if indeed they existed at all – they were wrong. Yet, given the way the story was worded, it was impossible for me to refute or challenge the claims at the time.

It was, however, a story on page 9 that was the straw which broke the camel's back. Bylined by the then unknown Toby Follett – together with Tom Baldwin – it was headlined 'File has practical value for agents'. The article began:

Michael Ashcroft is named in the files of the United States Drug Enforcement Administration because the information is thought to be of 'practical value' to their agents' investigations.

He is sufficiently important to be given his own index number on the Narcotics and Dangerous Drugs Information System (NADDIS), which, according to a confidential DEA memo seen by *The Times*, should not be 'cluttered' with useless information.

Last week *The Times* disclosed that Mr Ashcroft,

who has extensive business and political interests in Central America and the Caribbean, was named in four separate investigations into drug-trafficking and money-laundering. Senior Tories have tried to dismiss the report as a 'red herring', suggesting that he was referred to only in passing because of his prominent role in the Belize economy. Mr Ashcroft later said it was 'outrageous' to suggest he had been involved in any criminal activity.

Although there is no suggestion that the DEA plans to lay charges against him, senior officials within the organisation have confirmed that Mr Ashcroft's name, as well as businesses including the Belize Bank, have been tied to investigations dating back to 1989.

The memo from the DEA says that people on the NADDIS index should include those suspected of drug violations or connected to businesses and vessels suspected of involvement in the narcotics trade. It adds: 'Business firms or vessels which are just incidentally involved will not be indexed.'

The criteria for indexing also rules out 'officials of business firms' if they are not suspects or have not been 'contacted in the course of the investigations'. Yesterday, as the Tory leadership mounted a concerted effort to shore up Mr Ashcroft's position, the party treasurer spent most of the day locked in private meetings at Conservative Central Office.

At the same time, two Commons motions were tabled to increase pressure on Mr Hague ...

This story went further than before in suggesting, without anything to back it up, that I had been an important figure in the DEA agents' inquiries. As was to be characteristic of *The Times*'s campaign, these serious accusations were not properly put to me in advance of publication. A journalist from the newspaper had contacted David Hooper, my solicitor, the day before the article was printed. David had made the reasonable and proper request that any questions should be forwarded to me in writing so that they could be addressed fully. This request, as with countless others like them in the past and future, was turned down.

The article – as my legal team readily confirmed – had overstepped the mark by a long way. It was grossly defamatory and was designed to leave the reader in no doubt that the DEA believed that I was a suspected drugs runner – and a key suspect at that. The report was clearly saying that agents of the DEA suspected me of involvement in four separate investigations, and of drugs trafficking and money laundering. I was also perturbed by the claim that 'senior officials within the organisation have confirmed that Mr Ashcroft's name, as well as businesses including the Belize Bank, have been tied to investigations dating back to 1989'. This, I would later discover however, was false: *The Times*'s only source within the DEA was the abjectly inept Jonathan Randel.

On Tuesday, 20 July, between 9.40 a.m. and 10.58 a.m. local time, Jonathan Randel accessed six files from NADDIS which contained references to me. He printed off copies of the files on a DEA printer. For some reason, the DEA has always referred to these as the 'Dallas' documents. Randel then scanned this material on to a second computer within the DEA offices and sent these files as attachments by e-mail, again carelessly using the DEA's own system rather than his own. They were sent to jan.white@newsint. co.uk between 11.49 a.m. and 11.53 a.m. local time. Jan White worked as the secretary to Alastair Brett, the legal manager of Times Newspapers. Quite why Randel sent these documents to him is unclear, but it appears that the newspaper belatedly wanted from the horse's mouth a full record of the NADDIS documents that related to me. There was also at least one document relating to me that Follett, for some reason, did not have in his possession and this was contained in one of the files that Randel sent to *The Times* on 20 July.

Tom Baldwin had, early in the third week of July, made contact with Peter Bradley, the Labour MP for The Wrekin. Bradley, a self-styled champion of the left, was one of those odious, little-known MPs who will do virtually anything to get their name in the newspapers. A former public schoolboy, Bradley had profited from a career as a public relations/planning adviser to out-of-town superstores that were often built in Labour-run areas. His main claim to fame, however, was as a principal critic of Dame Shirley Porter, whose stewardship of Westminster Council had been overshadowed by scandal. He had only been elected as an MP for the first time in 1997 but he saw publicity as essential to promotion in the Labour Party.

On the evening of Tuesday, 19 July, Baldwin and Bradley were spotted huddled together on the terrace of the House of Commons. With the help of others at *The Times*, Baldwin had drafted a speech for Bradley using *The Times*'s in-house computer system. This draft was seen by most of the senior editorial team at *The Times* before its so-called author, Peter Bradley, had seen it himself. Baldwin ran through the draft with Bradley and showed him some of the DEA documents to which the speech referred. He tasked him with reading out extracts from the confidential NADDIS files in the House of Commons. As an MP, Bradley had the benefit of parliamentary privilege, which meant that he could not be the subject of a defamation action even if his claims were untrue. *The Times* – and indeed other media organisations – had qualified privilege in the reporting of his speech, provided any articles were fair and accurate and were not malicious. To ask an MP to make allegations in the House of Commons that a newspaper does not dare to make on its own is one of the oldest tricks in the journalist's book – and also one of the cheapest.

Bradley delivered 'his' speech – I suspect with some amendments of his own – to an attentive House of Commons on Tuesday, 20 July. At 11.41 a.m., Bradley stood up and said:

> I should like to raise some important issues before the summer recess – issues that some Conservative members may not wish to hear, but that need to be raised none the less.
>
> In recent weeks, there has been much interest and speculation about Mr Michael Ashcroft. Many allegations have been made. Many revelations have appeared in the daily papers about his status as a foreign funder of the Conservative Party, about his business dealings and

about his relationship with the previous Government. Throughout it all, the Leader of the Opposition has stood by Mr Ashcroft and said that he has no case to answer. Mr Ashcroft has conceded that his connections with the Conservative Party are causing it damage, but he still resolutely refuses to go.

May I remind the House who Michael Ashcroft is? He is a United Kingdom tax exile. His principal residence is in the United States of America. His principal business interests lie in Belize. He funds the Government party there – the People's United Party, which I understand has recently sought advice on joining the Socialist International. He is Belize's ambassador to the United Nations. He is a citizen of Belize; he is also a citizen of the Turks and Caicos Islands. As far as I know, he is a citizen of other places too. All those credentials are considered by the Leader of the Opposition to qualify him for his other job: treasurer of the United Kingdom's Conservative Party.

He then rehearsed the familiar innuendoes:

Mr Ashcroft is a man about whom our man in Belize warned the Foreign Office: there was, he said, a 'shadow over his reputation that ought not to be ignored' – of course, that shadow has been ignored by the Leader of the Opposition. Mr Ashcroft is a man whose business interests, according to a report by Rodney Gallagher, which was sponsored by the Foreign Office as part of its aid to Belize, were creating 'a growing sense of disquiet' in Belize – a sense of disquiet clearly not shared by the Leader of the Opposition.

Mr Ashcroft is a man whom our former high commissioner in Belize, Mr David Mackilligin, described last week as 'an object of suspicion to governments in the area, especially the Americans who have to cope with constant war against drug-runners and money-launderers.' He went on to write in a letter which appeared in *The Times*:

'he cannot escape responsibility for establishing a system that makes Belize a much more tempting target for drug-runners than it would be and for resisting efforts to regulate it properly in order presumably to maximise his company's profits'.

That is, apparently, what motivates Mr Michael Ashcroft – the bottom line. It is not political conviction; I have mentioned that he funds not only the Conservative Party, but the People's United Party in Belize. It is not personal loyalty. It is not public interest, but the ruthless pursuit of the bottom line. He has made money out of flags of convenience in Belize, which is known to have one of the worst safety records in the world. According to *The Independent* this morning, he has sold passports for profit. According to our Foreign Office diplomats, he is prepared to 'stir up trouble' for Britain in the Turks and Caicos Islands if he does not get his way.

Bradley now exploited parliamentary privilege in order to inten-sify the smearing:

In no fewer than ten of the 40-odd votes in the Unit-ed Nations since he has been Belize's ambassador there, Mr Ashcroft has voted against the United Kingdom. As I have said, he has opened the door in Belize to money-laundering and drug-trafficking through his interference in the regulation of its financial sector. The linking of Mi-chael Ashcroft to the drugs trade is the most alarming aspect.

On Sunday, Mr Ashcroft told the BBC that, although he was aware of one investigation undertaken by the Drug Enforcement Administration in the United States, he be-lieved that it had concluded in 1992 and that its principal interest was Belize, not him. To be caught up in one drugs investigation may be just bad luck – a big man in a small place at the wrong time – but there is more.

I have seen documents, which have also been seen by

The Times – files of the DEA, the FBI and the Bureau for International Narcotics and Law Enforcement Affairs. All refer to Michael Ashcroft and his business interests. I have no reason to believe that they are forgeries. They are taken from the files of United States investigation, intelligence and enforcement agencies. They make disturbing reading.

In 1989, Mr Ashcroft's name was linked to a DEA drug-trafficking inquiry that stretched across Europe, the United States and Canada, and involved the son of Jean Baptiste Andreani, who was immortalised, if that is the right word, in *The French Connection*. In 1992, a Thomas Ricke was arrested and jailed for laundering money, gained from organised crime, through Michael Ashcroft's Belize Bank. In 1993, the DEA conducted an investigation of Belize-linked businesses, half of which were connected to Michael Ashcroft – 12 of the 25-odd that it investigated had links with Michael Ashcroft.

At this point, some two-thirds of the way through his speech, Bradley was asked by Christopher Gill, the Conservative MP for Ludlow, to give way, but the Labour MP was having none of it. He continued:

In 1994, a DEA file reported observing Michael Ashcroft taking a flight from the United States to the Caribbean. It referred to 'possible air smuggling/money laundering activities under way by Michael Ashcroft'. It also reported that the plane was owned and piloted by two suspected drug traffickers.

In 1996, Mr Ashcroft was the subject of another investigation [by the DEA]. In 1997, a man arrested in Holland on suspicion of drug offences gave as his address the same address in Belize as Mr Ashcroft's principal company, Belize Holdings. These are serious matters.

I do not claim that Michael Ashcroft is guilty of any offence. I simply do not know, but nor does the Leader of the Opposition. However, he above all should be concerned about these allegations. The drip, drip, drip of disclosures is becoming a torrent that threatens to engulf the Conservative Party. It is extraordinary that the Leader of the Opposition has taken no action about it. After all, it was he who said just last year: 'We are not going to have in the future any of the kind of controversies that have dogged us in the past over funding.' He said it, but did he believe it and did he mean it?

If Michael Ashcroft were just another businessman, we would take little interest in him, but he wants to play a role in British public life, and that gives us legitimate interest in his affairs. That is why the Leader of the Opposition must refer him to the ethics and integrity committee that he established recently. That is why he should relieve him of his post as treasurer of the Conservative Party, and why he should consider returning to him the donations that he has made in recent years.

Michael Ashcroft says that he will not go. Only one man can decide his fate – the man who says that he runs the Conservative Party – but does he dare? Does he have the courage or even the authority to sack him, and can he afford to, given that Michael Ashcroft is the man who owns the Conservative Party?

The Conservative Party says that sleaze is a thing of the past, but it is running its [by-election] campaign in Eddisbury on money from Belize and tomorrow it will ask the people in that constituency for their trust. Does the Leader of the Opposition want it said that Michael Ashcroft is the man who defines the Conservative Party? This is the real test of his qualities of leadership. He has a big decision to make.

Bradley then sat down at 11.51 a.m., having rattled off his – or more accurately his *Times*-inspired – speech in just ten minutes and having ensured that *The Times* and every other media organisation had qualified privilege for the most scandalous claims against me.

Bradley had been allowed by *The Times* to deliver the speech without being informed that, by this stage, the newspaper knew that Sir Denis Thatcher and the London City Ballet had NADDIS references. *The Times* had deliberately kept this detail from the MP because it knew it would discredit its 'revelations'. Indeed, there was much humour within the walls of Wapping when the name of the London City Ballet came to light. 'I never realised the bulge in the tights was actually a stash [of drugs],' said one journalist at the time.

Bradley's speech was packed with smear and innuendo but was without substance. It contained an abundance of the favourite journalistic phrases such as 'linked to' and 'connected to' – the language that libel judges are all too familiar with and look upon with disdain. Bradley's phrase 'These are serious matters' was pompous drivel – perhaps a carefully rehearsed soundbite to provide newspapers with the option of using the word 'serious' – as of claims or allegations – in a headline. Bradley threw in, for good measure, a totally misleading claim against me – no doubt unchecked by him – from that morning's newspapers. 'According to *The Independent* this morning, he has sold passports for profit,' he told MPs. Bradley had tried, in just twelve words, to convey an image of me standing on a street corner flogging illegal passports to all and sundry.

Nothing could have been further from the truth. The reality of the situation was that one of my businesses, the Belize Bank, had provided, with the encouragement of the Belize Government, 'economic citizenship' packages. The Government – like many others around the world – wanted to offer incentives for wealthy individuals to invest in Belize and the packages, which included a passport, could be purchased – perfectly legally and above board – through several accredited suppliers. Similar packages are offered all over the world, including Switzerland, and are available for purchase from the world's most respected accountancy firms. Bradley had ended his speech by baiting William Hague and questioning whether he had the courage to sack me. As a self-styled champion of justice and fair play, Bradley ought to have been ashamed of himself. Here was a politician so desperate for publicity and so desperate to impress his Labour masters that he was encouraging a situation in which a man – just because he was a political opponent – was guilty until proven innocent.

Christopher Gill, no doubt much to his relief, eventually got his chance to speak to the House on the subject of commercial forestry. Despite having his mind on his address to MPs, Christopher was astute enough to spot Bradley's ruse and he could not resist pointing it out to the Commons. 'The House will understand that what the hon Gentleman has said was covered by Parliamentary privilege, but I did not hear him cite any specific charges that had been brought against Mr Ashcroft. I remind the House of the very important principle and tenet in British law that a man is innocent until proved otherwise. The hon Gentleman questioned the motives and motivation of Mr Ashcroft, but I hope that I shall not be out of order in questioning the hon Gentleman's motives. He spent 10 minutes giving us a lot of innuendo but, as far as I know, he was unable to substantiate that with any facts.'

A 'celebratory' dinner took place later that evening in the Churchill Room of the House of Commons which did nothing to hide the nature of the alliance between the newspaper and the Labour MP. Baldwin was the host, Bradley the guest of honour. Around the table were a number of other MPs, as well as Andrew Hood, a special adviser at the Foreign and Commonwealth Office and a close friend of Baldwin's. During the dinner, Peter Mandelson came over to congratulate Baldwin and Bradley on the wonderful work they had done for New Labour that day.

There are no prizes for guessing which speech *The Times* concentrated on the next morning. Indeed, it devoted the best part of five pages to 'The Ashcroft Affair' in its issue of Thursday, 21 July. It even quoted the deranged comments made later in the Commons by Dennis Skinner, the Labour MP – allegations that provoked uproar from MPs on both sides of the House. Once again speaking with the benefit of parliamentary privilege, he took it upon himself to intervene: 'The Tory Opposition are receiving £1 million a year from one of the biggest drug runners in the West.' As can be seen from this, Skinner's playful image as the so-called 'Beast of Bolsover' belies a deep streak of unpleasantness. Despite the preposterous nature of the comment, it was gleefully reported by *The Times* the next day.

However, Stothard and his fellow journalists on *The Times*, along with their stooge Bradley, had, once again, not been the only ones to be busy in the course of Wednesday, 20 July. I, too, had been holding meetings with my legal team because my patience had finally ended. I was no longer prepared to tolerate *The Times* and its sly and desperate campaign to discredit me. I had decided that enough was enough.

6 Fighting Back

'ENOUGH IS enough.' Thus I began my open letter to the editor of *The Times* dated 21 July 1999.

> When I agreed to have breakfast with you and Lord Bell six weeks ago, I listened carefully to your allegations and answered all the points you raised. You told me that I had given a good account of myself and I had expected to hear little more about it. How wrong I proved to be!
>
> Since that time, there has been an almost constant stream of inflammatory articles in *The Times* about me, about Belize, and about organisations with which I am connected.
>
> I have tried to be reasonable. My lawyers have written to you day after day asking you at least to have the decency to check the facts with me before you publish. You have consistently refused to do so.
>
> Instead, we have witnessed perhaps the most one-sided, partial and coloured account of anyone's affairs ever produced by a newspaper in a free country. You print deliberately selective quotes, you twist every detail and comment. You are the spin-doctor in this sorry saga.
>
> Everything that fails to fit the construction which you have chosen to place upon events is ignored, even official statements from the Government of Belize, the US State Department and the Governor of the Central Bank of Belize.

I went on to explain why I was taking no more:

Over the years, I have developed a thick skin and, until now, I have been able to ignore your allegations. But in the last 24 hours you have gone too far. As you know, I established Crimestoppers and I have been chairman of Action on Addiction [a charity set up to help drug addicts]. I do not condone crime, and in particular I do not condone drug-trafficking.

I have nothing to hide. On Sunday, my lawyers wrote to you asking you to publish the infamous DEA reports in full. You declined to do so. Instead, we were last night warned by one of your journalists that a Labour MP had been set up to ask questions in the House today about me. Step forward Peter Bradley.

This morning, you published more about me, making it perfectly clear to your readers what you consider my track record to be on both drug-trafficking and money-laundering. This was followed, as planned, by Peter Bradley's performance in the House of Commons.

This co-ordinated campaign – this conspiracy – to smear me at a crucial point in the run-up to an important by-election is disgusting.

I have asked myself the question, why is *The Times* doing this? Until last night, I was unable to find an answer. But I learn from one of your journalists that, following your failure to prevent Greg Dyke's recent appointment, you have told your colleagues that instead you intend to get me. I have no intention of allowing you to get me. I am this afternoon issuing a writ against you, your employers and two of your journalists.

The article I had chosen to sue the newspaper over was the one printed that morning – 21 July – headlined 'File has practical value for agents'. It was the article that was clearly intended to leave the reader with the impression that the Drug Enforcement Administration suspected me of being a drug runner and money launderer. My decision to seek damages had nothing to do with the collusion between the newspaper and Peter Bradley over the Labour MP's abuse of parliamentary privilege to level further allegations against me.

Stothard replied to me through the pages of his newspaper the next day in an open letter. His newspaper published both our letters side by side on page 5. Opposite the letters, taking up virtually the whole of page 4, was a verbatim record of Bradley's speech, composed with the help of *The Times*. Stothard wrote:

> Thank you for your unusual personal letter to me. Since you have released your letter to the press, I intend to do the same with this reply.
>
> I too recall our meeting last month. When Lord Bell asked me to see you for breakfast, I raised various points relating to your degree of financial and political control over the Conservative Party. You answered a number of my questions and, although you later chose to give on-the-record answers to other newspapers, *The Times* published the fullest possible account of your replies.
>
> Subsequently we received information and opinions about your business and political activities in Belize. Following normal journalistic practice, we conducted our investigations and asked you to respond to every substantial point in turn. It was striking that while you were frequently prepared to comment off-the-record you were almost never ready to give replies for publication.
>
> In these difficult circumstances we strove strongly for balance. I reject absolutely your characterisation of our reports as 'the most one-sided, partial and coloured account of anyone's affairs ever produced in a free country'. But this is not, perhaps, the best place for a history lesson on the British and American press.

He concluded:

> During wholly legitimate investigations into your position as Conservative Party treasurer, our reporters have been in

contact with many politicians and officials in Britain, the US and the Caribbean. Some have supported you; many have not. Among the latter are both the Labour MP who addressed aspects of your recent past in the Commons today and many senior Tories who have been publicly more reticent.

Today we have sent you a copy of one of the relevant documents upon which our continuing inquiries are based. This, and others which will also be available to us, will form the basis of a vigorous defence against your writ if you are determined that these matters should be aired in open court.

There has been no conspiracy. My personal view is that the Conservative Party has done itself no credit in this affair. I am far from alone in that opinion. But your attempt to connect our reports to the timing of the Eddisbury by-election is absurd – as is the contention that you are linked to our position on the next Director General of the BBC. The investigation has had – and still has – a momentum wholly of its own.

Stothard's reply was disingenuous and predictable. It was misleading to claim that I had been given every opportunity to reply – point by point – to the allegations made against me. My request to see the evidence and for the newspaper to publish in full the DEA reports that related to me had been rejected out of hand. For weeks, whenever the newspaper was doing a story on me the next day, it had tended to contact my office between 5 p.m. and 6 p.m. Journalists knew that, given my lifestyle, I was likely to be on the other side of the world and either difficult or impossible to contact. *The Times* did everything possible to ensure that I had insufficient time and information to make a full and detailed reply to its stories. There was also no admission in Stothard's letter of the way *The Times* had manipulated Bradley and parliamentary privilege for its own ends. Furthermore, it was the newspaper – not me – which was hiding behind anonymous sources who were making false claims and providing inaccurate information. Why was Stothard providing just one document – a partially redacted one at that? Why did he not have the courage to provide me with all the so-called evidence against me?

The newspaper's coverage of the events of Wednesday, 21 July matched Stothard's letter in its lack of honesty and its predictability. *The Times*'s front page was dominated by the story under the headline 'MP's onslaught against Ashcroft'. There were two prominent photographs showing William Hague and myself leaving a fundraising dinner at the Stafford Hotel in central London the previous night. For the first time, the newspaper also published a photograph of an extract from one of the DEA reports on me: one of those referred to by Bradley in his speech.

The story on page 1 began:

> Michael Ashcroft, the Tory Party treasurer, issued a writ against *The Times* yesterday hours after he had been named in Parliament in connection with a US Drug Enforcement Administration investigation into money-laundering and smuggling.
>
> Peter Bradley, Labour MP for The Wrekin, speaking in the House of Commons under parliamentary privilege, detailed a series of allegations against Mr Ashcroft based on official US documents.
>
> He quoted from a DEA report dated April 1994 saying Mr Ashcroft, who had recently given £3 million to the Tories, was observed boarding a flight from the US to the Caribbean. The documents, the existence of which was first disclosed by *The Times* last week, said the aircraft was piloted and owned by 'suspected drug traffickers', the MP added during an early morning debate. Mr Bradley went on to read the title of the report: 'Possible air smuggling/money laundering activities underway by Michael Ashcroft'.

It was thoroughly dishonest of *The Times* to suggest I had been 'named' in Parliament yet still make no mention of the central role that it had played in bringing this about. There was also an initial implication that I had sued as a result of Bradley's speech, which was also, of course, not the case.

I had, as a matter of courtesy, told William Hague about my decision to serve a writ. He was entirely supportive and indeed was quoted in *The Times* in its front-page story on what he had told the 1922 Committee of backbench Tory MPs. 'I am not going to allow people to be driven from positions in the party by smear and innuendo. We will now see whether Labour MPs have the courage to say outside the House what they had the cowardice to say inside.' As one might have guessed, there was a deafening silence from cowardly Labour MPs, including Bradley, once they stepped out of the House of Commons and, therefore, no longer had the protection of parliamentary privilege. In battle, I suspect Bradley would have been one of those who shouted 'charge' while running to the rear for his own safety.

In some ways, I was pleased that *The Times* had finally given me the chance to sue on a narrow, clear-cut issue. This enabled me to ring-fence the issue that I was seeking damages over and there would be no justification for the newspaper to bring in a host of other issues which would have prolonged the length of the legal action. I am a busy man and I wanted to devote my time and energies to growing my companies – not to fighting a High Court battle that, if it spiralled out of control, could have taken the best part of a year out of my life.

The article in *The Times* had provided the opportunity, in the words of my anxious fellow Tories, to 'do something'. A senior Tory MP later told me: 'There was a feeling of relief throughout the party when you served the writ. The campaign by *The Times* had made many people in the party feel a bit queasy: some were concerned because *The Times* was widely considered to be a reputable newspaper and they were worried in case there was "no smoke without fire".'

On 22 July 1999, the *Daily Telegraph* carried a much fairer report on the events written by George Jones and Robert Shrimsley. The story appeared under the headline 'Tory tycoon to sue over drug slurs: Ashcroft fights to clear his name'. It was only much later that I discovered that reporters in the newsroom of *The Times* had, that very morning, been debating their rival newspaper's headline. There was near universal agreement that the word 'slur' was definitely an accurate way to describe what I had been sub-jected to – as a result of *The Times*'s actions – the previous day.

Once I had served the writ, I was relishing the prospect of confronting the key figures in the High Court. After deciding to sue, I asked David Hooper, my solicitor: 'Who is the QC most likely to strike fear into *The Times* if the paper learned that he was representing me?' Without a moment's hesitation, David re-plied: 'George Carman.' Within hours I had acquired George's charismatic services at a time when he was widely regarded as the most formidable libel silk of his generation. He was a veteran of countless libel battles and I was particularly looking forward to witnessing someone as astute, flamboyant and devastating as George tearing into the likes of Peter Stothard and Tom Baldwin. I knew that George would cross-examine them in the most ruth-less manner and that – since I assumed that even this dubious duo would have to tell the truth under oath – it would be a joy to see their deceit exposed to the nation in the High Court.

Now, too, it was my opportunity to turn investigator. I and my legal team needed to find out which people were behind the campaign to discredit me and to what lengths they had gone to smear my name. I suspected that some of the tactics that had been used against me were unfair, even illegal, but nothing prepared me for the scale of dishonesty and criminality that I would eventually uncover.

Even when my fiercest business rivals have acted aggressively against me and my companies, I have never allowed such rivalries to turn to personal animosity. Matters did, however, become in-creasingly personal as I realised that some senior journalists and executives at *The Times* were determined to do all they could to bring me down – and were harming my livelihood at the same time. The newspaper was trying to do me down not with the qual-ity of its information but by the quantity of it. It was relying on endless column inches of disinformation, smear and smoke. By the mid-summer of 1999, all journalistic integrity had evapor-ated. On 22 July – the day after I served my writ – Michael Gove, a senior leader and comment writer on *The Times*, went on Radio 4's *Today* programme and was repeatedly asked by Ed Stourton, the presenter, whether *The Times* had passed the DEA reports to Peter Bradley. Time after time, he evaded the question, squirmed in his seat and prevaricated until eventually he said he did not know how Bradley had got hold of the DEA reports. My reaction at the time was that Gove was either lying or, alternatively, that he should not have been put on the programme to represent his newspaper if he did not know the answer to such a straightforward question. I initially suspected that it was the former, but I later learned – and not from Gove himself – that he had been recruited to go on the *Today* programme, even though he knew little about the story, because he was considered eloquent. However, due to his lack of knowledge of the ins and outs of the story, he put up a lamentable performance, and Stothard later went on to *The World at One* to try and repair the damage.

Some senior journalists were, however, as baffled by *The Times*'s campaign as I was. Boris Johnson, the editor of the *Spectator* and, later, the Conservative MP for Henley-on-Thames, poked fun at *The Times* and other media organisations which had sent reporters to Belize to try and get a story on me. In an article in the *Daily Telegraph* published on 21 July and headlined 'Show us the skeleton, boys – or catch the plane home', Boris wrote:

> Think of us, you BBC men, you Channel 4 honchos, when you raid the minibar tonight in the Radisson Fort George Hotel and head for an easy-skanking moonlight picnic on the Cays; think of us who pathetically scour your dispatches for something, *anything*, to explain the Ashcroft hysteria.
>
> What do we have, after a month of nudge-and-wink blackguarding by *The Times*? We know that this Ashcroft Johnny is jolly rich; that he has given roughly £3 million to the Tory party; and that he keeps his loot stashed in Belize, where he is a big noise. Apart from that, we have two-thirds of sod all.
>
> The gravest charge seems to be that he lobbied to pro-

tect his investment in Belize against tax by an incoming government. Is that a crime? Day after day we wait in London for the skeleton to tumble from the closet, clutching a bag of cocaine. Perhaps someone will send me a manila envelope containing a picture of Mr Ashcroft, arms round the shoulders of Mr Rankin' Dread, the senior Yardie. But until we receive better intelligence from Belize ... we are forced to conclude that the Conservative Party treasurer is the victim of an old-fashioned smear.

So he pays little tax in Britain: that's a bit rich coming from a paper owned by Rupert Murdoch. OK, so he's also Belize's ambassador to the UN. He was even on the delegation when Belize voted to outlaw the first strike of nuclear weapons – not exactly in line with UK policy, let alone Tory policy. You might think that was odd, or you might think that it was just the kind of useful job a buccaneering British patriot ought to have in his portfolio. Either way, how does it make him a crook?

... So I say to our chums [*The Times*'s journalists] on the beach in Belize: produce the smoking gun, that killer fact, that escrow account: or put a sock in it, because even Rupert Murdoch might begin to ask if your pina colada is justified.

IN HIS quest for fame, Toby Follett, *The Times*'s informant, had wanted his name on one or more of the newspaper's articles about me. This name appeared on the very article on which I decided to sue and Follett therefore found himself one of the defendants in my libel action. This disturbed him enormously and he became increasingly paranoid, imagining – incorrectly – that I had him under twenty-four-hour surveillance. To reassure him that he would be protected, Alastair Brett, the legal manager of *The Times*, even allowed Follett to stay at his house.

The Times was keen to mount a swift and vigorous defence to my libel action. However, after my writ had been served, its lawyers were dismayed to find that not a single journalist, other than John Bryant, had kept notes about what had happened. Bryant's own habit was to keep notes on the back of the day's news schedule. This meant they were dated and were, by definition, contemporaneous. The notes, however, recorded many things (including Bryant's reservations over stories about me) which the lawyers did not like and, in preparing the defence, they had to work around them. I later discovered – as a result of evidence presented to a US court by the Drug Enforcement Administration – that the newspaper gave Randel a return Delta Airlines ticket so that he could fly to London. Presumably, too, the newspaper hoped he would help sustain its editorial campaign against me. As Randel prepared to fly to London, he told his wife: 'Toby's in trouble. I need to go to London to help him out.' He failed to mention – or perhaps even to realise – that he would soon be in serious trouble himself.

The Times was prepared to spend good money on securing its only witness. Randel was put up at an expensive central London hotel, One Aldwych, where even then rooms cost £290 a night. The list of awards the hotel has won is almost as long as its main restaurant's formidable wine list. In May 2001, the *Toronto Globe and Mail* described it as 'the best hotel in the world'. More recently, in January 2005, the 105-room hotel, which has a fifty-six-foot swimming pool with underwater music, was chosen as one of 'The Best Hotels in the World for Location' by Condé Nast Traveller Gold List. Brett and his legal department arranged Randel's accommodation and his timetable, and they went to great lengths to keep the identity of the hotel a secret. Presumably their paranoia was still working overtime. Did they really think I was monitoring – even bugging – their every move and every conversation? Apparently so. The reality was that at that time I did not even know who Randel was, let alone where he was staying and why.

On 27 July, a clandestine meeting, with elaborate anti-surveillance precautions, took place at the Waldorf Hotel in central London. Tom Baldwin, the paper's deputy political editor, was considered too close to the story and too hot-headed and was excluded from the meeting. Alastair Brett, the legal manager of *The Times*, and Andrew Pierce, the paper's senior reporter, were charged with debriefing Randel, acting out the 'good cop/bad cop' scenario, while Heather Rogers, the newspaper's barrister, looked on. When asked why he was doing this, Randel said it was because it would be the making of him in Hollywood – he was convinced that he would move on to being a script writer and producer in Tinseltown. Pierce was unimpressed. 'This bloke is a flake,' he later concluded. In fact, when Randel admitted that he had used the DEA computer in his own office to download the documents, Pierce was unable to hide his despair at the man's naive behaviour and started banging his head against the table in front of him. On Saturday, 31 July, Randel flew back to Atlanta, arriving the same day. His hotel bill of £1,261.83, including phone calls, was picked up by Stephen Farrell, a reporter on *The Times*, using his Master-card. Farrell, who had been assigned to look after Randel while he was in London, recovered the money on his expenses.

US investigators were later to discover that on Monday, 2 August, the first working day after his return to America, Randel opened an account at an Atlanta branch of the Wachovia Bank, depositing a cheque from an unidentified source for $4,751. Two days later, on 4 August, a wire transfer for $3,218.20 (this would have equated to a sterling payment of £2,000) was transferred into the account from Follett's account at the Nationwide Building Society in Swindon, Wiltshire. DEA investigators uncovered this information when they visited the branch in Swindon to pursue their inquiries into Randel. Then, on 27 September, Randel received a further wire transfer from News International, the parent company of Times Newspapers, for $4,905. Eventually, it was established that *The Times* had paid Randel some £6,000, plus his travel and hotel expenses, and Randel had also received a further £2,000 from Follett. Just days after Follett had first walked into *The Times*'s offices hawking his material about me, Fulcrum had learned that he was selling information which the television production company had commissioned. Not surprisingly, Fulcrum – on Channel 4's behalf as well as its own – was unhappy about this and, after a three-way meeting between the parties, a written contract was struck whereby *The Times* paid £9,000 to reimburse Channel 4 for the expenses it had laid out, via Fulcrum, the production company, for Follett's trip to the United States. Follett was paid a further £25,000 by *The Times*, which he agreed to share with Randel. In short, Follett and Randel (the latter earned only some £30,000 a year) had achieved a nice little earner for selling the DEA's secrets – not to mention their own souls – to a newspaper that was devoid of principle, that was disrespectful of the law and that had long given up even any pretence of occupying the moral high ground.

I LODGED my detailed case against *The Times* in a legal document – the Particulars of Claim – on 4 August 1999. The claim was made against four defendants: Times Newspapers Ltd; Peter Stothard, the newspaper's editor; Toby Follett, the newspaper's informant; and Tom Baldwin, the newspaper's deputy political editor. Follett and Baldwin had been bylined on the article in question. My claim quoted extensively their story headlined 'File has practical value for agents', which had appeared on page 8 of the newspaper on 21 July. The claim was issued in the name of my counsel: George Carman QC, James Price QC and Mark Warby. It stated:

> In their natural and ordinary meanings the words complained of meant and were understood to mean that Michael Ashcroft:
>
>> is suspected, as a key suspect, on reasonable grounds by agents of the United States Drug Enforcement Administration in four separate investigations, of playing an important role in drug trafficking and drugs-related money-laundering; and/or
>>
>> is guilty, or very likely to be guilty, of such offences and/or is centrally (and not merely incidentally) involved in the narcotics trade, and as such is currently the target of DEA agents' investigations.

The claim declared that I was seeking damages, including aggravated damages, because 'as a result of the publication of the words complained of Mr Ashcroft has been gravely defamed, and has been caused anger and distress'. It went on to outline how the newspaper had chosen to ignore supportive comments from a range of relevant groups and organisations which had made it clear that I had never been accused of acting illegally and that I was not, and had never been, under investigation.

The claim also highlighted the lack of honesty from *The Times* and detailed how Michael Gove, its leader and comment writer, had been less than straightforward in his interview for Radio 4's *Today* programme about his newspaper's links with Peter Bradley, the Labour MP. 'Asked whether *The Times* had shown the documents to Mr Bradley Mr Gove repeatedly sought to evade that question, and to divert attention from the issue. Mr Gove concluded by giving the impression (which he must have known to be false) that *The Times* had not been instrumental in Mr Bradley seeing the documents, and was unaware of how he had done so. Mr Ashcroft will rely on this interview as an implicit admission that the conscience of *The Times* was affected by its conduct. TNL [Times Newspapers Ltd] and Mr Stothard only admitted helping Mr Bradley when Mr Stothard was driven to do so by Mr Bradley's own admission in an interview for Radio 4's *World at One* programme on 22 July 1999.'

I decided that, with so much misinformation flying around, I should put the record straight. I wrote an article which appeared in the *Daily Telegraph* on 24 July under the headline 'I'm an honourable man and I am staying put'. I wanted to redress the balance and, in particular, to refocus the public spotlight on my role as party Treasurer, which despite all the sensational headlines had been going rather well. I wrote:

> In an increasingly rare idle moment, I found myself yesterday imagining a scene in which Gene Hackman is asked to dust down Popeye Doyle's famous hat in preparation for the filming of *French Connection III*, in which he faces up to the deadly villain Limey One, a dark and sinister

drug runner who doubles as the Treasurer of the Conservative Party. I got as far as contemplating a car chase under the Hammersmith flyover before I was once again dragged back to reality.

Distinguishing between fact and fiction has become a preoccupation in the past few weeks. During this time, I have been on the receiving end of lies dressed up as fact, innuendo made to look like testament and the innocent cast as the dishonourable. I have been given cause to re-examine many aspects of my life but, thus far, with the exception of a little attention to a certain shirt, I am pleased to say that my friends have not seen the need for change.

I said that we had travelled a long way in the previous month, but that it was clear to me 'that the accusations which kicked off this campaign betray the true intent of those who continue to guide its progress'.

I stood accused variously of making a donation of £4 million to the Conservative Party, of guaranteeing its loans, of helping to increase its overdraft, and of funding it to the tune of £360,000 per month. It was implied that the party had become a rich man's plaything, and that I was that man. None of this is true.

Political parties need a great deal of money to make themselves heard in the fiercely competitive market place for the eyes and ears of the public – let alone for their hearts and minds. When I assumed responsibility for the party's finances just over a year ago, the truth of this statement could not have been more evident.

We had just fought a general election. Our overdraft at one time was hard against our £4 million limit and we had £3 million of pressing creditors. Today, our overdraft limit remains at £4 million, and we are comfortably within it. And we no longer have £3 million of pressing creditors. However, contrary to what some would have you believe, this improvement is not the result of a massive donation from me, nor indeed from any other donor.

The revival of the party's finances results from a steady and detailed programme of work involving almost 300 people throughout Britain. The irony is that we cannot rely simply upon the generosity of a small number of major donors. We need a broad base of giving in order to secure the party's future.

For the record, as a donor to the Conservative Party, I fulfil the spirit of Neill [a reference to the guidelines issued by Lord Neill's Committee on Standards in Public Life] in that I am a British citizen and I am entitled to vote in Britain.

I went on to indicate the true scale of my payments:

I make no secret of the fact that I have been a financial supporter of the Conservative Party since the 1980s, and that my donations, and donations from others related to me, have in that time totalled £3 million or so. I expect to make a further major commitment this year. But how could I not? I am perceived as a wealthy man. How can I ask others to give to the party if I do not give myself? Am I to say: 'I haven't given because *The Times* will say it doesn't look good'? I am proud of the fact that I am a Conservative. I am an 'all-weather' supporter and I intend to lead from the front.

My donations this year are likely to represent about 10 per cent of the party's income, but no amount of money gives me any say over policy. Nor would I want it. My aim in fundraising is to be able to approach a broad church for support. I do not get involved in policy matters.

The party's finances are in good shape, and they're getting better. This is, of course, good news for the Conservatives, but it is also good news for Britain. This country needs a strong, well-financed and effective Opposition in order to keep the Government on its toes.

It does not, however, take much imagination to conclude that there might well be those for whom a well-financed Opposition is not such a welcome development.

Destabilising the structure which will guarantee the future finances of the Conservative Party could in some circles be seen as a crafty wheeze, and my head as a significant prize. Rest assured that I intend to keep my head well away from anybody's trophy cabinet. I've got a job to do.

On the day my writ was issued, Dominic Kennedy, a reporter on *The Times*, was in Washington where he had gone to interview George Bruno, the former US Ambassador to Belize. Kennedy had been told that the diplomat would 'knife' me and deliver the 'silver bullet'. After his interview, Kennedy had to telephone his news desk and say that the outcome had been rather different. 'Bruno said that Ashcroft's a good bloke actually,' he reported. 'Did he?' came the reply from the news-desk executive. 'Well, that good bloke has just sued us.'

IT WAS time for others to show where their loyalties lay. Unsurprisingly, Peter Bradley, the Labour MP who had colluded with the newspaper to blacken my name, came out for *The Times* in an article in the *Independent* on 28 July headlined 'I retract nothing on Mr Ashcroft'. In a rambling and pompous article, Bradley made a pathetic attempt to justify his abuse of parliamentary privilege. 'It is no secret that, before I made my speech, I contacted *The Times* and asked if they had papers about the existence and content of which I had long been aware. I was right to ask and *The Times* was right to show me. I would not have spoken on the basis of hearsay. In the event I spoke on the basis of evidence,' he wrote. 'I knew the Tories would huff and puff about parliamentary privilege. But privilege is an essential feature of our democracy. It gives MPs the right to raise various issues in the public interest without fear or favour. It is upheld when MPs believe, like I did, that what they are saying is true. It is abused when what they are saying is false – as has been the case with those Tories who have since used it to smear my name.'

What Bradley did not do, however, was repeat the allegations without the benefit of parliamentary privilege. He had not been open in his speech to the House of Commons when he said, 'I have seen documents, which have also been seen by *The Times*.' In fact, he was being extremely economical with the truth, which was that he had been *supplied* with the documents by the newspaper in order to abuse parliamentary privilege. His statement had not revealed who had contacted whom or indeed that there had been any contact. His article posed more questions than it answered. How had Bradley 'long been aware' of the existence of the DEA documents about me in the build-up to his rambling speech in the House of Commons on 20 July? *The Times* itself had known nothing about the documents until Follett walked into its offices on Friday, 16 July. If Bradley had known about the documents well before this date, why had he not brought them to the public's attention earlier? Or was his claim simply, as I strongly suspect, a figment of his over-active imagination?

After my writ had been served, however, others came forward with statements which supported my legal action against the newspaper. George Bruno, US Ambassador to Belize from 1994 to 1997, told the *Guardian* that the American authorities had no evidence that I was linked to any illegal activities. In an interview published on 28 July, he said that references to me in DEA reports 'meant nothing'. Furthermore, he added: 'One must ask whether this is a politically motivated campaign. If there is anything against Mr Ashcroft, I have not seen the substance. This is a tempest in a teacup.' His comments could hardly have been more useful to my cause: George said that it would be wrong to assume that I was being investigated merely because my name appeared in DEA documents. 'I would question their validity. I would be highly sceptical of any news organisation having access to classified DEA documents ... DEA documents include details that could be nothing more than a DEA source pretending to be a friend of a powerful person,' he said. 'I don't know from where these stories came. But as someone once said, "Where's the meat?" I haven't seen any.' George could just as easily have made his comments to *The Times* if the newspaper, rather than rushing into print to blacken my name, had asked him and others in positions of responsibility just how easy it was to receive a mention in a DEA report. George's comments to the *Guardian*, predictably enough, went unreported by *The Times*.

It was Taki Theodoracopulos, the witty Greek newspaper columnist, who summed up the campaign against me entertainingly and succinctly in an article published in the *Spectator* on the same day. Taki devoted just three paragraphs to my libel action but nobody could accuse him of sitting on the fence:

> Which brings me to Michael Ashcroft. No, I've never met him and he has never offered me his private jet, but if he is forced to resign as Tory party treasurer it will be yet one more example of why the Tories deserve to disappear as a political party. Ashcroft has done absolutely nothing wrong except leave England in order to make his billions, and to employ 45,000 people. Bums like Peter Mandelson can go around making trouble for Ashcroft, but how many people has Mandelson ever given employment to? In fact, how many of Blair's cabinet have ever earned a living outside politics? How many have ever created jobs or employed people? None is the answer. The disgrace, of course, is that of *The Times* and the dirty work the newspaper has done to facilitate Labour's dirty tricks. Peter Stothard, the editor, has chosen innuendo and distortion when he wasn't libelling Michael Ashcroft.
>
> Stothard is the same little man who had his little wife write an article in the *Guardian* denying his cross-dressing [Stephen Glover had written in the *Spectator* that Stothard used to wear kaftans at Oxford].
>
> Stothard and his ilk are envious little creeps trying to destroy a self-made man by the most outrageous lies. If Ashcroft is involved in drugs because he owns banks in Belize, so is David Rockefeller and every other banker we

know. If Ashcroft is involved in drugs because he flies a private jet, so is every other private jet owner – the poor little Greek boy, too, as I plan to buy a share in one. This is what *The Times* has come down to. I hope a jury throws the book at Murdoch's catamites, and that Stothard is fired for disgracing a once good newspaper and for cross-dressing. But enough of such ugly and jealous people.

As summer 1999 turned to autumn, I was increasingly looking forward to my day in court: it could not come quickly enough. My legal team was busy throughout that time preparing our case and anticipating what would be the likely thrust of *The Times*'s defence. As part of the 'discovery' process when two sides are preparing for a defamation action, I finally got to see the DEA documents in early December. When my legal team and other advisers saw them, they could not believe how flimsy and inconsequential the newspaper's 'evidence' against me was.

I will explain, to the best of my knowledge and ability, how it seems I came to the attention of the DEA on several occasions. The only reason that I had a NADDIS record – and that *The Times* wrongly concluded that I must be a suspected criminal – is that the DEA monitors millions of innocent people as part of its wide-reaching and often indiscriminate fact-gathering process. Journalists from *The Times* had read the guidelines and become excited by suggestions that the NADDIS index should only include information of 'practical value' to their agents' investigations. However, far from giving NADDIS numbers only to suspects, the DEA gives them out routinely as an easy way of facilitating cross-referencing. The fact that an individual or a company or an organisation had a NADDIS number did not mean they were a suspected drug runner or money launderer – far from it.

In his speech to the Commons, Bradley had said that I was linked in 1989 to a 'drug-trafficking inquiry that stretched across Europe, the United States and Canada, and involved the son of Jean Baptiste Andreani, who was immortalised, if that is the right word, in *The French Connection*'. At this time, the Icelandic and Danish authorities were making routine checks of passengers who stopped off in Iceland on the 'North Atlantic route'. Iceland had, apparently, become a favoured meeting point halfway between northern Europe and the US for drug smugglers, and Operation Ice Track was launched to try to identify and catch the offenders.

My reasons for being in Iceland were straightforward. By 1989, I already had my first private plane but, unlike my present one, it did not have the range to fly across the whole of the Atlantic. I used therefore to stop off in Iceland either to refuel or, while I was working a great deal in America and Belize, to meet European business contacts. It was halfway for both of us. At this time, the ever vigilant DEA was monitoring the movements of executive jets to and from Iceland, and this meant that my plane and its passengers were given NADDIS numbers. My bad luck was to choose the same convenient location as a drug smuggler for business meetings. This may have been unfortunate for me but it was hardly a crime. However, it did account for me picking up a NADDIS number for the first time in my life.

Bradley had also gleefully told the Commons about my 'links' to the case of Thomas Ricke, the American jailed in 1992 for laundering money gained from organised crime. As already noted, an associate of Ricke's had deposited $25,000 for him with the Belize Bank, which I controlled through one of my companies. I did not know and had never heard of Ricke or any of his associates. No one has ever claimed that the bank or its staff was to blame. I was not a bank teller. It was absurd to suggest that I could be held responsible for verifying the propriety of a single transaction involving just one of the 40,000 savings accounts held by the bank at the time. Regardless of how responsible and thorough they are, large banks do occasionally handle the financial affairs of drug runners and criminals because every crook has a bank account and it is not always possible to know who is honest and who is not. Like it or not, most crooks in Britain will have an account with at least one high-street bank.

A DEA report of 1994, also referred to by Bradley in his speech, mentioned 'possible air smuggling/money laundering activities underway by Michael Ashcroft' relating to a flight of mine in the Caribbean. This is the easiest of all to explain. Occasionally, when my own aircraft was out of use, I used to charter a private plane to fly me around the Caribbean. On one occasion, I had flown in a private plane from Fort Lauderdale, Florida, to the Bahamas. It was my misfortune that the aircraft – which I had chosen at random from an advertisement – the aircraft's owner and one of the two pilots all had a NADDIS number. I had never met or even heard of the man who owned the plane, although I was to discover that he was called Victor Belote. This did not stop me, however, from receiving another unwelcome – but totally un-merited – DEA entry. In July 1999, the *Mail on Sunday*, unlike *The Times*, tracked down Belote. 'My business is being a lumber manufacturer, not smuggling cocaine,' he told the paper, adding that he was as 'straight as an arrow'.

I believe my name was initially brought to the notice of the DEA office in Belize for no other reason than that I was in-vesting heavily in the country and travelling extensively in the region. By Belizean standards, I was an extremely wealthy businessman and the millions of dollars that I was investing rep-resented an abnormally large amount. If I had been investing in a bigger and wealthier nation, such sums would not have been considered so unusual. The DEA office in Belize essentially sub-mitted a 'cuttings job' on me, mainly information gathered from newspaper articles and the internet that was in the public domain, to its Atlanta headquarters in 1994. As I have already indicated, at a later date Crimestoppers, my crime-fighting charity, and the London City Ballet, the height of respectability, would be given NADDIS numbers because of their links to me. The 'club' of unlikely NADDIS number holders also included Sir Denis Thatcher, who, I would contend, was as unlikely a drug smuggler as it is possible to find. Why, one might wonder, was *The Times* not running an article headlined 'Denis Thatcher named in drug agency probe' pointing out that the guidelines said the files should not be 'cluttered' with trivial information and that therefore he must be a suspect? The DEA was routinely giving utterly honest and respectable people like Denis and me a NADDIS number. It was blindingly obvious that the DEA was, for whatever rea-sons, less than exact in following its own guidelines. The way it operated clearly led to thousands and thousands of innocent people being given NADDIS numbers. How could *The Times* and Peter Bradley not see this? The DEA was, like many large organisations, prone to human error. Denis, rest his soul, was listed in DEA records as the 'son of former British PM Margaret Thatcher'.

As part of my lawyers' inquiries, they tracked down and interviewed a recently retired senior officer with the DEA. Tony Bocchichio, a man with twenty-five years' experience in the organisation, was able to explain how the DEA drew up its records. He said he found it ironic to learn that ADT, the large company I had built up in the United States and beyond, had a NADDIS number – because it supplied the security systems for many of the DEA offices across the US. He also said that Operation Ice Track, which had given me my first NADDIS number because I was flying in and out of Iceland, was a typical DEA operation – planes taking off from and landing in Reykjavik would have been cross-referenced to existing records. Tony Bocchichio, who had been in charge of 800 staff, considered it ridiculous that I had been linked to the Thomas Ricke investigation merely because there had been a deposit of money in my bank. The main thrust of the interviews that he gave my lawyers was that the allocation of a NADDIS number meant little, if anything. The phrase he used was that having a NADDIS number was 'less than circumstantial evidence'. He said that a NADDIS number was for reference only – he knew that congressmen and senators had been given NADDIS numbers. The officer added that God might have one if someone has used the name as an alias and it had featured in a DEA report.

My lawyers also worked out in September 1999 the extent of the resources that *The Times* had used. No fewer than twenty-three journalists on the paper had written or contributed to articles on me. Between 5 June and 27 July alone, the paper had carried an astonishing eighty-six separate articles and letters about me. Furthermore three journalists – Damian Whitworth, Dominic Kennedy and Paul Durman – had stayed a total of twenty-eight days in Belize. Never can a newspaper have spent so much money trying to find 'dirt' on an individual and yet found so little – in fact, nothing at all.

*

IN EARLY October, as the Conservative Party gathered in Blackpool for its annual party conference and my lawyers waited for *The
Times* to submit its defence to my action for defamation, something rather extraordinary happened. Peter Stothard, the editor
of *The Times*, ran an unprecedented full-page leader in his newspaper under his own name headlined 'Tories and Treasurer'.
I suspect that he was hoping he would be regarded by fellow
journalists as defiant, but I looked upon his article as the
desperate action of a desperate man, one which must have left
the majority of his readers thoroughly baffled. Indeed, I doubt
whether more than a small number bothered to reach the end
of his 3,000-word rant. It is virtually unheard of for any leader
article in a newspaper to be more than a few hundred words at
the most.

It went over much of the old ground already covered by
countless leader articles which Stothard had either written or commissioned earlier in the year. The article also had a sanctimonious
and condescending tone to it whereby Stothard implied that his
campaign against me was motivated by his desire to reform the
Conservative Party for the better. It began:

> When William Hague was elected as Conservative lead-
> er, he promised an open, accountable party and a break
> with the record of sleaze, scandal and unchecked foreign
> financing that had accompanied the catastrophic electoral
> defeat in 1997. This morning in Blackpool the people who
> make up the real Conservative Party have a rare chance to
> question those who rule their party and ask themselves if
> these promises have been kept.
>
> Members of the National Conservative Convention,
> senior representatives of those who raise Tory funds and
> rouse Tory voters at local level, are due to discuss 'house-
> keeping issues' before the main conference begins. Few
> politicians like to discuss the money that they rely on for
> their campaigns. But the Tories' heavy reliance today on

the wealth of one man, their Treasurer Michael Ashcroft, needs seriously to be discussed.

During the summer *The Times* set out a range of dis- quieting facts about Mr Ashcroft in a number of articles. In the opening days of this new political season, many Tory friends have tut-tutted to me about these investiga- tions. Why, they ask, should a newspaper editor of known conservative outlook, who has been a regular and mostly supportive attender of Tory conferences for 20 years, seem so opposed to a man who is pouring millions of pounds into the party in its present dire need? This question de- serves an answer. This is that answer: and members of the convention may care to consider it this morning as their meeting begins.

The article then went on to try to justify the newspaper's belief that it had been duty bound to look into the concerns of senior Conservatives about the extent to which I funded the party. Stothard sought to imply that the rejection of William Hague's recommendation that I should become a working peer was highly significant. He tried to imply, too, that I was preventing my party shaking off its reputation for sleaze and that I worked too closely for comfort with a supposedly corrupt government in Belize. He openly criticised the party for failing to investigate its Treasurer. Stothard moreover had the audacity to say that Michael Ancram, the Conservative Party Chairman, was wrong to suggest that the newspaper was waging a political campaign against me. 'Nothing could be further from the truth,' he wrote. He went on:

The only question over which I know we [Michael An- cram and him] disagree is whether, in the best interests of British politics and public life, Mr Ashcroft should be Treasurer of the Conservative Party.

Some of my Conservative friends say that they under- stand and even share my concerns but that I have simply made too much of them, that I have published too much over too short a time and acted in a way that is too far from the traditional *Times* character. My defence to such criticism, which I understand as well-meant, is threefold.

First, once we had begun our investigations, the information about Mr Ashcroft poured rapidly forth. Most of it was documented in official records; but each point had to be checked and, if it was of worthwhile public interest, prepared for publication. Allegations were carefully put to Mr Ashcroft for response and, although he almost never gave us an on-the-record reply, a very great deal of what we found was newsworthy; the resulting articles were newsworthy in the most literal sense that their content was new and, for the public good, worthy of publication.

Secondly, we were trying to alert the Tory leadership to an issue which was potentially seriously damaging to the party. If Mr Hague and Mr Ancram chose not to listen, our only option was to keep speaking out, more often than we might have liked.

Thirdly, in presenting an investigation boldly, we were acting firmly within a *Times* tradition. In 1967, to take an example from a different area of public interest, William Rees-Mogg's *Times* investigated what became a notorious police corruption case at Scotland Yard. 'The method of revelation bordered on the sensational,' commented the Metropolitan Police Commissioner, Robert Mark. 'It read more like the *People* or the *News of the World* than *The Times*.' And so it did. And it was right that it did. As another editor of *The Times* wrote in 1852 in response to repeated attacks by the British Government: 'The press lives by disclosures.' Then, as today, *The Times* lives by disclosures.

Stothard then went on to call for a debate within the party on its own funding before rounding off his article – one of the longest opinion pieces ever submitted by an editor to his own newspaper – with what I can only assume was meant to be a rallying call to his rapidly dwindling rump of Tory supporters.

Let me end with a warning of muddied waters. Not all of those criticising our interest in Mr Ashcroft deserve as sympathetic a reply as this has been intended to be. There are those rival newspapers which, in the search for a competitive advantage and short-sighted favour with the party hierarchy, would rather parrot party propaganda than behave as a candid friend. There are the Tory authors of that propaganda who, whether they believe in Mr Ashcroft's suitability to be Treasurer or not, have decided to bury their heads in the Blackpool sand and kick out wildly at whomsoever brings an unwelcome message. And there is Mr Ashcroft himself, who has chosen to issue his writ for libel.

Some of Mr Ashcroft's supporters have expressed the hope that this writ will stop us writing about him. That, I must tell them, is an empty hope. We will continue to investigate the Treasurer's affairs and publish what is relevant and new in the public interest. Today the volunteers of the Conservative Party can directly confront what their leaders would rather forget. And afterwards they must continue that confrontation – and take the inevitable criticism for speaking more loudly than is their wont – if their party is to be reformed and ready to govern Britain again.

Stothard's self-serving diatribe was of course predictable in that I had always expected that he would use the start of the Conservative Party conference to try to find a way to embarrass me. So it had been with a certain amount of trepidation that I opened my copy of *The Times* on the first Monday of the conference in my room at the Imperial Hotel. I had a variety of reactions to Stothard's article. My initial one, even before reading the article, was that if he needed a full page he must be concerned by the weakness of his newspaper's case against me. After reading through it, I could see the main purpose was the few lines in which he said he was *not* accusing me of being involved in drugs and money laundering. This claim took my breath away because this was clearly now going to be at the centre of his defence. Coming as it did just days before the defence was due to be submitted, it was a crass attempt to build the newspaper's case in the public arena rather than in confidential pleadings.

What were these 'disquieting facts' that *The Times* had revealed about me? 'Facts' such as Gordon Baker, the then British High Commissioner in Belize, revealing in 1997 that 'rumours do cast a shadow over his reputation', though not providing anything to justify such a statement? 'Facts' such as *The Times* repeatedly misleading its readers about the ludicrously exaggerated size of my donations to the Conservative Party even though they had been repeatedly told their information was wrong?

On reflection I was annoyed, too, that he should be making a final plea to the party hierarchy to dismiss me when it was already clear that William Hague and other senior party members had given me a vote of support on the basis of my work as Treasurer. Furthermore, I was incensed by the number of inaccuracies in the piece. Indeed, the claim that the newspaper had 'carefully put' its allegations to me almost made me choke on my breakfast. As I have shown, reporters from *The Times* had repeatedly ignored my requests for time to answer the claims against me. On the article I sued on, for example, the newspaper had rejected my reasonable request that any questions should be put in writing. How, too, could Stothard seek to compare the allegations his newspaper had used against me based on no evidence at all with *The Times*'s investigation into genuine corruption at Scotland Yard in the 1960s? Finally, I found it galling that someone as petty and unreliable as Stothard should have the nerve to portray himself as a 'candid friend' and a courageous protector of both the Tory Party and the public. For Stothard to claim that his paper was speaking out 'more often than we might have liked' was humbug. If his message was, as he suggested, directed at William Hague and Michael Ancram, Stothard could have written a private letter to them rather than involve the entire readership of his newspaper.

There was, however, much comfort to be gained from Stothard's article. Two strands ran through the article: an overwhelming sense of desperation which encouraged me to pursue my libel action ever more vigorously, and an overriding impression

that senior party officials had privately been telling the editor of
The Times that his campaign was ill conceived and misguided.
Furthermore, it gave my lawyers a strong, advance indication
of the nature of the newspaper's 'public interest' defence to my
defamation action. As I began wandering around the conference,
other journalists approached me to discuss the article, and their
conclusion was – in the words of one of them – that 'Stothard was
putting up the white flag.'

By chance, that day senior officials from the constituencies
were debating a resolution on whether the Conservative Party
should start to elect its treasurer. Stothard had referred to this in
his article in an attempt to persuade officials to support the new
move. I was therefore delighted when the resolution was crushingly
defeated. The meeting was chaired by Robin Hodgson, chairman
of the convention and head of the voluntary party, who delivered
a cracking speech in my support. Stothard's article had not had its
desired effect and was quickly forgotten amid the hurly-burly of
party conference.

PETER STOTHARD was not the only member of staff on the
newspaper with a burning desire to do me down. Tom Baldwin,
who at the time was the newspaper's deputy political editor, had
also become passionate about the 'Get Ashcroft' campaign. I eventually decided to look into his background and was horrified by
what I discovered.

I found not only that Baldwin was a binge drinker but also that
he was a habitual user of cocaine, the Class A recreational drug.
The more I delved into his past, the more apparent it became that
he was a prime candidate for a lengthy visit to both Alcoholics
Anonymous and Narcotics Anonymous. Baldwin would not be
the first, nor the last, journalist with a drink problem. However,
what I found utterly distasteful and hypocritical was that the journalist from *The Times* who had pursued me the most vigorously
should himself be a heavy and regular cocaine user. It was beyond
irony that I, who had no interest in or connection with illegal
recreational drugs, was being hounded by an addictive personality

who used a Class A drug so much himself that he was fuelling the illegal market for the drug traffickers and money launderers that he claimed to be targeting.

I had met Baldwin only fleetingly at various Conservative Party functions, but the more I learned about him the more I came to agree with the assessment of a senior Conservative MP who has had many dealings with political journalists over the years. The MP told me: 'Tom Baldwin is a clever man but he is not an honest man. I don't believe his principal objective as a journalist is to get at the truth: I think he just wants to have a good story and he doesn't mind if it is true or not provided it puts his name on the front page. He is the journalist I would trust least of any journalist I know.'

The Times's legal manager, Alastair Brett, also appeared to be taking an unusually close interest in me. I have never met Brett. I do, however, have a high regard for his ability, under any circumstances, to try to defend the indefensible. I have an equally low opinion of his integrity. He is a lawyer prepared to resort to discreditable tactics to obtain information that is beneficial to his newspaper. My inquiries into his practices have revealed that in the course of his work as *The Times*'s lawyer he has, at best, exhibited extremely poor professional judgement.

This was certainly true of his conduct in the case of *Carmen Proetta* v *Times Newspapers*. Proetta had been a witness to the SAS shooting of three IRA terrorists in Gilbraltar in 1988 and she brought a libel action against the newspaper group over a story in the *Sunday Times* which criticised her reliability as a witness. In the build-up to the hearing, as both sides submitted argument on the admissibility of evidence, the courts issued two judgements that were critical of the legal department that Brett headed.

In a judgement handed down on 21 February 1991, Mr Justice Drake criticised the way Brett and others had handled an aspect of the newspaper's defence. Joseph Wilkins, a convicted criminal awaiting trial on drugs charges, had offered to give evidence for the newspaper against Proetta but only in return for a payment – to his sister. Payment was agreed, and made. This obviously undermined the worth of Wilkins's evidence considerably. Brett was less than candid about these events, and tried to disguise the payment. In his judgement Mr Justice Drake said: 'It is conceded that Wilkins is a man with an appalling record, and it appears from documents that I have seen that Wilkins asked for payment in return for giving the statement and that the defendants, after the statement was given, did pay £2,000 to Wilkins's sister at his request, which they falsely described as a consultancy fee.'

Six days later, on 27 February, three Court of Appeal judges ruled on the *Sunday Times*'s appeal. They noted how the payment to Wilkins's sister was 'euphemistically referred to in affidavits on behalf of the defendants as a "consultancy fee". It did not feature in their bill of costs. In the event, £1,000 was paid to the sister in December 1989 and a further £1,000 in March 1990. Legal assistance was also afforded to Wilkins by the defendants in regard to his appeal against conviction [for drug offences].' So Brett had arranged for substantial payments to be made to the sister of a man, already garlanded with convictions for fraud, counterfeiting and drug running, to secure his evidence and had even offered to commit the *Sunday Times*'s legal resources to assisting him in overturning his latest conviction. Later in 1990, as the Court of Appeal noted, Wilkins had managed to escape from HM Prison Parkhurst and had gone on the run.

Brett's behaviour came under further scrutiny when the *Sunday Times* was criticised by *Hard News*, a self-appointed television watchdog on newspapers' journalistic standards, for the way it defended libel proceedings. He financed his own legal action against Channel 4 and *Hard News*, in respect of the edition broadcast on 16 June 1991. In January 1994, Brett, then aged forty-three, won 'substantial damages' against the programme but in announcing the result in the *Sunday Times* effectively shot himself in the foot.

For the same story in the *Sunday Times* that announced Brett's 'victory' against *Hard News* also reported his admission that he had made payments totalling £3,000 to a potential witness in the case (Joseph Wilkins, who was not named by the newspaper). Curiously, the payments to Wilkins had somehow risen from £2,000 to £3,000, suggesting that the newspaper's original evidence to the courts in 1991 had been false. On 23 January

1994, the *Sunday Times* concluded its report on how Brett had received compensation, an apology and his legal costs with these two deeply embarrassing paragraphs:

> Yesterday Brett admitted that, with hindsight, he had been wrong to pay a total of £3,000 to the sister of a convicted drug smuggler whom he had been advised to see by leading counsel. He had agreed to the payments (subject to being given an opportunity to check the truth of the information) during prison visits while making important inquiries to defend the libel action.
>
> Brett said: 'I never offered money to criminals: they demanded it from me, and with the exception of one case nothing was ever paid. My problem was that in order to get to the truth behind Proetta, I had to make a snap decision how to deal with the demand for money by a man who could clearly give highly relevant information about Proetta's background.'

So, other than the ranting, misguided and obsessional Stothard, two principal members of the rival team were an alcohol-and-cocaine-fuelled, hypocritical political journalist and an in-house lawyer with appalling judgement who was prepared to pay a criminal thousands of pounds for evidence. It was good to know the sort of people I was up against.

THE TIMES submitted its defence on 7 October 1999. In layman's terms it was a 'kitchen sink' defence in that the newspaper threw anything and everything into it that could cast some doubt on my integrity. This was no surprise, when the only evidence it had from the DEA was a few documents which of course I had at that stage yet to see, but which failed to substantiate the story published. We concluded that the defence was an attempt to cloud the issue and broaden the scope of the future hearing. It came up with a range of arguments suggesting its story was justified, true, privileged and, in any case, not defamatory.

The defence referred to a series of articles carried by *The Times* – not just the one I was suing over – and claimed: 'In publishing those articles, *The Times* was exercising its right of freedom of expression to publish matters of a legitimate public interest.' Furthermore, it denied my claim that the article I had sued on alleged that I was 'guilty' or 'very likely to be guilty' of drug trafficking or money laundering, or that I was even thought to be a 'key suspect'. Finally, for good measure the newspaper also relied on the so-called 'Reynolds defence', a novel and complicated issue that arose from a Court of Appeal ruling the previous year. *The Times* was now citing the 1998 ruling to claim that its report was published after it had done everything possible to verify the story and therefore had a degree of protection from my defamation claim. The newspaper stressed the importance of the fact that I had been listed on four separate occasions on the DEA's Narcotics and Dangerous Drugs Information System (NADDIS). This, the newspaper claimed, meant that the information about me 'was deemed to have practical value for DEA investigations'.

Just a day later, on 8 October, I met with my legal team in London to consider our tactics now that the newspaper had submitted its defence. Both I and my legal team were confident and upbeat. *The Times*'s defence had been weak and predictable and had not thrown up anything we had not expected. George Carman warned me, however, that the case would become a war of attrition and that our primary objective in the run-up to the hearing should be to remove as much extraneous material as possible from the defence. I had sued on a matter that we could manage. I have a life – professionally, socially and politically. I had neither the time nor the desire to litigate on a whole series of irrelevant areas. However, on the fundamental allegations of drug running and money laundering, I had to do what I had to do.

James Price was adamant that the hearing must concentrate on the drug-running and money-laundering allegations, whereas *The Times* would continue to want to widen the scope of the case. James said there were strong grounds for thinking that a judge would strike out everything in the defence except the drugs and money-laundering matters. He advised that an application for summary judgement could also be made whereby a judge would be asked to decide the issue without a trial – to rule that there was nothing in the defence which was substantive enough to require putting before a jury. I decided to go down this route because, if successful, it had the major advantage of fast-tracking my legal action.

By early October, we had also established that *The Times*'s original article had been printed within hours of the arrival in the newspaper's offices of Toby Follett – a researcher who was unknown to them at the time. Far from the newspaper giving me ample time to respond, it had not even given its own journalists sufficient time to analyse and check out the significance of the DEA documents that Follett was providing.

By 16 November, my lawyers had submitted a thirty-seven-page reply to the newspaper's defence, which answered points raised by *The Times*. In the response, my legal team fiercely disputed the newspaper's claims point by point and said that 'the plea of justification is untenable and illegitimate and ought to be struck out'. Similarly, we denied that the newspaper's claims were true, or were subject to any claim of privilege such as the 'Reynolds' defence. We insisted again that *The Times* had intended to allege that I was involved in, or suspected of involvement in, drug running and money laundering. We stressed that the DEA's methods of preparing NADDIS records had become unscientific and lax. It was clear that those drawing up the records had long ago abandoned the direction under the DEA guidelines that the NADDIS index should not be cluttered with 'information of no practical value'. By 1984, for instance, there were NADDIS files on more than one and a half million people, including congressmen, clergymen and foreign dignitaries. By 1991, the DEA had amassed more than two and a half million names on the NADDIS database. By 1999, the figure was five million. Either huge percentages of the population in the US and other countries were suddenly making a living out of drug running and money laundering, or the register had become overloaded with innocuous data. It did not take a genius to conclude that it was the latter.

It was not until 1 December 1999 – a fortnight after my lawyers had submitted my reply to the newspaper's defence – that we were finally sent the DEA documents about me which *The Times* had in its possession. We had been asking for them repeatedly for months, receiving a variety of unconvincing reasons for their non-production. Given what was (and was not) in the documents, I had no doubt that this lengthy delay was deliberate. If the newspaper had possessed what it thought was a 'killer fact', I am sure the documents would have been handed over much earlier. As it was, *The Times* was clearly nervous about delivering its rag-bag of documents, fearing – quite rightly as it turned out – that, when they saw them, my lawyers would find the 'evidence' against me to be laughably weak.

The Times's legal team introduced the documents with an accompanying witness statement from Rupert Earle, the out-of-house solicitor acting for the newspaper. Earle did not identify the source of the information from the DEA – Jonathan Randel – but he did admit that *The Times* had paid him £6,000. Earle said: 'I am told the source received the sum of £5,000 from *The Times*, which went to reimburse him for his work and the expenses he had incurred (including travel, telephone calls and communications, and public information database access, which ran to several thousand dollars). He received a further £1,000 from *The Times* for additional work undertaken at its request.'

I was to discover later that the line that Earle had been fed was a joke. History was repeating itself, with *The Times* paying an informant for information, then dressing it up as something else. At the time, though, I knew little about the criminality, or even the identity, of the so-called reliable and authoritative source. There was still much that I needed to find out if I was to get to the bottom of what had led to 'The Ashcroft Affair'.

7 The Need to Settle

AS THE two sets of lawyers exchanged countless letters, I was becoming increasingly aware that time was not on my side. Whereas I was keen that my libel claim should be heard as quickly as possible, *The Times* wanted to proceed at a more leisurely pace. I suspect that *The Times* hoped that if it had more time its team of private investigators and journalists would be able to gather the evidence needed to support the accusations it had already made. It was still searching for the 'silver bullet' which it hoped would bring me down.

As the newspaper's delaying tactics burgeoned, my greatest fear was that the date of the libel hearing would be fixed for the second half of 2000. This would be heard at the worst possible time – in the run-up to the general election expected the following spring. Indeed, I simply could not allow this to happen – nor would it have been fair to the Conservative Party or William Hague. I could not, just as the electorate was deciding which party to vote for, expose the Tories to the sort of headlines that the hearing would inevitably throw up. The newspaper was going to be represented by Geoffrey Robertson QC, who was no slouch as an advocate. Although I had nothing to hide, it was inevitable that the press would glean some sensational soundbites from Robertson's opening speech and from the questions he put to witnesses in cross-examination.

My legal team knew that I was anxious to proceed with the fastest possible timetable for my legal action. However, the issue of obtaining an early hearing was complicated by the fact that Mr Justice Morland, the judge appointed to the case, and some of the lawyers involved, including George Carman QC, were involved in the High Court libel battle between Neil Hamilton, the former Conservative minister, and Mohamed al-Fayed, the owner of Harrods. The case had opened on 14 November 1999 and was expected to last several weeks.

I will put the timing of my libel battle into further context. It had also been made clear to me that the whole matter of revisiting my peerage nomination was on hold until my defamation action had been resolved. Furthermore, I knew that the Belize Government had put my name forward for a knighthood as part of the New Year's Honours List to be announced on 1 January 2000. However, Said Musa, the Prime Minister of Belize, had been asked by the Labour Government in Britain to defer the nomination while my peerage nomination was still under consideration. The Prime Minister of Belize had agreed to the request but only on the basis that the knighthood appeared in the Queen's Birthday Honours List in June 2000.

My business interests were being seriously damaged by *The Times*'s campaign against me. The adverse publicity – and the fear among shareholders and other investors that there might be some truth to the claims against me – meant that millions of pounds had been wiped off the value of my public company, the Carlisle Group, during the summer and autumn of 1999. Even more importantly, renewing the worldwide banking facilities for my companies was becoming increasingly difficult. Not surprisingly, large lenders are extremely wary of providing loans to anyone 'linked' to drug smuggling or money laundering. I found it hard to persuade some bankers and investors that a newspaper with a history as formidable as that of *The Times* could conduct such a campaign without there being any truth in its claims about my involvement in such activities. I guess some – including a minority of my colleagues in the Conservative Party – believed in the old adage that perhaps there was no smoke without fire (the very conclusion reached by others, no less wrongly, when my company ADT was sued by Laidlaw eight years earlier). In short, I was under pressure on a number of fronts to settle.

On the other hand, I was prepared to reach an agreement with *The Times* only if it resulted in the accusations against me being withdrawn and my reputation being publicly restored. *The Times* had not produced any evidence against me that caused me a moment's concern, but when an unlikely opportunity presented itself to reach an out-of-court settlement I was prepared to listen. Enter, out of the blue, my old friend Jeff Randall, the senior and experienced business journalist with a fat contacts book who had interviewed me the previous July. Past jobs that he has held include business editor of the *Sunday Times* and editor of *Sunday Business*. He is currently business editor of the BBC. I have known Jeff more years than I can remember – ever since he was a young reporter on *Financial Weekly* magazine. Over the years, he and I had built up a mutual trust and respect for each other.

When I was in the middle of my libel battle, Jeff was the editor of *Sunday Business* and he would sometimes ring me at the end of the week for a chat that was often angled towards his getting a story for his newspaper. By chance, during a telephone conversation with him one day – on Friday, 26 November 1999 – Jeff told me that he was attending Rupert Murdoch's Christmas drinks party the following week. 'Is there any message that you'd like me to give him?' he asked mischievously. I thought about it and said: 'Tell Rupert Murdoch that I think if the two of us were to sit down face to face alone and discuss this [my legal action], I think we could sort it out.'

Jeff duly attended the party at Rupert's apartment in St James's the following week on the evening of Thursday, 2 December, where one of the other guests was Peter Stothard. The political movers and shakers who were attending ranged from Baroness Thatcher to Gordon Brown, from William Hague to Peter Mandelson. Even before arriving at the party, Jeff had told Rupert that he might be able to help him over my libel action. When Jeff arrived, Mandelson was waiting to speak to Murdoch, but when the party host saw Jeff he ushered him to a quieter part of the room to speak with him privately. 'Great,' said Rupert. 'Invite Michael here. We'll sit down and have a cup of tea.' Then he added: 'Let's keep this *tight*.' Jeff did not waste any time in relaying Rupert's positive response back to me. He rang me up on his way home from the party and said: 'I saw Rupert and passed on your message.' He added that I had an appointment at Rupert's home in London in just two days' time – at 3.30 p.m. Even at that early stage, I thought a settlement was possible, if not likely, because I was convinced that I would be able to make Rupert an offer he would find difficult to refuse.

I had never met Rupert before, but I knew he was a tough operator who combined a passion for newspapers with a sense of the bottom line, both financially and journalistically. I believed that the terms I was prepared to offer were generous. Indeed, I had crafted them in a form which I was convinced would encourage Rupert to impose them on *The Times*. This, however, was a tricky area: when Rupert bought the newspaper in 1976 he had given an undertaking to preserve the editorial independence of *The Times* and he could face criticism if he broke it.

I flew to Britain from America and, fortified by a breakfast of kippers, I met with my legal team in a conference room at the Petersham Hotel in Richmond, Surrey, on Saturday, 4 December. I decided to keep my appointment with Rupert so secret that I did not even inform my lawyers during our four-hour meeting, at which I received a full review of the case. George Carman joined us for the second half of the meeting, arriving by taxi from his home in nearby Wimbledon. (It was only later that I learned the reason for this – his failing health caused by prostate cancer.) This meant that when I saw Rupert later that day I was up to date on exactly where we stood. I did not tell George or any of the legal team that I was meeting Rupert because I did not want to take the risk that they would tell me it was inadvisable or inappropriate. Instead, I felt I had to go with my own gut instincts. I later learned that Rupert had taken a similar approach and had not even told Stothard that he was seeing me.

I visited Rupert at his London apartment. We spent the first forty-five minutes of our meeting discussing the world in general and exchanging small talk. I enjoyed his company: he was charming, well informed and witty. Then, as we sat together in his drawing room sipping tea, we got down to the business in hand. I said: 'Rupert, I am going to propose a deal that you will not find difficult to accept. Although I want a page-one retraction, I am not looking for a humiliating climb-down from *The Times* and I am not looking for your paper to pay my costs.' I explained that

I wanted a clear and unequivocal recognition that the newspaper had no evidence that I, or any of my companies, had even come under suspicion of drug running or money laundering. I said, however, that I was also willing to pad out any statement with an acknowledgement that it was legitimate for the newspaper to delve into the area that it had investigated.

During my meeting with Rupert, I passed on some information about one of his journalists. I told him that Tom Baldwin, then *The Times*'s deputy political editor, was a regular cocaine user and questioned whether this was the sort of person suitable for employment on the newspaper. Incidentally, I see that Baldwin is still employed by *The Times*. Perhaps I should not be surprised: in recent years, the newspaper has never minded hiring people who break the law, although I suspect that standards are higher under Robert Thomson, the newspaper's straight-shooting current editor.

I liked Rupert's style and, as you might expect from two pragmatic businessmen, we swiftly thrashed out the basis of a resolution. I detected that privately Rupert felt his newspaper had pushed the issue too far without the evidence to back it up, although he did not spell these feelings out to me. He agreed that *The Times* would draw a line under 'The Ashcroft Affair' and print a front-page retraction to that effect if, in turn, I brought my legal action to a close. At the end of the business part of our meeting, which took less than half an hour, we left it that I would send him a draft of what I would like to see on the front page. I came away from his apartment convinced that Rupert wanted this subject off the agenda and that it would only be a matter of time before we reached agreement on the wording of the text. Unlike Stothard, Rupert was a man I felt *could* be trusted.

I still did not inform my legal team even at this point. I was confident that Rupert was not going to bring in his lawyers and I knew that the moment our teams of solicitors and barristers were involved things could get out of hand. Over the next two days, Rupert and I exchanged faxes after I had initially sent him a draft of the statement that I wanted *The Times* to carry. Our brief debate on the precise wording of the statement was entirely courteous and professional.

My application for summary judgement had been due to be heard on Monday, 13 December. However, with the Hamilton–Fayed case looking as though it would continue right up to Christmas, *The Times*'s legal team made an application to have the summary-judgement application postponed. Among other problems, Geoffrey Robertson QC, who was acting for *The Times*, had a holiday planned over Christmas and the New Year in Australasia, where he wanted to see in the new millennium. On Tuesday, 7 December, senior lawyers representing myself and *The Times* gathered in Court 13 at the High Court in the Strand, unaware that a possible out-of-court settlement was being negotiated elsewhere in the city. The lawyers, including my team led by George Carman QC and *The Times*'s led by Heather Rogers, met before Mr Justice Morland at 10 a.m., half an hour before the latest session of the Hamilton–Fayed hearing was due to begin in the same courtroom. George presented our case, asking Mr Justice Morland to hold the summary-judgement hearing either on 13 December or, if that was not possible, before Christmas. The judge, however, turned down the request and set the date for the preliminary hearing in February 2000. Unknown to all of us at the time, George's prostate cancer, held at bay with medication for several years, had returned with a vengeance. With his health failing, I am sure that he was not at his persuasive best. I remain convinced that George, in perfect health and on top of his game, would have triumphed, enabling my claim to be heard at the early date I needed.

The successful attempt by lawyers for *The Times* to drag matters out was terrible news for me. We could have a summary-judgement hearing in February but success was not guaranteed, or the case could linger on until a trial in the autumn of 2000, during the build-up to the next general election. Whatever course the case now took, the cloud of doubt would continue to hang over me. My position had been severely weakened. It was time to finalise Plan B – my out-of-court settlement with Rupert Murdoch.

At the time that my legal team was facing its setback in the High Court, Rupert Murdoch and I were edging ever closer to agreement on the wording of a front-page statement that would settle the dispute. I had faxed him a second draft of the proposed statement which was shorter and more succinct. In a brief conversation with him, it was evident that the two of us had reached an agreement. Rupert now said that he would have to clear it with his editor. In a later telephone conversation, Rupert told me that he was having some difficulty with Stothard, who wanted some further changes. I could not live with the majority of the proposals that Stothard wanted. In particular, Stothard wanted to draw a line, *not* under 'The Ashcroft Affair', but under the litigation: this would have enabled him to carry on smearing me. However, I won the day on this point and, by Wednesday afternoon (8 December), we had agreed a wording acceptable to both parties. We concluded that my writ against *The Times* and its journalists should wither on the vine rather than bring lawyers together to end the action formally.

When it comes to negotiating the settlement of a libel action, timing is everything. If I had held out longer, I felt confident that I would eventually have obtained an apology, damages and my costs. However, because I, largely for the sake of the Conservative Party, needed a quick settlement I had to agree – somewhat reluctantly – not only to waive any damages but also to pick up the bill for my own costs.

It was now time for Stothard to transform from newspaper editor to spin doctor, delivering a performance worthy of Alastair Campbell, the former press secretary to Tony Blair. Stothard's reaction to the news of the settlement in the east London offices of his newspaper was, once again, entirely predictable. He told his colleagues that he had won a great victory and that I had backed down.

As agreed, *The Times* ran its page 1 retraction, which appeared in its issue of Thursday, 9 December, just five days after Rupert Murdoch and I had first met. It was headlined 'The Times and Michael Ashcroft' and it read:

> In the past six months *The Times* has reported extensively
> on the business and political interests of the Conservative

Party Treasurer, Michael Ashcroft. During that period *The Times* has questioned the suitability of Mr Ashcroft to be both Treasurer and the most substantial donor to the Conservative Party, and has challenged the dependence of Her Majesty's Opposition upon the wealth of one man.

Mr Ashcroft has a British passport but has lived and worked abroad for more than a decade, not only as a businessman but, for part of the time, as the Permanent Representative to the United Nations for the Central American Commonwealth state of Belize. The issues raised by *The Times* have resulted in a substantive and useful debate on foreign donations to political parties.

In the course of its inquiries – and in its view acting in the public interest of disclosing relevant facts about those in public life – *The Times* published details of US Drug Enforcement Administration files in which Mr Ashcroft's name is mentioned. Mr Ashcroft issued a writ for libel, alleging that *The Times* had implied that he was under serious suspicion of involvement in drug trafficking and money laundering.

The Times is pleased to confirm that it has no evidence that Mr Ashcroft or any of his companies have ever been suspected of money laundering or drug-related crimes.

Mr Ashcroft has told *The Times* that he recognises the public concern about foreign funding of British politics, and that he intends to reorganise his affairs in order to return to live in Britain. *The Times* applauds this. He will continue with his work to raise funds for the Conservative Party from the largest possible number of donors, including both the wealthy and the less well-off. The openness and accountability of political funding by all parties will remain a central issue for investigation and comment by *The Times*.

With this statement *The Times* intends to draw a line under 'The Ashcroft Affair'. Litigation between the parties has been settled to mutual satisfaction, with each side bearing its own costs.

Aged ten weeks with my mother.

Aged six months with my father.

TOP LEFT: Dressing up as a soldier, aged four, in Nyasaland. TOP RIGHT: Learning to ride in St Anne's-on-Sea, 1950. BOTTOM: With my mother and Mary the nanny after Patricia's christening in Nyasaland, 1951.

TOP: Family portrait, Burnley, 1956. BOTTOM LEFT: In the Cathedral grounds at Norwich School, 1956. BOTTOM RIGHT: Anyone for tennis? With my father Eric, British Honduras, 1956.

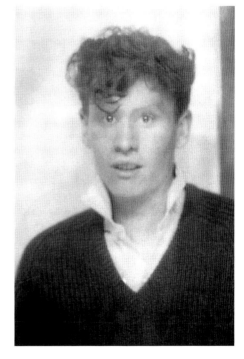

TOP: Aged eleven (circled), Norwich School, 1956. BOTTOM LEFT: With my best friend, David Sabben, British Honduras, circa 1955. BOTTOM RIGHT: A student at Mid-Essex Technical College in Chelmsford, 1966.

"THE NEXT STRANGE ANIMAL IS THE
ENTREPRENEUR WHO LIVES BY INITIATIVE
AND TAKING RISKS."

TOP: Launching my business in High Wycombe, 1972. BOTTOM: This cartoon made me laugh because it sums up what an unusual species we entrepreneurs are.

TOP: Chairman of ADT, 1992. BOTTOM: Not exactly an average night at the dogs: Wembley, circa 1988.

TOP: Deep in conversation with Diana, Princess of Wales, Washington DC, October 1990. BOTTOM LEFT: My son Andrew, dressed as an original ADT (American District Telegraph) boy, on the same evening. BOTTOM RIGHT: Standing next to the Princess at the same event.

TOP: At the launch of the crime-fighting charity Community Action Trust (now Crimestoppers) with Sir Peter Imbert (now Lord Imbert), then the Metropolitan Police Commissioner (left); Douglas Hurd (now Lord Hurd), then the Home Secretary (second from right); and Shaw Taylor, the television presenter (far right) in 1988. BOTTOM: Margaret Thatcher doing what she does best.

TOP: Conservative Party Conference, Blackpool, 1999. BOTTOM: *The Guardian*'s David Austin adds to the Government's embarrassment at having to pay my legal costs (June 2003).

TOP: Meeting leaders of the Tamil Tigers in Sri Lanka with Michael Ancram in 2003. A photograph from the meeting later unexpectedly turned up on the rebel fighters' website. BOTTOM: Michael Ancram and I meet Afghan warlord Ismail Khan, 2004.

Harrogate, April Fool's Day, 2000.

TOP: With William Hague, 2000. BOTTOM LEFT: David Austin (*The Guardian*) demonstrates that it is possible to find humour in the subject of tax (May 2001). BOTTOM RIGHT: Nicola Jennings (*The Guardian*) caricatures the altercation with Clare Short (June 2001).

TOP: With Seb (now Lord) Coe: a great Olympian and a great friend. BOTTOM LEFT: Invested as Chancellor of APU. BOTTOM RIGHT: Taking the oath in the House of Lords, 2000.

Leaving Conservative Central Office after election night, 2001 – soon after my quadruple heart by-pass.

However, Stothard's public statements on the day that his newspaper carried its retraction did not give me confidence that he was being gracious or that he considered our dispute over. He told Radio 4's *PM* programme: 'I was completely happy with this statement. It was a withdrawal of Mr Ashcroft's libel action, no correction, no apology, no payment of costs. It was hardly a statement which was imposed on an unwilling editor.' The truth was that two pragmatic men – Rupert Murdoch and I – had reached a practical decision that avoided the need for continuing costly and time-consuming legal action. I only found out much later that the settlement also effectively ended John Bryant's career on *The Times*. For the previous five months, Stothard had resented the fact that his deputy editor had been entirely right when he warned that I would sue over the DEA documents if such information was used recklessly in a story. Although he had needed Bryant on board for the legal action, he now told Murdoch and Les Hinton, News International's executive chairman, that he considered him to be 'hostile' and could no longer work with him. Bryant therefore left the paper shortly after the settlement, another innocent victim of the newspaper's campaign against me.

News of a settlement was welcomed by the stock market. During the day – 9 December – shares in my public company, Carlisle Holdings, rose from £6.90 to £8.70. This was welcome news for shareholders, myself included. Indeed, it meant the value of my personal holdings increased by £70 million in a matter of hours. Yet I had reservations about the settlement too, primarily that it deprived me of my day – of victory – in the High Court.

The settlement received widespread coverage in national newspapers. However, it was the way that another old detractor of mine, *Private Eye*, picked up on the story that gave me a chuckle. Lord Gnome's spoof leader in the Christmas Eve edition, 1999, read:

I am happy to announce that a settlement has been reached in the dispute between my newspaper and Mr Cashcroft, treasurer of the Conservative Party and UN Ambassador of the Republic of Selize.

At an informal drinks party aboard my aeroplane, Mr Cashcroft and I both agreed that it is unhelpful for newspapers to go prying into the affairs of very rich businessmen who choose to live abroad for the purposes of avoiding tax and who use their money to wield political influence.

We have, therefore, agreed to draw a line under this unfortunate affair.

Meanwhile, my editor Mr Stopwork has my fullest confidence, as he seeks alternative employment in what is a very tough market.

I do not think I realised at the time quite how much George Carman had been looking forward to the trial and how disappointed he was that I had settled my action. However, in February 2001, just a month after his death from cancer, Karen Phillips, his devoted companion, wrote a lengthy article about George's extraordinary life for the *Mail on Sunday*. She said: 'It was during quiet meals together that we would discuss his more private work. Believe it or not, the courtroom dramas were often not as interesting as the cases which settled before they got there. I know that George was in some ways disappointed that his client Michael Ashcroft, who had sued *The Times*, reached a settlement with Rupert Murdoch. Central to the action were suggestions that Ashcroft – now Lord Ashcroft, the Tory Party treasurer – was somehow involved in drug running. George had discovered that one of the key defence witnesses was himself a little too personally involved in the "drugs industry". He was looking forward with relish to that particular piece of cross-examination. Sadly, it was not to be.' From what Karen says about George's zest for the case, I think Tom Baldwin should feel he had a lucky let-off in not having to give evidence under oath.

THROUGHOUT MY battle with *The Times*, I had another inquiry hanging over me. This was the Marine Accident Investigation Branch (MAIB) inquiry into the sinking of the *Rema* on

25 April 1998, with the loss of four lives.

The inquiry, which began on 16 June 1999, was published on 17 February the following year, less than two months after I had settled my legal action against *The Times*. The report must have made disappointing reading for the Stothard and Blair teams. It showed that the *Rema* had been fully seaworthy on her departure from Berwick-upon-Tweed and that all her certificates were valid. Yet somehow – and it was not possible even with underwater video footage to establish exactly how – 769 tonnes of water had seeped into the hold without the crew being aware of it. An underwater survey had been carried out on the wreck in June 1998. It showed that the vessel was upright and intact, but with evidence of 'soft contact bow damage'. When the ship sank bow first, her cargo had shifted forward and forced its way out of the forward hatches, thereby spilling on to the seabed. The ship had sunk so quickly that the crew had no time to escape.

The investigation put forward eight possible reasons for the sinking – including the deliberate scuttling of the vessel – but each was rejected in turn for lack of evidence. The International Merchant Marine Registry of Belize (IMMARBE) was given four recommendations, but these partly related to general safety proposals that it was hoped would apply to the international community. For example, it proposed the fitting of hold bilge alarms in all single-hold vessels to avert a similar tragedy. I was relieved by the report's findings, but certainly not surprised. In short, the sinking of the *Rema* was simply a tragic accident at sea for which nobody was to blame. Although I was not surprised by the report's findings, I was satisfied by them. Irresponsible journalists and opportunist Labour politicians had used the deaths of four seamen to attack me and the Conservative Party. Now that I had been exonerated, there was not a squeak of contrition.

WITH THE settlement of my litigation against *The Times* and with the official report showing that I had no culpability for the loss of the *Rema*, my name was put forward again by William Hague for a working peerage. With the exception of the *Rema*, the other obstacles had been technical and capable of near-instant resolution. I needed, for instance, to resign my role as Belize's Ambassador to the United Nations.

I had been appointed as Belize's Permanent Representative to the United Nations in 1998, an honorary position bestowed by the Belize Government. While performing this role, I was effectively a civil servant: I and other permanent representatives had to vote as instructed by the Belize Government. This role should have been uncontroversial. After all, Belize is part of the Commonwealth; the Queen is its head of state; Belizean nationals are permitted to be members of the Privy Council in the UK; a Belizean citizen can be a member of the British House of Lords; Belizean citizens living in the UK are able to vote in British elections; and Belizean citizens living in the UK can contribute towards UK political parties. Where was the demonstrable conflict of interest between my role for the Belize Government and my role for the Conservative Party? And if there was any conflict of interest on a specific point, I would do what any individual does in such a position and not participate in a particular set of decisions or debates.

The role had, however, become controversial and eventually I chose to relinquish it. This disappointed me a great deal and I felt I had been the victim of some petty-minded attitudes. Yet I had to be pragmatic: I could have fought it, but it would have delayed my peerage still further. Even now, I remain an itinerant ambassador for Belize.

So, with all obstacles removed, approval of my nomination for a peerage should have been automatic. Some senior figures in the party felt strongly – even more strongly than me – that I was being treated unacceptably badly over my peerage nomination. One of them – James Arbuthnot, the party's Chief Whip – felt so outraged by the whole episode that he, unprompted by either William or me, arranged a meeting with Sir Richard Wilson, the Cabinet Secretary, to complain. 'I spent an hour with the Cabinet Secretary,' James later told me. 'I just wanted to tell him that I thought what was happening to you was grotesquely unfair and utterly intolerable. I demolished the arguments against you one by one.'

Unfortunately for me, fairness is not something that New Labour has ever considered to be a priority. Tony Blair wrote to William on 3 March 2000, indicating that my nomination for a peerage had been turned down a second time by the Honours Scrutiny Committee, the cross-party committee consisting of Lord Hurd of Westwell (Conservative), Baroness Dean of Thornton-le-Fylde (Labour) and Lord Thomson of Monifieth (Liberal Democrat), who was its chairman.

To the unsuspecting, it seemed as if I had been judged by the great and the good and found wanting. Once again, it was not quite as it seemed. Lord Thomson is the former Labour MP George Thomson, whose daughter Caroline married Roger Liddle, a friend of Peter Mandelson. As Brenda Dean, Baroness Dean had previously been the leader of Sogat, the printers' union, from 1985 to 1991. Neither Lord Thomson nor Baroness Dean was likely to look upon me sympathetically – indeed, some might say that for me to be judged by this pair, despite the moderating influence of Lord Hurd, was akin to jury tampering. In any case, Blair was trying to hide behind the committee when, in fact, he was personally blocking my nomination: a letter he enclosed from Lord Thomson did not support the Prime Minister's claim that my nomination had been rejected – it was no more than a request for clarification of certain points.

It did not surprise me when the news of my rejection was leaked to Tom Baldwin of *The Times*. The newspaper's main front-page story of 24 March 2000 was headlined 'Peerage for Ashcroft vetoed again'. *The Times* and Labour MPs could hardly contain their glee. Peter Bradley, the newspaper's lapdog rent-a-quote Labour MP, said: 'Sooner or later, the Tories are going to have to ask themselves whether the cash Mr Ashcroft provides is worth the humiliation which comes with it. Yet again they have showed themselves to be a party without scruples and with a leader without judgement and – thanks to the vigilance of the scrutiny committee – a treasurer without a peerage.'

There were no legitimate grounds for the rejection of my peerage and William was as furious as I was disappointed. In the absence of valid objections, the Prime Minister of the day should make the appointment of working peerages as individual party leaders request (provided those leaders do not exceed their quota of appointments). In the case of my working peerage, William believed that this was a constitutional issue: Blair had asked him to nominate people to work for Her Majesty's Opposition in the House of Lords and now the Prime Minister was refusing, without good reason, to make the appointments that William had requested.

With little time left to resolve the issue, William had to ring Blair during a summit of European leaders in Lisbon, informing the Prime Minister's aides that it was 'urgent'. William complained furiously to Blair, telling him it was 'disgraceful' that his recommendation had been turned down without good cause. He demanded that Blair reconsider and warned the Prime Minister that he saw this as a major constitutional issue. It was, admittedly, hardly the best time for the leader of the Opposition to telephone the Prime Minister, but it was the only possible time. In the face of William's protests, Blair backed down and I got my peerage. It meant that within the space of three months, and amid relentless pressure and controversy, I had received a knighthood and a peerage. Peter Bradley, the Labour MP, was less than delighted and quipped: 'At the rate Ashcroft is going, he will be a member of the Royal Family by Christmas.' It is the only comment Bradley has ever uttered that has made me smile.

Yet even now that my peerage had been granted, things were not straightforward – there would still be an unpleasant sting in the tail. Exactly a week after *The Times* had reported that my peerage had been vetoed a second time, the newspaper was forced to concede that it had been granted. The front-page story that it ran on 31 March 2000 was headlined 'A peerage with strings for Ashcroft'. It reported:

> Michael Ashcroft was finally named as a peer last night, but only after being forced to accept unprecedented conditions before he can take his seat in the House of Lords.
> The billionaire Conservative treasurer made it on to a list of 33 new working peers after giving the cross-party

honours vetting panel an assurance that he will come back to live in Britain this year.

Mr Ashcroft, who has given more than £3 million to the Tory party since the election, as well as loans of up to £2 million at any one time, also complied two days ago with its request to give up his post as Belizean Ambassador at the United Nations.

It is believed to be the first time such strings have been attached to a peerage, and the decision to give him the honour in such controversial circumstances provoked a political storm last night, with even senior Tories voicing dismay and disbelief at the arrangement.

Viscount Cranborne, the former Tory leader of the Lords and longstanding opponent of Mr Ashcroft, called it 'an affront to the dignity and standing' of the party and Parliament. He said: 'I regard the award of a peerage as primarily the award of a right to become a member of the British Parliament and that implies that the recipient is worthy and already satisfies all the criteria which we would expect. As far as I know, it is unprecedented for conditions to be set before anybody can become a peer. It reminds me of the way medieval Popes made their nephews into cardinals' ...

The announcement of a peerage is intended to be a dignified affair: my elevation to the Upper House was made, as tradition dictates, with the briefest of statements in the *London Gazette* of Thursday, 30 March 2000. Under the heading 'life peers', my name was second in alphabetical order in the list of barons, and the six words read: 'Michael Ashcroft, Chairman, Carlisle Holdings Ltd'.

New Labour decided, however, that this was far too dignified and understated. If Tony Blair was being forced to recognise my peerage, he would do so with the worst possible grace. On April Fool's Day, the story of William's telephone calls was leaked to several Sunday-newspaper journalists. It meant that, once again, I found myself at the centre of a fabricated controversy.

The headlines in the weekend newspapers included 'Hague inter-rupted summit to beg for Ashcroft peerage' in the *Sunday Times* and 'Hague begged Blair for Ashcroft peerage' in the *Independent on Sunday*. The *Sunday Times* even quoted the publicity-seeking Peter Bradley as saying: 'You have to wonder why Hague was so utterly desperate to secure the peerage right now.' William found it unbelievable that the contents of his private and confidential phone call to Blair should be leaked in this manner and that his words should be twisted to suggest that he (William) had not only been pleading but had been in the wrong.

That weekend I gave an interview to Joe Murphy, political editor of the *Sunday Telegraph*. This caused controversy too, but for different reasons. The newspaper led its front page with the headline 'Tory treasurer: I will be Lord Ashcroft of Belize'. Joe reported that I wanted to adopt the title Baron Ashcroft of Belize in 'an extraordinary gesture of defiance to critics who opposed his peerage'. He also wrote, perfectly accurately, that I had assured the Belize Government that I would use my influence in the House of Lords to defend the country's interests abroad.

William and other senior officials in the party thought that to be called Lord Ashcroft of Belize was imprudent. When William was asked about the choice of title on GMTV that Sunday morning, he said: 'I think that was a little joke he was having and I think it should be taken as a joke rather than written up as a genu-inely serious story.' In fact, I was totally serious about my desire to be Lord Ashcroft of Belize. Ideally, I would have liked to have reflected my affection for Belize in my title. I learned, however, that there have to be exceptional reasons if the location of the title is not in the UK and this would have involved protracted nego-tiations with the Foreign and Commonwealth Office. This could have delayed my investiture still further, so eventually I agreed that, for once, I should be less confrontational. I therefore took the pragmatic approach and adopted the title of Lord Ashcroft of Chichester. I had no overriding affinity with any particular town in Britain, so I chose the place of my birth.

I am deeply indebted to William that he pursued the issue of my peerage so vigorously. I am indebted to him, too, for his loyalty to me throughout my battle with *The Times*. There had been one Sunday in the summer of 1999 – 18 July – when virtually all the newspapers were full of negative stories about my working life and my private life. As I looked at the press cuttings spread in front of me, I was at my lowest. I felt depressed for myself and the party. I thought to myself: how much longer can William sustain this sort of relentless pressure? As I was pondering these difficulties, I received a mid-morning telephone call from William. When I was asked to come to the phone to speak to him, I thought, 'This has to be William saying to me that we have to release the pressure: that it is time for me to stand down.' So I picked up the receiver rather apprehensively – if he was going to ask me to resign, I was going to accept my fate. William, however, was in good spirits and said to me: 'Ffion and I are up in Yorkshire looking at all the papers. We just want you to know that you have the best wishes of both of us because it can't be very easy for you or your family at the moment.' And that was his only message. William had not made a single mention of his own or the party's difficulties, or the political pressures that he was under. If my friendship with William and Ffion had not been totally cemented at that time, then it was after that telephone call. The Hagues came up trumps.

Shortly after receiving my peerage, I went into the chamber of the House of Lords and saw Viscount Cranborne, my adversary within the Tory Party who had been anything but helpful during my attempt to get a working peerage, sitting on the front bench reserved for Privy Councillors. I stood in front of him waiting for him to look up, and when he did I said: 'Robert, I am here. Perhaps we should have lunch together?' There was no response from the man who once described himself as an 'ill-trained spaniel'. Nor, it seems, will there be any future opportunity for us to make up. My sternest critic, who has since succeeded his father as Marquess of Salisbury, is currently on indefinite 'leave of absence' from the House as a protest against the introduction of new rules on the declaration of business interests in 2001. No doubt Salisbury, who characterised the new rules as 'onerous', is relieved that *The Times* never investigated his business and personal life in the same way that he had encouraged the newspaper to explore mine.

I gave my maiden speech in the House of Lords on 12 December 2000, in a foreign affairs debate. In my speech, I made a plea for the Government not to abandon its responsibilities to Britain's four remaining overseas territories in the Caribbean: Anguilla, the British Virgin Islands, Montserrat and the Turks and Caicos Islands. I also took the opportunity to denounce drug trafficking in the area. 'The Caribbean overseas territories are not drug-producing countries, but they do sit astride some of the most prolific drug trafficking routes in the world. The threat of powerful, organised crime is ever present. Those who deal in drugs are a cancer on the societies in which they operate.'

THE TIMES had said it was willing to draw a line under 'The Ashcroft Affair', but it quickly emerged that the axis of Peter Stothard, Tom Baldwin and Alastair Brett were not prepared to bring an end to their personal hostilities. Bizarrely, they even seemed to think that the libel settlement had weakened my hand and that it had given them a greater licence to target me further.

As soon as I realised that there were going to be continuing attempts to smear me, I decided to go on the offensive. I wanted to piece together the full story of what had happened to me. After the libel-action settlement with Rupert Murdoch in December 1999, I was prepared to let bygones be bygones and I did not have a vengeful attitude towards *The Times* and its senior staff. However, once I was aware that the unscrupulous trio of Stothard, Baldwin and Brett were not prepared to accept that they had enjoyed a lucky escape as a result of the agreed settlement, I decided to raise the stakes a little and to scrutinise the full extent of their appalling behaviour. At the height of our legal battle, *The Times* had employed Forensic Investigative Associates (FIA), a London-based firm, to help defend my action against the newspaper. The company is chaired by Lord Armstrong of Ilminster who, as Robert Armstrong, had been a career civil servant, becoming Cabinet Secretary in 1979 and head of the Civil Service in 1981. To this day, Armstrong is best known for a delightful phrase uttered during the *Spycatcher* trial in Australia when he admitted that he had been 'economical with the truth'.

In the autumn of 1999 – when it still looked as though *The Times* and I were heading for a High Court battle – Armstrong had approached the newspaper saying that he believed his company could help it defend my legal action. He was confident that his well-connected staff could gather material in the US and Central America that could be used against me. *The Times* agreed to hire FIA, knowing that the company would inevitably run up a substantial bill for its services.

The private investigator who made many of the inquiries into my personal and business lives was Jessica De Grazia, a former leading New York City prosecutor who started working for FIA after she came to live and work in Britain. De Grazia, who is the author of a 1991 book entitled *DEA: The War Against Drugs*, knew that her job was to dig for 'dirt' on me. As part of this process, she telephoned and e-mailed former British and American military and diplomatic officials in an attempt to obtain damaging information about me (one of them was kind enough to e-mail me both her sly requests for help and his dignified replies). Among the issues that she decided to scrutinise was the sale of my American house two years earlier. When I sold ADT to Tyco in 1997, I no longer needed a house in Boca Raton, Florida. Dennis Kozlowski, then Tyco's chief executive and chairman, did, however, need a property there because he intended to relocate Tyco to the former, but enlarged, ADT headquarters. I therefore agreed to sell him my house, and, because I was going to be away on business, I paid a nominal fee of $100 so that my wife Susi could act as my agent in the sale. She in turn transferred it at completion to Kozlowski for the agreed price of $2.5 million which was at, or fractionally below, the market value of the property. Although to an outsider this transaction might have looked odd, it was entirely innocent and above board. Had I not been away on business, I would have conducted the sale myself and would not have transferred the property to my wife.

I found out that John Moscow, a friend of De Grazia and former colleague of hers in the New York District Attorney's office, had been looking into the house deal. Moscow was now working as an Assistant District Attorney in New York. As part of his inquiries, he summoned senior Tyco executives to explain the apparently unusual house sale, and they in turn alerted me to what was happening. I discovered, quite by chance but from an impeccable source, that it was De Grazia who had drawn the Boca Raton property deal to his attention. Indeed, at a conference in Miami, Florida, on 17 February 2000, he spoke with a journalist friend of mine who he was unaware had anything to do with me. Moscow chatted with my contact shortly after delivering an early-morning presentation along with two others on the subject of 'The Bank of New York, the Fight Against Money Laundering and Organised Crime in the US and the Americas'. The investigative journalist went to speak to Moscow during the 10.15 a.m. coffee break because he had known him as a result of his (Moscow's) investigations into the worldwide collapse of the BCCI bank. When my contact asked if he was working on anything interesting, Moscow told him he had been 'looking into a house – sold by Michael Ashcroft to Tyco – for a friend of mine'. This, at least, explained why Moscow was delving into the deal even though it was so trivial that it would be outside his normal remit. Furthermore, this had happened in Florida, well out of his 'normal' jurisdiction. On his return to London from America, the journalist, learning that his editor was interested in running something about the investigation in his newspaper, rang Moscow, only for Moscow to insist that any story could harm, or even end, the investigation into the deal. So nothing ever appeared in the British newspaper.

De Grazia had clearly scrutinised the details of the property deal and had wrongly assumed that something odd was afoot. Perhaps it was because of the apparent transfer to my wife in her maiden name Susan Anstey – a name she uses to this day on her passport and on the electoral register. Indeed, in early 2000, as I now looked into the sale of my house, I discovered something I had not known before: that the property had not been sold to Dennis Kozlowski personally, as I had always thought, but to Tyco. At this stage, I took advice on whether I should have declared the transaction and I was told that I had, in fact, acted entirely properly by not doing so because it was part of a 'competitive process' exempt from disclosure.

So here was De Grazia, someone who had been – or possibly even still was – on the payroll of *The Times*, calling in favours from contacts just to cause trouble for me. What alarmed me most about all this was that it was happening several weeks after I had settled my action with *The Times* and when it had agreed to draw a line under 'The Ashcroft Affair'. I tried to get to the bottom of it all through my lawyers, but FIA and *The Times* repeatedly refused to answer straightforward questions, and I eventually decided to let the matter rest.

The Times never ran any articles about the sale of my Florida house, presumably because it was satisfied that all was above board. However, shortly after Kozlowski's arrest, this transaction came back to haunt me for a second time. In June 2002, the New York District Attorney's office leaked information to American journalists that it was looking into some of Kozlowski's property transactions, including the house deal that he had negotiated with me. The District Attorney's office was trying to make this non-event house sale – a transaction that it had already examined two years earlier and on which it had taken no action – look as though it was a key part of its investigation.

I was, however, concerned to learn at the end of March 2000 that Peter Stothard needed to take several months off from his job as editor of *The Times* for chemotherapy for a rare, but treatable, form of cancer of the pancreas. Concerned about rumours apparently spreading through the industry that he was being replaced because of his dispute with me, he called an impromptu staff meeting in the news room on 29 March. 'It is wrong for me, wrong for *The Times* and wrong for the owners of *The Times* to allow the allegation to stand that I have been eased out of the editor's chair, even temporarily, at the instigation of Mr Ashcroft, his acolytes and satellites,' he said. While I was sorry to learn that Stothard had health problems, I was perturbed that the tone of his speech provided further evidence that he did not think our battle was over. Moreover, it confirmed to me that he was someone who enjoyed dishing dirt but was thin-skinned about what other people thought about him.

Incredibly, about a year after our agreed settlement and when Stothard was off for several months on sick leave, Ben Preston, his deputy and a friend of Tom Baldwin, sent Dominic Kennedy to Belize to go over all the old subjects again. It was a deeply unpleasant experience – as well as a total breach of the deal with Rupert Murdoch – to have someone back on my home turf, where I felt relaxed and safe, on a speculative assignment trying to dig up 'dirt' all over again. It was impossible for a journalist engaged in such activities not to be noticed, nor for those who were approached not to draw their own conclusions about why they were being questioned. I was furious that the newspaper was not prepared to keep to the agreement that I had reached with its proprietor. I seriously considered suing News International, the company which owned *The Times*, for breach of contract – an action which would have put Rupert Murdoch into the witness box.

For the most part, the exchange of letters between my lawyers and those from *The Times* was deadly serious and formal, but occasionally I could not resist winding up Alastair Brett. I had heard from several sources that Brett was becoming increasingly paranoid and was even convinced that I was using a team of private investigators to trace his every move, along with the activities of the reporting team that had been looking into my affairs. This was, of course, nonsense, but early in 2001 I discovered that Brett had started holding meetings about me in the corridor because he believed that I had bugged his own office at News International. This was because Brett had persuaded himself that the office cleaners at *The Times* must have been employed by one of my companies. He became convinced that these cleaners came armed with bugs, especially for the telephones. 'Ashcroft appears to know everything we're doing,' he complained to colleagues. On another occasion, at the height of his paranoia, he even seriously talked about getting a 'lead-lined office', which he understood would prevent me from bugging him.

On 2 February 2001, David Hooper, my solicitor, wrote a letter to Brett in which he referred to – and dismissed – a suggestion that I had been using private detectives to monitor Dominic Kennedy, a reporter on the newspaper. David wrote: 'Coming from

The Times, which has employed numerous private detectives to poke around into our client's affairs, I find such a statement a little rich. It also has a ring of paranoia to it. Next you will be telling me that your office has been bugged and that you have to hold your meetings in the corridor instead!'

I would love to have been a fly on the wall of Brett's office when he read that last sentence – I suspect it caused him to splutter over his morning coffee. In his reply of 7 February, Brett made an early reference to our baiting of him. Before going on to other issues, he wrote: 'As regards meetings in our corridors because we are paranoid about being bugged – how right you are!!'

THE DRUG Enforcement Administration had been alerted, by the US Embassy in London, to the fact that some of its classified files had been leaked. Such a breach of security is a serious matter and at some point the DEA launched an investigation to try to identify the culprit. Jonathan Randel was challenged in December 1999. He resigned his position immediately and walked out. The DEA continued a criminal investigation, however, and its investigators also seized the hard drives on his work computer. They studied all the information that he had accessed throughout 1999 and found he had been downloading data on a wide range of people – other than me – whose names must have been supplied by Toby Follett and/or *The Times*. This activity continued throughout the latter half of 1999 following the commencement of my legal action against *The Times*, and involved Randel making dozens of queries to DEA databases, not only about me but about other prominent UK citizens. I do not know who else was targeted in this way, presumably at the behest of *The Times*, or what the results may have been. Randel was certainly not acting on Follett's requests during this period, for we were to learn that the pressure of events had become too much for him and he had fallen ill. Randel was eventually arrested in the car park of his local shopping mall on 11 July 2001 and indicted.

As the date of Randel's hearing approached, my legal team received a letter from the US Department of Justice dated 4

January 2002, informing them that I had been given a six-digit Victim Identification Number. I suspect that those who have known me well over the years would have found it hard to imagine a more unlikely 'victim' but it showed that the authorities in America were taking the case seriously. I hoped that it would soon be Randel and those of his associates who had broken the law who would receive an even more unwanted number – a prisoner number.

Eventually, Stephen Sadow, Randel's expensive attorney, entered into a plea-bargaining deal in which his client admitted guilt in response to a newly negotiated additional indictment. There was then a delay for various expert reports before he was sentenced. One of the expert witnesses chosen to give evidence was Michael Sissons, the senior consultant to Peters Fraser & Dunlop, the leading writers' agency in Europe which represents some 1,000 media clients. At the time he gave evidence, I had never met Michael although I knew him by reputation as a result of his role as chairman and managing director of Peters Fraser & Dunlop for thirty years from 1965. Michael was asked to give evidence in his role as an expert on damaged or tainted copyright – that is, where the value of written material has been affected by theft, damage or other misfortune. Michael flew from Britain to Atlanta to give evidence assessing the 'commercial value' of the leaked documents – the 'news value' of the material rather than the more serious damage it had done to the DEA. It seemed a difficult task but he put the value at not less than £10,000 and not more than £30,000: a figure the judge later decided was 'speculative' and too high, preferring to estimate the value at between $10,000 and $30,000 (by coincidence the same valuation as Michael's, but in dollars rather than pounds).

However, it was Michael's independent assessment of *The Times*'s behaviour that I found especially interesting. In his written evidence to the court based on the articles that the newspaper had published, he said:

> *The Times* was heavily engaged in a vendetta against Michael Ashcroft, which might be said to have become

something of an obsession with its editor Peter Stothard. This was in fact more to do with their wish to discredit the Conservative Party under the leadership of William Hague, than Mr Ashcroft (now Lord Ashcroft) himself. I would go so far as to say that there would have been little interest in Mr Ashcroft without his connection and substantial contribution to the Conservative Party. The advent of these documents must have seemed like manna from heaven.

In his statement, Michael condemned the behaviour of the newspaper:

> I will make one final point which doesn't strictly attach to the value of the material *per se* but rather to the position and behaviour of the legal department of Times Newspapers Ltd in this matter. As I have suggested above, the only situation in which a legal advisor to *The Times* could properly have given his assent to the use of the DEA documents would have been that they were in the public domain. Otherwise both he and the editor of *The Times* were fully aware of the disgraceful circumstances attached to this material and to which I have referred above in consideration of my own theoretical position in this matter. Does it then follow that *The Times* was complicit in this alleged felony and was indeed compounding it?

Another to give evidence to the court in the summer of 2002 was Martin Pracht, a special agent with the DEA who had worked with the organisation for nineteen years. He told the court that there were special procedures in place to deal with communications and disclosures to the media and that Randel had not followed them. He also revealed that an investigation into a public figure – such as myself – would be carried out by a Sensitive Activity Review Committee (SARC). There was, however, no SARC investigation – or indeed any other inquiry – into me or my affairs. He said he had never seen sensitive DEA material disclosed in the way Randel had done – and then published in a foreign newspaper. Martin Pracht spoke, too, of how the disclosures by Randel would have a detrimental effect on the DEA's relationship with the UK and other countries. 'They [other countries] have to allow us to put people in their country,' he said. Overall, his evidence relating to the way Randel had acted was damning.

The offence that Randel was charged with is so serious that it carries a theoretical maximum penalty of ten years in jail and a fine of up to $250,000, though these would be imposed only on a repeat offender. Alastair Brett, the legal manager of Times Newspapers, submitted a witness statement to the Atlanta court on 8 August 2002. He was responding to the written evidence of Michael Sissons and set out to defend *The Times*'s behaviour, but he was oddly reticent about his own role. When Michael Sissons was shown Brett's statement at the hearing he pointed out, 'He is not, as I understand it, significantly defending, or otherwise, his behaviour ... There's no way in the world that *The Times* would have gone through with this exercise and published confidently these [stories] until the writ from Ashcroft arrived without Alastair Brett ... being centrally involved in that.'

In his statement, Brett had the gall to sing the praises of Randel, whom he had met in July 1999. 'He struck me as a principled young man with strong convictions and a genuine belief that powerful people with things to hide should on occasion be exposed to greater public scrutiny.' Extraordinarily, this was said of a dishonest wretch who was happy to feed the names of anyone into a confidential computer, without knowing who they were or what they had done. Additionally that person was then – in return for money – prepared to pass on confidential information about those people without knowing how the information would be used or who would receive it. Furthermore, he was reckless in his failure to protect the identity of fellow DEA agents, thereby endangering their lives. Brett tried to play down the newspaper's payments to Randel, saying, 'TNL [Times Newspapers Ltd] did no more than pay Mr Randel for his expenses and his time.' This was an outrageously disingenuous claim: Randel was being paid for his confidential information about me on the DEA database that he was willing to pass on without any consideration of the enormity of his betrayal or the repercussions from it. Finally, the suggestion that I was a man with something to hide was sheer lunacy. There was nothing to hide. Until *The Times*'s story was published, I did not even know that my name appeared in DEA records. When I did know, far from seeking to suppress such information, I urged *The Times* to publish it in full. Talk about pot, kettle and black – it was *The Times* which had sought to hide the facts, not me.

Before Randel was sentenced, I, too, wrote to the court where the case was being heard and detailed the distress that Randel had caused me, my family and my companies. In pressing for a serious penalty, I concluded: 'As the DEA has itself recognised in the Court, a system which captures the names of the honest within precisely the same database as that designed to ensnare the names of the dishonest would, in the wrong hands, be a very dangerous weapon indeed. Mr Randel's hands were, without doubt, the wrong hands. His actions deserve appropriate punishment, if only as an example to the countless others who also act as custodians of the security of the Nation.'

In jailing him for a year on 9 January 2003, US District Judge Richard W. Story acknowledged that Randel had previously led an exemplary life that had enabled him to obtain a responsible job. 'You worked, for goodness sake, for the Drug Enforcement Administration,' he said.

> On the other hand, having worked in that agency, you probably had a better appreciation than I do of the work of the agency, the dangers associated with work within the agency, and the grave concern that I think any citizen would have about the leaking of information from that agency to the public. Anything that would affect the security of officers and of the operations of the agency would be of tremendous concern, I think, to any law-abiding citizen in this country.
>
> This is a very serious crime. In my view it is a very serious offence because of the risk that comes with it, and

part of that risk is because of the position that you are in
... And for any person within the agency to take it upon
himself to leak information poses a tremendous risk; and
that's what, to me, makes this a particularly serious offence ...

And the risk that you created here was tremendous.
Fortunately, this is like the drunk driver who gets home
without killing somebody: nobody got run over or killed,
and we're thankful for that; but you should never have
gotten in the car driving and drinking. No agent was
killed as a result of the information that was leaked and
no investigation was compromised, but the risk that was
created was certainly there. And that is of grave concern.

And that's the reason that, in my view, incarceration
is appropriate in this case. I do think that it is appropriate
with a crime of this type, and it is my judgement that you
be committed in the custody of the Bureau of Prisons for
a term of 12 months.

Randel was also told he would be put on probation for three years
upon his release and he was fined the equivalent of £1,200.

There was a mixed reaction from the two sides to Randel's
one-year jail sentence. Alastair Brett told the *Guardian*: 'The
judge's sentence on this man is monstrous. Journalists talk to all
sorts of people like MI5, MI6, customs, and we don't expect them
to be banged up for it. His lawyer thinks he has a good case to
appeal. We did pay money to Mr Randel but it was a research
fee.' Brett's comments brought back echoes of the Carmen Proetta
libel action more than a decade earlier when he had called a £3,000
payment to a convicted criminal, via his sister, a 'consultancy fee'.
Now a payment of £6,000 to another criminal was being dressed
up as a 'research fee'. While other people seek to learn from their
mistakes, Brett repeats them and seems to learn nothing at all.

I was extremely pleased when I was told that Randel had been
imprisoned. For here was an educated but thoroughly dishonest
man who, even though he did not know me and was aware that
there was no evidence that I was a criminal, had been prepared

to help to try to destroy me and my reputation. Furthermore, here was a man who was prepared to risk the lives of courageous DEA agents, some of whom were working under cover in the most dangerous circumstances imaginable to bring some of the world's most evil criminals to justice. Randel was a stupid and dangerous menace. Incidentally, I am told that he had always been unpopular at the DEA because of his arrogance and his misguided belief that he was somehow superior to his colleagues.

I was equally pleased with the carefully worded press release from the US Attorney's Office which made it absolutely clear that, first, Randel had been paid for his information – not simply for his expenses and lost earnings as *The Times* had tried to claim – and, second, that I had never been suspected of any crime by the DEA. 'From February, 1999, to September, 1999, Randel provided DEA-sensitive information about an individual to an overseas-based company in exchange for money,' the press release said. 'Specifically, Randel repeatedly provided sensitive DEA information about a British citizen named Michael Ashcroft to The London Times, a newspaper based in England. The British citizen, Ashcroft, who was not under investigation by the DEA, and has never been charged with any crime, held a significant political and business position in England, and was of interest to the publication.' I could not have worded the press release better if I had written it myself. *The Times*'s shameful skulduggery had finally been publicly exposed.

Shortly after Randel was sentenced, Michael Sissons wrote about his experiences in Atlanta in a fascinating article in the *Daily Telegraph* published on 7 February 2003 and headlined 'Ashcroft and The Times: questions that won't go away'. He explained why he had been puzzled when he studied the DEA documents relating to me and my companies which *The Times* had obtained:

I had one problem with the material from Atlanta: I couldn't find a vestige of evidence that was actually damaging to Ashcroft. I rang Randy Chartash, the assistant US attorney who had briefed me, for an assurance that I had seen all the relevant material. Mr Chartash insisted there was nothing more.

To reassure me, he arranged for a briefing by the senior DEA agent involved and the administration's lawyer. We gathered in the US attorney's office on the eve of the court hearing in Atlanta in August. I then understood why the DEA was in such an unforgiving mood.

'The first thing you've got to understand is that we're dealing with the scum of the earth,' I was told. 'The people you'll meet in these files would kill you as soon as look at you ...'

Through his contacts with the DEA, Michael was also able to shed light on the damage that the Randel-inspired articles in *The Times* had done to the DEA's work and reputation, and to the international war on drugs barons. Michael said that confidential relationships between the DEA and other international agencies were vital, but Randel's dirty work had caused untold harm to them. 'There had been consternation at Scotland Yard at the Randel leaks,' he wrote. 'Indeed, the head of the DEA's international division had been dispatched post-haste to London and Moscow to allay misgivings in the intelligence community. The last thing the DEA had expected was for a responsible employee to pass secret files to a foreign newspaper. And when I was taken through the files in detail, I could understand why. On virtually every page were details that could identify sources and agents in highly dangerous situations. In short, this was as irresponsible and damaging as it could be. Leaving aside my naïve and old-fashioned belief that *The Times* had no business using them, I couldn't help wondering what critical judgement had been applied to their content.'

Michael was in no doubt that the sorry episode warranted further police inquiries in Britain and America. He was incensed that *The Times* had sought to portray Randel as 'principled' and its own actions as in the public interest. In his article, he reviewed Alastair Brett's August 2002 statement to the Atlanta court. Brett had not only spoken of Randel's 'high-minded concern' but had gone on to claim that he had known people 'with access to far more sensitive material' who believed it to be right that classified information should be passed on, 'so long as this does not put people's lives at risk or compromise ongoing operations'. Michael wrote: 'So does Mr Brett's argument hold up? In a word, no. First, at no point has it been shown that Ashcroft had "things to hide". Moreover during the investigation into the misuse of its records, it emerged that Randel had trawled the names of further prominent figures in British public life and others who might have been connected with Ashcroft. At whose behest, and on what terms? The Federal authorities believe there is a prima facie case on both sides of the Atlantic that further criminal offences could have been committed. Certainly, Mr Brett's high-minded concern [in 1999] about not putting "lives at risk" sits uncomfortably with the damning assessment of the judge in Randel's case.'

On the same day that Michael's article was published, *Private Eye* also picked up on the story, warning that the newly knighted Sir Peter Stothard and Alastair Brett were now likely to come under scrutiny from American investigators. 'With a successful conviction under its belt the DEA is keen to press on,' the magazine reported. 'Incredible though it may seem, Stothard himself could find himself charged with bribing a US official, a very serious offence indeed. It is hoped that this dreadful prospect doesn't take the edge off his investiture at the palace.'

THERE IS one aspect of the Randel hearing that deserves greater scrutiny and that is the witness statement prepared in his defence by Alastair Brett, the legal manager of Times Newspapers. Quite apart from trying to portray Randel as a courageous hero, there was something far more worrying about Brett's witness statement: it was fundamentally untrue. For in his signed statement Brett claimed that Follett did not reveal Randel's identity to *The Times* until on or after 21 July 1999, the day when I served my writ against the newspaper. Brett wrote: 'At this stage, Mr Follett identified Mr Randel as his source and we decided to ask Mr Randel to come over to London for a few days to assist TNL in its defence.'

Two years later, my lawyers made these points to the Atlanta court about what Brett had told it. The points went unanswered by Randel's lawyers.

> Brett's statement to this court is contradicted by Brett's own prior statements; the statements of *The Times*'s outside solicitor Rupert Earle; and the findings of DEA Inspector James T. Akagi, who testified before this court on August 8, 2002. To begin with, in a Defence document filed in connection with ... Michael Ashcroft's 1999 libel action against *The Times*, Brett previously stated that on July 16, 1999 'Andrew Pierce, a senior Times journalist, spoke to Mr Follett's confidential source and satisfied himself that the source was reliable and authoritative, and that the documents shown to *The Times* were genuine' ... Also, in a witness statement dated December 1, 1999 ... Rupert Earle ... stated that 'The DEA source [Randel] had been authenticated' by *The Times* by '5.30pm on 16 July 1999'. Finally, DEA Inspector James T. Akagi testified at the August 8, 2002 Loss Amount hearing before this court in Randel's criminal case that 'On July 20, 1999, from approximately 9.40am to 10.58am Mr Randel queried or accessed NADDIS, specifically 6 files within NADDIS. And then on that same date, from 11.49am to 11.53am ... e-mailed [the files] to an e-mail address in the United Kingdom that reads as janwhite@newsint.co.uk.

It is understandable, perhaps, that *The Times* had been keen to confirm Randel's identity, given the fact that within hours of Follett's arrival at the paper's offices a story was being prepared for publication the next day. Even *The Times* would have wanted to satisfy itself that the information was from an authentic source and that the documents were not fake.

In addition, Brett made other misleading claims in his witness statement, about *The Times*'s policy on paying for confidential information and paying sources and about the nature of the payments made to Randel. He even went so far as to claim that the information *The Times* had bought from Randel could have been obtained through a Freedom of Information request – a ludicrous thing to say, as he could easily have found out.

What Brett thought he was doing when he said these things to the US court is anyone's guess, but this string of false or misleading statements does him absolutely no credit. What I do know is that Brett was at one point so worried about his actions that he confided to a colleague: 'I could get struck off for this.' At the very least, on the publication of this book and of the evidence against him that it contains, I trust that even someone as stubborn as Brett will have the decency to admit his professional failings. I trust that Baldwin, too, will have the good grace to admit his professional failings now that I have exposed his illegal activities in the drugs world – which is common knowledge in the Westminster village – and the hypocrisy of his behaviour.

THE TIMES'S willingness to rely on criminals was not restricted to its dealings with Follett, the DEA and the US legal system. I eventually discovered that in the summer of 1999, at the height of our dispute, the newspaper had hired the services of a so-called private investigator called Gavin Singfield. Singfield had been working as a self-employed 'business consultant' and 'research analyst' for ten years. By November 1999, he had set up Corporate Risk Consultants Ltd, of which he was a director and the sole shareholder, providing 'risk assessment and corporate research services'. The newspaper had wanted to access details about my payments to the Conservative Party's bank account, but needed the safety of 'deniability'.

The Times is certainly not the only national newspaper that routinely uses private detectives to obtain illegal information. The man in the street would be appalled if he knew how often it goes on and how easy it is to obtain information on an individual, famous or unknown. If private detectives are used sparingly by newspapers, it is usually because of budget restraints rather than because of moral concerns. Private detectives can, either through their own knowledge of computer systems or by sub-contracting, find out all sorts of confidential information on an individual in a matter of hours. It might cost a newspaper £100 to ask a private detective to 'pull' – that is the phrase normally used by journalists – an individual's ex-directory telephone number. Similar amounts are charged to gain a print-out of a credit card, which can prove lucrative for the private detective if, as is usual these days, an individual has more than one credit card. I am told £200 is about the going rate, too, to obtain someone's confidential medical records or an itemised print-out of someone's calls from a given phone for a three-month period. Journalists are just a telephone call away from obtaining all this information on an individual and more because most experienced news reporters have a private detective with whom they have a relationship of mutual trust.

Some information is harder to obtain and therefore a journalist has to pay more for it. Most private detectives are unable to obtain banking or income tax records by breaking into a secure computer system and they therefore have to impersonate the individual involved and 'blag' information from staff using a combination of cunning and genuine data that they have obtained. They provide accurate information – the individual's birthday, National Insurance number and the like – to bank or Inland Revenue staff to persuade them that they are who they say they are. Such information is more costly because it is more difficult to obtain and the penalties are greater if the private detective is caught. To obtain difficult bank or Inland Revenue records might cost a newspaper hundreds, even thousands, of pounds and it might take several days, even weeks, to obtain. Buying illegal information for a journalist can be like a supermarket shopper buying soap powder – discounted bulk rates mean the more you buy, the cheaper the product becomes.

In November 1995, the *Sunday Times* – *The Times*'s sister newspaper – ran a story headlined 'For sale: your secret medical records for £150'. The story began: 'Confidential medical records of politicians, celebrities and millions of other National Health Service patients can be bought on the information black market for £150. The contents of the files, comprising patients' most personal health details dating back 30 years, are being sold to order

by high-street detective agencies advertising in the Yellow Pages.'
With inflation, the going rate is now £200. There was no mention
in the *Sunday Times* article of how adept journalists in general and
reporters working for Times Newspapers in particular are at using private detectives to obtain confidential information. I have,
however, been sent a copy of a memo in which a journalist from
the *Sunday Times* is ordering illegal 'credit/bank checks' on an MP.
Within twenty-four hours, the reporter had the information – in
the form of Barclaycard payments – from a colleague, who had
obviously used a private detective.

Gavin Singfield is not a sophisticated computer hacker and he
did *The Times*'s dirty work, not by a technical breach of computer
security, but by out-and-out con-artistry. No one at *The Times*
would have been crass enough to ask Singfield to break the law
but they would have known that he would have to do so to obtain the information that their newspaper required. Stothard, like
most editors, would have been protected from such dirty work
and would almost certainly not even have been told the details of
what was going on. Under section 5 of the Data Protection Act
of 1984, it was a criminal offence to procure an unauthorised disclosure of data and to sell data so obtained, unless it could be
proved that this was done in the public interest.

Singfield was asked by the newspaper to uncover information
on my recent donations to the Conservative Party. *The Times* was
presumably hoping to find out that the details I had given about
the size of my donations were wrong. The fact that the newspaper
was using a private detective showed that it doubted the earlier
information supplied by the Conservative Party about the size of
my donations. I am sure *The Times* hoped to prove that the original information provided by its sources in the Party – that I was
donating up to £360,000 a month – was accurate.

Singfield 'blagged' his way into the Conservative Party's banking records held by the Drummonds branch of the Royal Bank
of Scotland and was able to establish payments of £83,000 a
month – that is £1 million a year. The donations consisted of
money from my personal savings which were sent through one
of my accounts in Belize to the Conservative Party. I had learned,

from an impeccable source during my visit to the Conservative Party conference in October 1999, that the newspaper already had these details. However, the source also told me that *The Times* was worried about using the information because it was quite clear it could have been obtained only through unlawful means.

The newspaper, however, eventually used this information in November 1999, a month before the settlement of my legal action against *The Times*. It chose to use it at a time when the Conservative Party was already on the ropes. On Saturday, 20 November, Lord Archer of Weston-super-Mare had withdrawn as the Tory candidate for mayor of London after the *News of the World* tricked him into admitting he had asked a friend to lie for him during his successful libel action against the *Daily Star* thirteen years earlier. Two days later, Scotland Yard revealed that it was investigating Lord Archer over the allegations. With the Tories in difficulty, *The Times* decided that this was an opportune moment to dress up some largely old information about my funding for the party and spin it to try to make life awkward for William Hague and me.

At this point, the information had come into Tom Baldwin's possession. He wanted to muddy the waters, to obscure its dubious origin, and he was also keen to create as much havoc for the Conservative Party as possible. He therefore took the rare, almost unheard-of, step of giving the details about my funding to two other senior journalists on rival newspapers – the *Guardian* and the *Independent*. Shortly after 5 p.m. on 23 November – the day before the story was published – Conservative Central Office was bombarded with calls to its press office from these three newspapers. The next day the three papers ran similar stories. It was, predictably, *The Times* that gave the story the most prominent display. 'Tories admit taking £1m "foreign" cash' was the paper's front-page headline. It was a peach of a headline even by *The Times*'s low standards. Far from admitting something new, the party was confirming the levels and sources of my donations that were already widely known.

Baldwin's story began: 'The Conservative Party admitted last night that £1 million a year is being channelled into its bank accounts by its treasurer Michael Ashcroft through a secretive trust based in Belize. The donations, in sums of up to £250,000, appear to be in breach of new rules on personal funding of political parties, as well as throwing a question mark over William Hague's promise more than two years ago that he would not take foreign money.' Baldwin's standards of journalism were as shoddy as ever. The Conservative Party did not admit that money was being 'channelled' through a 'secretive trust'; these were his sensational and misleading words, rather than the party's considered and accurate ones. There were no 'new rules' – rather recommendations from Lord Neill's Committee on Standards in Public Life that had yet to come into effect.

The *Independent* also carried a front-page story by Andrew Grice, its political editor, headlined 'Hague pledge on foreign donors "broken" by £666,000 Ashcroft gift'. The *Guardian*'s front-page story written by David Hencke, the newspaper's Westminster correspondent, was headlined 'Tory rage over new Ashcroft disclosure'.

So, not only had Baldwin sought to disguise the source of the story but he had also managed to get maximum impact for the disclosure and to cause maximum embarrassment to the Conservative Party. Alastair Campbell and Baldwin's many friends in the Labour Party will have been well pleased with his day's work. In fact, the whole episode was a fuss about nothing. As Michael Ancram, the Conservative Party Chairman, pointed out, the payments were fully in accordance with the party's policy of the previous two years. The party had made it clear that it would operate by its existing guidelines until Parliament introduced new ones based on the recommendations of Lord Neill's committee.

Michael's revelations that the party had called in Scotland Yard to investigate how the security of private bank accounts had been breached also figured prominently in the newspapers of 24 November. 'Tories call for bank leaks probe' was the front-page headline in the *Financial Times*, while the *Daily Mail* led its front page with a story headlined 'Yard in hunt for Tory bank hackers'. *The Times* was the exception to the rule and – for some reason – did not carry a word about the police inquiry into the leaks. Knowing what I do now, it is not hard to see why the newspaper did not want to highlight the prospect of police scrutiny of the security leak.

My response was to write an article for the *Independent* in which I, once again, sought to put the record straight following an unprovoked attack by *The Times*. I pointed out that both I and the party had acted entirely properly and that the important issue was not where the money had come from but who *owned* the money that was being donated. I finished the article with the words: 'One last question. There is another man who, like me, is self made; who, like me, travels extensively in support of those interests; who, like me, no longer resides in the country of his birth; and who, like me, has assets and influence in a number of countries. His name is Rupert Murdoch, a man who has, without doubt, made a major and, I would argue positive, contribution to Britain. To attack him for the way he runs his life would be absurd. So why is one of his newspapers attacking me for the way I run mine?' Little did I know when I wrote those words that I would be sipping tea with Rupert at his London home just days later.

As my displeasure at the behaviour of *The Times* and its journalists grew throughout 2000, I resolved to try to get to the bottom of this specific breach of banking security. To me it was beyond the pale that somebody was willing and able to obtain details of the Conservative Party's bank accounts. If individuals were willing to do this, they were surely willing to go to virtually any lengths to harm the party and me. When I began my inquiries, I was unaware that *The Times* had played such a central role. Investigations carried out at the request of one of my companies were extensive and costly, but I was helped by senior figures from within the newspaper who disapproved of their employer's immorality.

By the summer of 2000, I was convinced that Gavin Singfield had played a pivotal role in obtaining confidential information from the Conservative Party's bank account. At this point, my interest was aroused by an article in the *Guardian* by Kevin Maguire, a former *Daily Mirror* journalist (he is now back working for that paper). Kevin was well aware of some of the illegal activities that private investigators routinely carried out for journalists. Since Singfield had not been the *Guardian*'s source for its story on my company's donations to the Conservative Party – this role had been performed by Baldwin – Kevin felt entitled to look into the activities of the private investigator. On one occasion, Singfield had allowed Kevin into his home and discussed accusations against him relating to stories that had appeared in newspapers based on a 'telephone blag' or impersonation. This included the scam used, years earlier, to obtain the tax records of Lord Levy, Tony Blair's Middle East envoy. 'I don't need this,' Singfield initially told the journalist, adding that he had not been contacted by investigators looking into the security breaches. Singfield later made a series of phone calls to Kevin in which he asked if he had been identified as having been involved in the Levy case and my own case and in which he offered to give the journalist a further interview. Later still, however, he simply denied any involvement in any attempt to obtain information in either case.

Kevin also wrote a witty and informative article in the *New Statesman* magazine revealing some of the tricks of the trade in which journalists employ impersonators and private investigators to obtain confidential information. 'Meet Gavin. A former thespian who lives in (let's say) Sussex, he now makes a lot more money than he did treading the boards. A brilliant mimic, his voices are superb. So good, in fact, that if he rang, you would be unlikely to know if it was whoever he was that day or just plain old Gavin,' Kevin wrote.

> Say hello to Jonathan. Those in the know say that he's not quite as convincing as Gavin, but he can be pretty convincing as a lawyer, accountant or assistant to a high-profile public figure …
>
> Bank and mortgage arrangements, credit card statements and itemised phone bills: Gavin and Jonathan can get them. These boys do their homework, memorising dates of birth, maiden names, addresses and anything else that a well-trained or mildly suspicious employee might ask. Tricks of the trade include ringing at lunchtime when, with half the staff away and the other

half looking forward to a break, a person's guard is often down.

Singfield had the impudence to report Kevin to the Press Complaints Commission, the press watchdog, on the grounds that his privacy had been invaded – a complaint that was, not surprisingly, rejected.

By the end of June 2000, it was our turn to confront Singfield about his activities and to explore whether he might be willing to divulge information about his work for News International, the parent company of *The Times* and the *Sunday Times*. A letter dated 30 June from Jeffrey Green Russell, solicitors to the Belize Bank, was sent by courier to Singfield's home in Horsham, West Sussex. It read:

> Last year, details of certain transfers of funds made by our client on behalf of a customer were reported in several British newspapers. These details were confidential and should at all times have remained confidential.
>
> We have information and evidence which indicate that you played a significant part in the process which led to the publication of this confidential information. We do not condone your actions and we explicitly reserve all our client's rights and all their customer's rights to take whatever action is found to be appropriate.
>
> Nevertheless, it is fair to say that both our client and their customer are more concerned with the process that led to the breach of confidentiality than they are with the mechanics of the breach and those who may have played a part in that exercise.
>
> Pending the commencement of proceedings, we are writing to offer you the opportunity of a without prejudice meeting to establish whether there may be an alternative, and perhaps less costly, means of resolving matters.
>
> If you would like to explore this route perhaps you would care to telephone the writer. In the absence of any communication, we will press on with current plans.

Inevitably, I suppose, Singfield denied any involvement in or knowledge of the scam in a lengthy exchange of letters between my company's solicitors and the private investigator and, later, his solicitors Lewis Silkin. Singfield did, however, make contact with Alastair Brett, the legal manager of *The Times*. Some neutral observers might say this was a strange action for someone who supposedly had no knowledge of the security leak that had led to a story in the newspaper. Singfield and his solicitor eventually spent five months stonewalling straightforward questions that anybody without something to hide would willingly have answered. Stothard remained equally evasive about the episode. When pressed by the Conservative Party about the breaches of security, he chose his words extremely carefully when he said: '*The Times*, in common with other newspapers, does not reveal the identity of its sources and will never do so. We have not asked for any illegal acts to be carried out, and would not condone such behaviour.' Stothard was subsequently interviewed by John Humphrys for the Radio 4 *Today* programme in which he was, at best, economical with the truth and, at worst, a blatant liar. 'This information came in the normal course of our inquiries. We did nothing illegal to obtain it ... We got this information in the absolutely normal way ... You're a journalist, and you know that if information is passed to you ... if you're told scraps of information ... you are not precisely sure where it came from right at the beginning of the chain. No one is precisely sure where a bit of information originally came from.' This was Stothard's lowest point in a catalogue of increasingly shabby dealings. He either knew where the information had come from or knew that the law must have been broken to obtain such information and was turning a blind eye to the detail so that he could deny knowledge or responsibility. Either way he behaved abominably and failed to live up to his responsibilities as the editor of a once great newspaper.

SOMEONE AT Times Newspapers had also decided to look into my tax affairs. They worked in league with a private investigator who had, in turn, breached the security of the Inland Revenue, gaining access to information about my tax returns. In a sting similar to that conducted by another newspaper on Norman Lamont when he was Chancellor of the Exchequer, a con-artist made telephone calls to staff at different tax offices and thereby gradually garnered information about my tax returns. This information was then published in the *Sunday Times* – the same newspaper that just eight months earlier had published confidential information relating to the tax returns of Lord Levy, the Labour Party fundraiser. This information had been obtained in June 2000 by a man impersonating Lord Levy in two calls to the Inland Revenue.

The author of the article in the *Sunday Times* about my tax returns was none other than Nick Rufford, an investigative journalist whose undignified treatment of Dr David Kelly, the scientist who took his own life after leaking information to the media in the build-up to the war in Iraq, was scrutinised by the Hutton inquiry of 2003–4. In his report into the scientist's death, Lord Hutton recounted how Rufford had confronted Dr Kelly in the garden of his Oxfordshire home eight days before he died, but the journalist was not criticised over his behaviour. Rufford is now the newspaper's motoring editor – not perhaps the best position in which to take advantage of his much vaunted contacts in the security services.

Rufford's story appeared in the *Sunday Times* of 18 February 2001, under the headline 'Ashcroft faces new questions over tax'. It began: 'The role of Lord Ashcroft, the Conservative party treasurer, was under scrutiny last night as it emerged that he was still a tax exile, months after he was said to be returning from abroad to live in Britain. Ashcroft, who is playing an increasingly high-profile role in the party's affairs, paid no income tax in the financial year to April 2000 and declared himself non-resident for tax purposes, according to the most recent Inland Revenue records.' The newspaper provided detailed information about my tax affairs, including the fact that they were handled by a little-known unit of the Inland Revenue called the Financial Intermediary Claims Office (FICO), based in Bootle, Merseyside.

It was clear that somebody had illegally obtained details of my tax returns in tactics similar to those used against Lord Levy.

This was confirmed to me by Sir Nick Montagu, the chairman of the Inland Revenue. In a letter written on 7 March 2002, he told me that he had seen the article and that his first concern had been whether the information had come from the Inland Revenue. He had established that its office in Bootle had received telephone calls during the week leading up to the publication of the *Sunday Times*'s article from someone purporting to be me. The caller was able to quote correctly my unique taxpayer reference number, which is not a matter of public record and is generally shown only on certain correspondence between the Inland Revenue and individual customers. He also had accurate details about a small tax repayment I had received. Sir Nick Montagu wrote:

> It is now clear that the caller was masquerading as you, and I am extremely sorry that we failed to spot as bogus someone who was able to give a reference number which matched your name and who displayed some familiarity with your affairs. We have marked your files to make clear that you will not be calling us in person, and that any caller purporting to be you should therefore be treated as suspicious. We are also looking into our security procedures to see if they need tightening.
>
> We believe there may have been other bogus calls before those referred to above, and we are continuing our efforts to establish the precise chain of events from our internal security systems. Meanwhile, I have asked my Departmental Security Officer to pass the details of the calls to the Information Commissioner for investigation into an apparent breach of the Data Protection Act. He did so on 1 March.

A year later, I learned from an investigating officer acting for the Information Commissioner that five calls had been received between 9 and 14 February 2001 from someone who purported to be me, but efforts to trace the person or persons responsible had 'proved fruitless'.

The man who had been impersonating me was clearly good

at his role and none of those he had called had been suspicious: he fitted together each new piece of information about my tax returns as if he were doing a jigsaw. One of those he telephoned was an experienced Inland Revenue operator who knew exactly the questions to ask in order to verify the authenticity of the caller. She told Inland Revenue investigators looking into the breach of security: 'Having worked for the Revenue for such a length of time, one has a sixth sense about bogus calls, and when something is not quite right, but this call gave me no cause for concern. The caller made reference to a tax repayment and was able to quote the exact amount involved and wished to know the breakdown – to which years this amount referred to. I gave him this information. There was no other information requested and the call was terminated. Other than the voice being that of a well-spoken person, and an older person, there was nothing distinctive about it.'

PETER STOTHARD was eventually demoted from his position as editor of *The Times* by Rupert Murdoch. He became editor of the *Times Literary Supplement*, a specialist weekly magazine with a much smaller circulation. His demotion came little more than two years after being told by his proprietor to print a front-page retraction about me – one that made it clear that neither he nor his newspaper had any evidence that I was linked to drug trafficking or money laundering. It is a disappointing end to a once-promising career. Stothard was eventually knighted in 2003: in my opinion, for services to New Labour – notably for targeting me – rather than for any noble contribution to the world of journalism, a profession that he helped to corrupt.

I heard that Stothard was standing down as editor a fortnight after meeting him, quite by chance, at a charity function at the Natural History Museum in west London. We initially exchanged pleasantries, but Stothard quickly began threatening me, telling me that if I did not stop making inquiries into the source of the leaks against me – notably Jonathan Randel – 'we [*The Times*] could start on you all over again'. I never take kindly to being threatened, but to be talked to like this by Stothard, who had behaved so badly himself, made me extremely cross. It also made me more determined than ever to get to the bottom of all the skulduggery in which *The Times* and its associates had indulged during their campaign against me. It was against this unhappy backdrop that I wrote to Stothard summarising my disappointment at his behaviour over the previous three years.

Stretching to three pages and dated 27 February 2002, the letter told him that he had made fundamental errors of judgement in his dealings with me. 'You listened too attentively to the whispering which accompanied my appointment as Treasurer and, worse, you gave public expression to it,' I wrote.

My word is important to me. In business, I depend upon my reputation. In choosing to stain my character and damage my reputation, *The Times* picked a fight from which I had no wish to walk away.

Unfortunately for me, I had others to consider. My loyalty to William Hague and my overall concern for the Party obliged me to contemplate a settlement of the litigation, even though it would deprive me of the opportunity to clear my name in public. Both of us know full well how the case would have played out had it reached the courtroom.

Imagine my reaction, therefore, when I realised that 'drawing a line under the Ashcroft affair' was proving so unpalatable for some Times Newspapers employees that I had to endure continuing smears and snide innuendo. Imagine my humour at the news that *The Times* had once again despatched Dominic Kennedy to Belize to rake over the same old ground.

Insult was added to injury when a number of letters of complaint to your Legal Manager were responded to with belligerence rather than understanding.

I would commend you to consider some of the facts.

I am accused of a number of things – including an involvement in drugs – by a journalist whose cocaine habit is the talk of the Lobby, and who has been assisted in his endeavours by an unattractive alliance which includes a New Labour spin doctor and a blueblood Tory grandee who wished to settle a score against William Hague.

There are no prizes for identifying the three unnamed men – Tom Baldwin, Alastair Campbell, a close friend of Baldwin whose role in this story I shall return to later, and Viscount Cranborne.

It is suggested that I am guilty of impropriety on the basis of a contorted analysis of documents which have been acquired by Dr Jonathan Randel, a US Government official.

I then discover that a con-artist called Gavin Singfield has been commissioned ... to commit a number of criminal offences, including the acquisition of certain banking information. Furthermore, I learn that this banking information is consciously held back for months by *The Times* until Jeffrey Archer's resignation [as the Conservative candidate for mayor of London], at which point it is shared with other newspapers in the hope that it will finally unseat me ...

Make no mistake, my commitment to the agreement that I reached personally with Rupert Murdoch remains rock solid, but other agencies have taken a wider interest. At the same time, malign influences within your own organisation remain both suspicious of me and uncommitted to the settlement agreement. I cannot ignore that.

You will also appreciate that I cannot and will not ignore the other very real factors which remain at play, few, if any, of which are now within my control. Influence I may have, but I am in no mood to extend to others the courtesies which they have so consistently denied me.

My letter may appear ungracious to an editor who was standing down, but my patience with and tolerance of Stothard had long run out. Alastair Brett, for one, did not welcome or enjoy the letter. He received it on the way to Stothard's leaving party at the editor's home in Swiss Cottage, north London. Brett walked into the drinks party carrying a briefcase containing my letter. As he moved round the room, he repeatedly pulled the letter from his briefcase and shouted in a deranged voice, 'Fucking Ashcroft!' When Robert Thomson, the new editor of *The Times*, later demanded an explanation of the points I had raised, Brett produced a reply that rivalled *War and Peace* in length.

Stothard did not reply to my letter. This duty was left to Les Hinton, the executive chairman of News International who, while not agreeing with all the points I had made, acknowledged that it was time for the newspaper to move on. Although Rupert Murdoch and Les Hinton are honourable men, I did not trust *The Times* at all and I therefore felt my own inquiries into the story ought to be pursued. The incident of the con-artist trying to extract information from the Royal Bank of Scotland was not isolated. I also discovered that someone had got hold of the landline telephone records of a colleague of mine, while the Belize Bank was targeted by another 'blagger' who tried, unsuccessfully, to obtain further confidential information relating to me and my companies. I was never able to prove who carried out these intrusions, but I certainly have my suspicions and I would not be surprised if *The Times* had some involvement in these incidents too.

Knowing, as I do, quite how often newspapers use private investigators, I was amused to read this article in *Private Eye* on 10 December 2003:

> Red faces all around Fleet Street after a raid on a private detective by investigating officers from the information commissioner found incriminating details of scores of tabloid hacks having paid a private eye to break the law.
>
> Ex-directory phone numbers, numbers of family and friends, vehicle licence traces and criminal record investigations – all illegal under the data protection act, all commissioned by journalists whose papers claim to support the right to reasonable privacy.
>
> This may explain why when a Met detective was arrested on corruption charges there was not a squeak out

of the press. But the names of the victims and the reporters and photographers who were clients are all detailed. Prosecutions will follow as sure as night follows day or as desperate hacks follow celebs ...

There are three footnotes to my battle with *The Times*. Early in 2003, Francis Maude, the former Conservative minister, asked me to help finance his new initiative C-Change, a Conservative think tank. I realised that Michael Gove was a key member of the think tank (he has since become its chairman) – the same Michael Gove who had written some less than flattering things about me in his role as a senior leader and comment writer on *The Times*. It was also the same Michael Gove who had been put up to appear on Radio 4's *Today* programme the day after I had served my writ against the newspaper but, in the face of relentless questioning, had turned out to be unaware that his newspaper had passed the DEA's reports on me to Peter Bradley, the Labour MP. I explained to Francis that Michael and I had a 'past', but that if we had lunch I thought we would be able to resolve our difficulties. Michael and I duly dined at the House of Lords and discussed the Radio 4 programme in which he, rather unconvincingly, had tried to justify his stand. However, I explained that I had a high regard for his journalistic abilities and his ambitions to become a Conservative MP. I told him that, concerning his radio interview, I was willing to accept that perhaps he had merely been a good trouper for his employer and I was prepared to let the matter rest. I have since supported C-Change, and I received a letter in the summer of 2003 asking if I wanted to take on a greater role and join the board – an invitation that I did not take up. In May 2005 Michael was duly elected MP for Surrey Heath, a safe Tory seat. When he was originally chosen as prospective parliamentary candidate I wrote him a letter of congratulations, and now that he is an MP I wish him a long and successful political career.

The second footnote concerns Tom Baldwin's cocaine habit, which regrettably seems to have become more serious in recent years. Indeed, during the Conservative Party conference in October 2001, he put Peter Stothard's suite at the Imperial Hotel to 'good' use when his editor was unable to make it to the conference as planned. In the company of two journalist colleagues – Giles Coren and Alice Miles – Baldwin snorted lines of cocaine from the glass coffee table in Stothard's suite. I certainly have no evidence that his colleagues took the drug, but I am told that Baldwin's appetite for it was voracious and also that at least one colleague reprimanded him for his stupidity, saying: 'What the hell do you think you are doing, Tom?' Such is Baldwin's craving for the drug that he had taken the not inconsiderable risk of smuggling cocaine through the hotel's high-level security in order to feed his habit.

More recently Baldwin, who now enjoys the grand title of associate editor of *The Times*, has shown signs of developing a further condition – kleptomania. At the Conservative Party conference in October 2004, he was a guest at a party given by Lord Hesketh at his room in the Highcliff Hotel in Bournemouth. How did Baldwin show his gratitude for such generous hospitality and for the opportunity to drink with senior politicians and fellow journalists? By slipping off unnoticed into the night without so much as a thank-you, clasping an already opened bottle of Pol Roger champagne. The next morning, a sheepish Baldwin, who had been the worse for wear the previous night after an evening of heavy drinking, admitted to stealing the bubbly. When later asked by a fellow journalist if he would at least have the good grace to reimburse Lord Hesketh for the champagne, he was not keen to discuss the incident. 'I'm not getting into this,' he told the *Evening Standard*'s diary. 'If Lord Hesketh wants to ring me about it, he can.' The incident was first revealed by Stephen Glover in his column in the *Spectator* on 16 October 2004. Initially, the columnist considered the incident – 'hardly the grossest sort of theft' – not worthy of inclusion in his column. 'And then I considered what would have happened if a politician – say a member of the shadow Cabinet – had been caught doing what Baldwin did,' he wrote. 'Newspapers would have mentioned it, probably including Mr Baldwin's, and some might have got quite worked up about it. Journalists should not expect politicians to observe higher standards of behaviour that they do themselves.'

The third footnote relates to some wonderful double standards displayed by Baldwin's employer, *The Times*. In November 2003, the newspaper had the audacity to criticise Clive Soley, a Labour MP, for using parliamentary privilege to name someone he claimed was guilty of sexual harassment. The newspaper got on its high horse and complained about the abuse of this 'ancient privilege'. I could not resist writing a tongue-in-cheek letter to Les Hinton, the executive chairman of News International, to poke fun at the hypocrisy of it all. I told him that I noted with great interest *The Times*'s indignation and asked if he did not think that Tom Baldwin writing Peter Bradley's speech on an internal computer was an equal abuse of the privilege. I received a charming letter back from Les saying that he did not know anything about the matter I had referred to, and adding: 'It would be interesting to catch up soon to chat about the rapidly changing world of Conservative politics.' Les is a good man and I look forward to enjoying a gossipy lunch with him soon.

8 The Money Man

I HAVE so far largely overlooked the huge and central task of being party Treasurer. I have been silent about the scale of the problem that I discovered at Smith Square. Silent, too, about the work that I, with the help of others, had to do to repair weaknesses and failings. I wanted to put the Conservative Party in a financial position not only to fight a general election, but to survive it and regroup afterwards.

William Hague's outstanding leadership qualities had reinvigorated my interest in and commitment to the party, both of which had faded under John Major. It was a great honour to be asked to be Treasurer in June 1998. I took my responsibilities extremely seriously and did everything that I could to deliver for William during my three years in the role. When I took on the position, I hoped and expected that William would become an exceptional statesman. Having sold my company, ADT, to Tyco in 1997, I had more time to devote to the party than in previous years. I was determined not to fail as Treasurer for the sake of the party and of William, as well as for my own pride.

When I accepted the invitation to become Deputy Treasurer and, just months later, Treasurer, I was unaware of the scale of the problems. I knew that the party had fought an expensive but unsuccessful election campaign the previous year, but I had no idea that it had spent money that it simply did not have. After I was appointed Treasurer, Cecil Parkinson, the party Chairman, told me that income was about £6 million a year and expenditure was £14 million a year. 'You are what?' I replied in sheer disbelief, in a tone of voice that Mary must have heard from Joseph. It was an incredible position: in simple terms the money coming in was well under half the amount being spent. There was more bad news: once all the bills had been paid from the election campaign

– including a formidable bill from the advertising agency M & C Saatchi of some £15 million – the party's working overdraft was teetering on the edge of its £4 million maximum. If the party had been a company I had been thinking of taking over, I could not have considered it even the sort of business for which I would have paid $1 or £1. It was beyond hope: a financial basket case. Furthermore, the party was out of power and likely to be in the wilderness for some time. Morale was low and there did not seem any good reason for previously high-giving donors to continue their generous level of financial support.

While I was working on the financial restructuring, Archie Norman was doing a similar job on the organisational restructuring in order to enable the party to campaign more effectively. Archie, who was the new Deputy Chairman and chief executive of the party under William, was a talented man and a bundle of energy. He disliked the creaking structure of Conservative Central Office and the archaic set-up in the constituencies: one of his first tasks was to rip down many of the internal walls in Smith Square and make it more open plan. Like me, he had a business background – he had been a successful chief executive of the Asda supermarket chain – but we had different styles and ways of dealing with people. He often seemed to have too much on his plate and too many outside distractions. He also had an unfortunate habit of putting other people's backs up. His critics saw him as a bull in a china shop and felt that he lacked political skills – he undoubtedly made enemies. On top of this, his early speeches in the House of Commons and his initial skirmishes with Labour MPs did not go down particularly well. I had a soft spot for Archie, but he would probably have achieved even more if he had adopted a less confrontational style. He eventually stepped down as Deputy Chairman and chief executive of the party in June 1999, when I was just a year into my role as Treasurer, in order to become front-bench spokesman on Foreign and Commonwealth Affairs.

A close friend of mine, Cecil wanted someone as Treasurer whom he could trust. He also wanted me to apply commercial principles to the party's finances and to be as ruthless as if I had been turning around a failing company. So I set out to reduce overheads as rapidly as possible and to increase revenue equally quickly by finding new sources of income. Savings were made, including unpopular redundancies at Conservative Central Office. I needed some good people around me. I was fortunate to have inherited David Prior, then the Conservative MP for North Norfolk. Initially he was appointed by William Hague as Vice Chairman and deputy chief executive to Archie Norman. However, after Archie's departure, David stepped up to become Deputy Chairman and chief executive. He is an astute operator and was the unsung hero of Conservative Central Office during William's time as leader. I quickly established a strong working relationship with him. The party's ultimate decision-making body is a board of seventeen members – representatives from the voluntary, political and professional sections of the party – which meets once a month. At that time, it proved not to be the decisive body that the circumstances cried out for.

I felt that I had to lead from the front. As I have already pointed out, it would have been difficult for me to approach others for donations without making my own financial contribution. So in my first year as Treasurer I donated £1 million to the party and, at various times, lent up to £3 million more to ease cash-flow difficulties. I think, however, that my own wealth was a disadvantage rather than an advantage. I am certain that some donors felt that, if push came to shove, I would always pick up the tab for whatever bills arrived. These donors were therefore not as generous as they might have been.

I decided initially to concentrate on balancing the books and worry later about how on earth I was going to raise a fighting fund of £15 million to contest the next general election. In the short term, my aim was to cut the party's expenditure to £10 million a year while accepting that there would be several one-off costs, including redundancy payments, in order to get down to that level. Job losses and cost cutting are never popular, but in this case they were vital. I insisted on significant reductions in expenditure across the board, including expenses.

When I became Treasurer, the scenes in the accounts department on the third floor of 34 Smith Square were chaotic.

There were literally baskets of cheques waiting to be sent out to cover unpaid bills, but they had not been dispatched because they would have pushed us over our agreed overdraft limit. One senior finance officer had found the whole situation so depressing and overwhelming that he had walked out overnight. I found that too many people – nearly eighty in total – were in possession of party credit cards. These were being used so freely that many officials did not even bother to submit expense claims for scrutiny. I decided that every credit card should be removed in order to make staff more accountable for their spending.

I made my point at one board meeting by bringing in the huge pile of monthly receipts from one senior official which included a £400 bill from Stringfellow's nightclub in central London. I am no prude and I hope the official and those with him greatly enjoyed the lap-dancing entertainment that was on offer that night; however, I did not feel this was an appropriate use of party funds. How could I ask supporters to work hard up and down the country, or to make donations, if this was the sort of activity that the party's income would be spent on? I will spare the official's blushes by not identifying him, but suffice to say he no longer works at Conservative Central Office. There were many other receipts of a 'doubtful' nature that had been automatically paid. Nobody had been taking responsibility for the bills that were piling up.

I wanted a culture change and was helped – and hindered in turn – by the fact that under the new party constitution, introduced in March 1998, board members had unlimited liability for any party debts. This resulted in board members being aware of the need for savings, but the perilous state of the party's finances led to one or two of them panicking and seeking indemnity insurance in respect of any bankruptcy proceedings. This was neither possible nor desirable and I did not support the proposal, which was eventually defeated.

I could see that we needed to broaden the donor base in order to bring income up towards the same level as expenditure. I felt it was too risky for the party to rely on the generosity of a few large donors. If such donors died, became disillusioned with the party or hit hard times, this would cause acute financial difficulties for us. I was responsible for two significant initiatives. First, I created and developed a wider range of donor clubs where groups of people pledged to give a certain amount of money to the party each month. There was Team 1000 where members agreed to donate a minimum of £1,000 a year, the Frontbench Club where the pledge went up to £5,000 a year and the Renaissance Forum where the promise was £10,000 a year. There was also a series of events and initiatives aimed at encouraging people to join the clubs.

Secondly, I encouraged, partly by a programme of direct-mail appeals, the membership scheme to be linked directly to Conservative Central Office rather than the local party. This meant that as association membership declined the central membership increased, while the total number of members remained fairly static. The benefit of this was to enable modern marketing techniques to be used to raise money for the party. Many of these people who joined the party centrally also donated money, bringing a new and much needed revenue stream. This, however, caused some tensions with the constituency associations, who were reluctant to relinquish their powers. I think, too, because of some of the poor financial regulation of previous years, the associations felt that Conservative Central Office was a black hole where money disappeared, never to be seen again.

I like to think that the changes I made transformed the party's dated fundraising machine for the better – changes which are still being built upon to this day. I brought in a small, hard-working and loyal team of professional fundraisers to do the work that was needed – three able people who knew how I operated. However, I still had to tolerate aspects of the job which I found tedious. The worst part of my role was undoubtedly the monthly board meetings, held in a gloomy office at Smith Square, which started at 2 p.m. and were often still going on at 7 p.m.

During my time as Treasurer, I had to put up with some harsh treatment from the party's bankers, the Royal Bank of Scotland. The bank, which had allowed the party under John Major's leadership to build up an overdraft of £19 million, had initially capped the overdraft under William's leadership at £4 million. Yet, shortly after I took over as Treasurer, the bank wanted to cap the overdraft at £2 million. After some lengthy and tense negotiating, the party won the right to reduce its overdraft limit by £250,000 a quarter. This meant that we were reducing it over a space of two years rather than overnight, as the bank had unrealistically demanded. I felt that the Royal Bank of Scotland's tactics were unnecessarily 'hard ball': they were neither generous with their interest rate nor slow to add fees to our account whenever they could. The tough approach of the bank did, however, convince some within the party of the seriousness of the financial difficulties that we faced.

I made some interesting discoveries along the way. In the past, the constituencies had loaned the party a total of £3.6 million, but this had been placed in a separate bank account where the only benefit to the party was the modest deposit rate on the money. So I organised a letter to all the constituency associations informing them that – unless they objected – the party was going to use this money as short-term working capital. As a consequence, their loans would become unsecured. Most associations agreed, but I still have a mental note of the associations which withdrew money totalling £600,000 and were not prepared to help their party at its time of need. The money did not buy us out of a crisis but it did buy us time.

After I had been Treasurer for a year, we had an annual loss of just under £2 million – which I considered satisfactory bearing in mind my starting position. My role as Treasurer had been further weakened by the Labour Party's announcement that it would voluntarily disclose the name of donors who gave more than £5,000. This put pressure on the Conservative Party to do the same at a time when more and more donors were seeking anonymity so that they would not be scrutinised by the media. William Hague decided that the Conservative Party ought to come into line. He got the transparency that he wanted but I lost several of my largest donors. Those who had previously given tens of thousands of pounds a year were now only prepared to write out cheques for £4,999 in order to preserve their anonymity.

It had taken a while to pull back from the brink of insolvency. Once we had turned our fortunes around, we were in a position to contemplate the push that would be needed to raise the general election fighting fund. By the end of my second year as Treasurer, the party was back on an even keel with annual expenditure and income matching each other at around £10 million. Indeed, in the annual report for the year ending 31 March 2000, the party actually showed a tiny surplus – of £4,000 – compared with a deficit of £1.9 million the previous year.

The combination of my role as party Treasurer and my battle with *The Times* meant that it was impossible for me to be as hands on with my companies as I would have liked. I had to become an absent shepherd for many of my businesses and rely on other people. When I eventually took a more direct role in handling my business affairs after standing down as Treasurer in 2001, I discovered that my companies had enjoyed a mixed record in my absence. Some had done well with little or no involvement from me, while others had performed disastrously. Although it is a difficult figure to quantify, I suspect my three years as Treasurer cost me more than £100 million in lost capital value: money that I would have made if I had retained tighter control over my businesses. Once I resigned as Treasurer, I had to devote a considerable amount of time and energy to ensuring that all my companies were back to performing at their best. Indeed, that became my prime focus for the first year after I had stepped down.

My final year as Treasurer was the most difficult and the most challenging. Not only did I want to provide William with a fighting fund of £15 million for the general election, but I was determined to leave my successor in a strong position too. Initially, we had a chicken-and-egg situation with regard to the general election. As party Chairman, Michael Ancram wanted to know how much money he had at his disposal so that he could plan his campaign. The problem from my point of view was that he wanted to know a full year in advance, yet most of the funding comes in during the immediate run-up to polling day. It would, therefore, have been imprudent of me to give the go-ahead for him to spend £15 million when there was no way of seeing where the money would be coming from. I already had it in the back of my mind that, if the Labour Party won the election, I would not remain as Treasurer. If this happened, I wanted to leave my successor in a position where he or she had money to pay bills after the 2001 election at a time when there is, inevitably, a decline in donations. If Labour won and William stood down as party leader, I did not want to resign as Treasurer feeling guilty that I had left my successor in a mess. For a long time, I could not see how we would be able to raise more than £7.5 million. This caused a certain amount of unease because Michael, and indeed William himself, felt it was simply not enough to fund a vigorous and effective election campaign.

Yet just when I needed a stroke of luck in the New Year of 2001, I received it. Stuart Wheeler, a businessman and a known Euro-sceptic, came forward with a donation of £5 million. It was the largest single donation ever given to a political party and it came completely out of the blue. It was so unexpected that if, the day before, someone had asked me to produce a list of ten people who might give the party £5 million, Stuart – who had made his money from IG Index, the betting company – would not have been on the list. He donated money for the same reason that I did: because he wanted to support William Hague and give him the best possible chance of winning the forthcoming election. I will always be grateful to him for his generosity in the party's – and indeed my own – hour of need. This donation meant I could lift my confidence level about how much would be raised for the election to £12.5 million. Indeed, on further reflection, I threw caution to the wind and told the party's board that it could plan to spend the entire £15 million that it had always hoped to have at its disposal.

At this point, a group of three donors were leading Michael Ancram to believe that they would together put up £5 million, but I was extremely sceptical. I suspected the individuals involved talked a better game than they played. My intuition proved correct and the donation never materialised. As the election drew closer, I had borrowed a total of £5 million for the party without knowing exactly how some of this money would be repaid.

There is no doubt that the Conservative Party's election campaign got off to a promising start. We had a large and effective poster campaign, which I paid for, early in 2001 with the theme 'You pay the taxes ... so where are the nurses/teachers/etc?' It was designed by Yellow M, the Edinburgh-based advertising agency. The advertising campaign was considered a success and I seized on its popularity to deliver a number of presentations to donors and potential donors in January and February which generated substantial further funding. There was one major presentation at Conservative Central Office on 30 January at which William Hague, Amanda Platell, his press secretary, and Stephen Gilbert, the party's field operations director, outlined our election plans and posters to our biggest donors. It was a great success and raised a considerable amount of money for the party. With hindsight, although Yellow M's advertising campaign was clever and well received, voters may not have been ready for the message that the Labour Party was failing to deliver. Perhaps it was one election campaign too soon.

Events in politics can move quickly. The outbreak of foot and mouth in Britain in February 2001 delayed the election. At the time, we had been expecting it to be held in May, but there were also rumours that it might be as early as April. In the end, it was not held until June. We were determined not to be caught on the hop and we devised a 'first twenty-four hours' campaign to ensure that we seized the initiative. Within an hour or so of the election being called, William Hague was in a helicopter at Battersea heliport in south London and he visited three target seats that afternoon. The first week of the campaign was a great success for the Tories and there was hardly a political pundit in the country who did not consider we had got the better of the early skirmishes with Labour.

William had managed to do a clever job in forcing the Government to delay the election, thereby putting them on the back foot. Politically, this was a good thing and it also enabled the Tories to attack the Government over its handling of the crisis. However, the delay added a further £1 million to the Conservative Party's election bill – one of the biggest extra costs was that we had leased a private plane for William to travel the country which had to be kept for a further month at a cost of about £250,000.

The Conservative Party's spring conference in Harrogate in early March had been the intended initial launch of the election campaign. The revised election date, however, meant we had an extra month to kill and some senior figures in the party chose to fill it with internal mischief. There were tensions between, on the one side, William Hague's camp and, on the other side, the camps of Michael Portillo, the Shadow Chancellor of the Exchequer, and Francis Maude, the Shadow Foreign Secretary. I suspected that, without the blessing of Michael or Francis, some of their senior supporters were trying to undermine William in the hope that their man would emerge victorious in a subsequent leadership battle. There were also tensions between the Portillo and Maude camps and Amanda Platell, because they believed – wrongly I think – that she was trying to undermine Michael's and Francis's future leadership ambitions. This meant that, by the time the election campaign was launched, we were in a weaker position than a month earlier. Once it was under way, however, everyone rallied to the cause: Michael and Francis became joint spokesmen for our election effort and both men did an energetic and efficient job.

In the weeks immediately before the election, there was a strong belief throughout the Conservative Party that, even if we did not win the election, we would substantially reduce Labour's majority. As soon as campaigning started in earnest, we had two great strengths: our strategy had been skilfully planned and executed, and William displayed immense enthusiasm and stamina on the campaign trail.

As the election approached, I calculated that in order to meet the £15 million fighting fund and to leave my successor in a good position, I would personally have to write out a cheque for £4 million. This was an uncomfortably large amount and I was not happy with such a situation: in particular I did not want there to be a fresh wave of allegations claiming that the party was the 'plaything' of the Treasurer. I did not think lightning could strike twice, but a matter of days before election day, after all the commitments to spend had been made, Sir John Paul Getty II, the philanthropist, came forward and made a donation of £5 million. This was my 'get out of jail' card.

I was able to meet the spending pledge. I was also able to repay the loans (where promised, with interest) after the election, although most of those who had lent money were generous enough to leave a little bit behind for the party. I never had to write a cheque for any of the £4 million that I had feared having to contribute. When William resigned as leader after his general election defeat in June 2001, I too stepped down, in the knowledge that I was leaving the party's finances in a far sounder position than I had inherited them. I went with a sigh of relief because not only had the pressures of raising the money been lifted, but I had been suffering from poor health. For once in my life, I needed a break to recharge my batteries.

My three years as Treasurer of the party I had supported since I was old enough to vote had been anything but straightforward. I was pleased, though, that my efforts were acknowledged by those who were in a position to know exactly what I had been able to achieve. I received several generous messages of thanks and support after I announced that I was standing down as Treasurer. They included one from Eddy Shah, the businessman who had launched *Today* as the first national colour newspaper in 1986. His e-mail, dated 17 September 2001, read: 'Dear Michael, I think the Party now needs you as much as it did when William was leader. You made the place buzz and your organisational skills put the Party on a sound financial footing. You also brought in a semblance of real common sense and reality in the real world which the politicos seem to have picked up on. We really do need you. I hope you will reconsider and stay as Party Treasurer. Regards, Eddy.'

IT GOES against the grain to admit publicly any failings in my health. I do not like to give the impression of weakness to a business or political rival and it is for this reason that I have always kept any health problems to myself. This book, however, seems an appropriate time to come clean about a couple of medical issues.

I have been a diabetic since my early forties but I am usually able to stabilise the condition through medication. Just over a year into my stint as party Treasurer, however, I began suffering from a second and more serious medical problem. Since October 2000 – and in the run-up to the general election – I had been having attacks of Menière's disease, a disorder which, from time to time, leads to a rupturing of the membrane in the inner ear resulting in vertigo and vomiting. To compound this new health problem, my diabetes was also proving difficult to control. My first attack of Menière's disease came when I was due to travel from London to the north of England to address a gathering of regional Conservative Party chairmen. I woke up in the morning with my eyes flickering uncontrollably and unable to hold my balance enough to walk. Furthermore, I was vomiting and retching, and I found myself clinging to the edge of the lavatory seat. It was a terrifying experience but I had some sea-sickness pills handy which I instinctively took. Fortunately, I later discovered, this was the right thing to do. I crawled into the shower cubicle and washed myself as I sat on the floor. Eventually, I managed to get out of the shower and reached for my phone. I rang my driver, who came and helped me to dress. He then assisted me to the car and I slept in the passenger seat, fully reclined and with my head on a pillow, as we drove up the M1. By the time we reached our destination, I was well enough to have a lunch and to give a talk afterwards to nearly 200 party activists. It was only later that I saw a doctor who diagnosed Menière's disease. I had another attack after my mother's eightieth-birthday party in London. I was trying to hail a taxi with my younger son Andrew when I began stumbling all over the place. The unfortunate thing was that, just as I needed to get back home urgently, several taxi drivers would not stop, presumably because they wrongly assumed that I was drunk.

It was just when William Hague needed me most that I was struck down with a third, and even more acute, health problem. As a result of my diabetes, I had decided many years earlier to spend two days of every year having a full medical check-up on the basis that, if there was anything wrong with me, I would rather know about it as soon as possible and try to take measures to deal with it.

It was during my routine annual medical shortly before Christmas 2000 that doctors found that I needed some urgent 'plumbing'. Two of my arteries were 90 per cent blocked and another two were 75 per cent blocked: I was well on the way to a disaster. I was immediately put on medication, including blood thinners, and I was naturally extremely concerned. I initially hoped to postpone surgery until after the election, but I was told that, if I did this, I might well not be around after the election to have the required operation. There was little alternative but to go along with my doctor's recommendation. So I arranged for surgery as soon as it was practical and spent time getting my affairs in order. In the first week of February 2001, and having worked the tables at the party's Winter Ball at Planet 2000 in London, I told my various contacts that I was going to take a short safari, supposedly in one of the world's most remote spots where there was no mobile-phone reception. After explaining why telephone calls would not be returned for a few days, I went into hospital on Thursday, 9 February, and underwent a quadruple heart-bypass operation the next day.

I had chosen to have the operation on Friday so that I would be in intensive care on Saturday and Sunday, when fewer people would be trying to reach me on work-related matters. However, business – most notably my role of fundraising for the party – had to go on. So on Monday, 12 February – three days after my operation – my mobile phone was switched back on in my private hospital room and I continued the schmoozing and cajoling for party funds that I had been forced to interrupt at the end of the previous week. My first few days back in contact with donors were hectic: from 16 February not only did those making donations over £5,000 a year have to be identified but the amount they had given also had to be quantified (previously the Conservative Party's voluntary code had identified those donating more than £5,000 without giving the amount). So I was busy working from my hospital bed trying to collect substantial last-minute sums from generous but publicity-shy donors. I left hospital on Thursday, 15 February and took my plane to Acapulco where my yacht was waiting for me. I spent the next two weeks anchored in Acapulco harbour where I was fully operational, except for having to take my medication and carry out the recommended daily exercises.

At the time, nobody in the party was aware that I was below par. I never once considered stepping down as party Treasurer because – particularly with the election near – I saw the concerns over my health as a problem to overcome rather than one that was going to defeat me. In the weeks after the surgery, a few people remarked that I seemed to have lost weight, which I put down to a particularly nasty bout of food poisoning. William himself only found out many months later after he had stood down as leader and I had resigned as Treasurer. As we were relaxing beside a swimming pool on a summer's day, he noticed the rather impressive scar on my chest and I decided to tell him what had happened. William was astonished that he had worked so closely with me and had not picked up that something so serious was wrong. I am glad that I managed to keep my health difficulties from William and the team as the election approached. I was determined that I should not be seen as a weak link and I did not want William to worry about me when he had quite enough on his plate.

If a business rival reads this book and thinks that I am now past my best and a soft touch, he or she will be disappointed. My diabetes is back under control, my quadruple bypass has been a complete success and I take drugs which have stabilised the Menière's disease. Touch wood, I have not had an attack for two years. There is plenty of life in the old dog yet.

AS TREASURER I had wanted to do as much as possible for William and the party. I also wanted to lead from the front in terms of donations, so during my three years in the role I gave about £6 million to the party. Over the years, the size of my financial support to the party has been linked to my opinion of the party leader. The fact that I gave more under William's leadership than under all previous leaders I have supported put together indicates how much I rated him – and how much I desperately wanted him to succeed. Sadly, the eight-to-ten-year programme that I envisaged for William – which was to have ended with him becoming Prime Minister – was brought to a halt at half-time by the election result of June 2001. I had calculated before the election that for William to be able to stay on as leader the party needed to win eighty more seats than at the previous election. In fact, the Labour Party won 413 seats and we, the Tories, won just 166. It was a comprehensive and overwhelming defeat by any standards and we had gained just a single seat on our utterly dismal total of 165 recorded in 1997.

On the morning after election night, I was one of a group of some eight people from William's election team who saw him and his wife Ffion at Smith Square when he returned from his constituency. We all gathered in William's office: the others present included Michael Ancram, the party Chairman, and James Arbuthnot, our Chief Whip. Out of affection and loyalty, many in the group wanted him to remain leader – some indefinitely, others for a matter of months – but I knew this was not the right decision for him or the party. The scale of the election defeat meant that it was not a credible proposition for him to continue as leader: he could not realistically stand up every day in the House of Commons to fight the Conservative Party's corner knowing that this result would constantly be thrown back at him. William, who was exhausted but composed, had already come to the conclusion that he was going to stand down. I thought that at his age time was on his side and that if he stood down he could still come back to play a senior role for the party. If he remained ambitious, his time would come again – even as leader of the party for an improbable second time.

I was the first voice within the group to agree with William that he should resign, and I was supported by James Arbuthnot. There is absolutely no doubt in my mind that resigning with his dignity intact was the right decision. His reputation – not to mention his bank balance – has subsequently been enhanced further. I remain hopeful that he will play a senior role in the party again. Ffion was always a fantastic support for William and would have made a delightful 'first lady'. She is exceptionally bright, witty, great company and a wonderful companion for her husband. I still see William and Ffion, and I remain enormously fond of them. I have no doubt that we will be friends for life.

9 Taking on New Labour

THE ATTACK on me by the Labour Government in 1999 took place on both sides of the Atlantic. As well as helping their ally *The Times* to smear me, my political opponents also tried to harm me financially. My tax arrangement agreed in 1990 with the Belize Government became the battleground between myself and the Labour Government. I first became aware that I had a potentially troublesome issue brewing in the spring of 1999 when Ralph Fonseca, a senior minister in the Belize Government, told me: 'We are having problems with the British Government.' He was referring to the issue of whether Belize should receive debt relief under the Commonwealth Debt Initiative (CDI) announced by Britain in 1997. On that occasion Clare Short, the International Development Secretary, had declared that Britain was prepared to cancel debts paid by poorer Commonwealth countries, provided extra resources were used to reduce poverty.

Following the visit of a delegation from the Department for International Development (DFID) to Belize in April 1999, the British Government decided not to grant Belize debt relief under CDI. This was a considerable sum of money to a country as small as Belize, amounting to around £10 million. The Government spelt out its reason for this in a letter to Ralph Fonseca, then the Minister for Budget Management, Investment and Trade, from Tim David, the British High Commissioner to Belize, in September 1999. Somehow the Labour Government – halfway through my tenure as party Treasurer – seemed to be blaming me for the decision to withhold debt relief. The letter from David (to avoid any confusion, this is his surname – he is most definitely a member of the away team) cast doubt on Belize's commitment to pro-poor policies because it had granted large-scale tax exemptions to my company, Carlisle Holdings. In a second letter, clearly pointed at my company again and also written in September, David extended an invitation from the British Government to the Belize Government to attend seminars on 'The Future of Taxation Reform'. It was obvious that I had a new fight on my hands. The Labour Government was evidently prepared to withhold millions of pounds in debt relief from the poor in order to renew its attempts to 'Get Ashcroft'.

It soon became apparent that the British Government hoped to blackmail the Belize Government into reneging on the deal it had made with my company in 1990 giving it a tax break for thirty years. The British Government amorally tried to suggest that the debt relief was conditional on the Belize Government revoking its agreement. Short was at the forefront of the attempt by New Labour to undermine my position. Tim David, in his role as British High Commissioner to Belize, had been persuaded to take up the cudgels on behalf of the Labour Government. To this day, I have met Short on only one occasion. It was about a year after Labour came to power in 1997 and three of us had dinner at an Italian restaurant in London. The third person present was Bowen Wells, the then Conservative MP for Hertford and Stortford and the chairman of the International Development Select Committee. He had arranged the gathering because he knew I had some strong views on how the Commonwealth Development Corporation was losing its way and not fulfilling its objectives. As far as I can recall, Short was good company and it was a pleasant evening. It seems, however, that Short's view of me was less generous.

The level of Short's animosity towards me became apparent when she attended a meeting of the World Trade Organisation in Seattle in the late autumn of 1999. At the event, she had a conversation with Ralph Fonseca, the Belizean politician, in which she referred to me as a 'scumbag' – Short seemed unaware that Ralph and I go back many years. Ralph, who had been taken aback by the personal nature of her attack on me, duly relayed the conversation to me.

I was so annoyed by Short's unflattering remark about me that I asked Kevin Bays, my solicitor, to write to Short's lawyers protesting about her outrageous behaviour. The letter referred simply to Short's use of the word 'scumbag', but it did not, however, mention where it had been said, on what occasion, when or to whom. Lawyers for the Department for International Development wrote back denying that Short had said any such thing. However, when David Hencke, a journalist on the *Guardian* picked up the story – again not knowing where the comment had been made or to whom – he was briefed by a Department for International Development official who denied that Short had called me 'a scumbag *at the World Trade Organisation in Seattle*'. I put that briefing down to Short having too much information about the incident for her own good: in her attempt to deny the comment she had effectively confirmed it.

Short repeatedly took a butter-would-not-melt-in-her-mouth approach to the whole issue. She not only continued to deny the offensive comment but she also denied that her attitude to Belize was politically motivated. For the next year or so, she also made a series of disingenuous claims such as 'We have no interest whatsoever in Michael Ashcroft. Our concern is with the poor of Belize.'

There was no way that I was prepared to relinquish my company's carefully negotiated and totally legitimate tax concessions without a considerable fight. I was going to oppose the Labour Government in every way that I could. I was worried that a large and powerful nation (Britain) would put undue and unfair pressure on a smaller, weaker nation (Belize) to capitulate. I made it clear to both governments early on that if they wanted to take me on then I was going to contest it all the way.

The British Government leaned on the Belize Government to appoint expert tax consultants to look at two areas which they hoped would adversely affect me: tax exemptions for Public Investment Companies (PICs) – which was the status of my company Carlisle Holdings – and the regulation of offshore financial services. I have already detailed how the tax concessions for Carlisle Holdings came to be set up and I should stress that the requirements to become a PIC were, and are, stringent. The concept behind the legislation was to encourage large, well-regulated investment vehicles for the purposes of promoting overseas investment in Belize. One of the key requirements of PIC status is that the company's shares must be listed on an approved international stock exchange. To date, only two companies have obtained PIC status – Carlisle Holdings and a smaller company, Sonisa, which I have nothing to do with.

Clare Short, however, adopted an aggressive and bullying attitude towards the Belize Government from the outset. I am reliably informed that on 29 February 2000, she wrote a letter to Said Musa, the Prime Minister of Belize, in which she expressed surprise that the UK's offer of debt relief was causing so much 'trouble'. She said that in order to move the CDI review further forward the British Government needed to 'explore' two areas with the Belize Government: the regulation of large-scale tax exemptions and the regulation of offshore financial services. Those who have seen the letter tell me it was effectively an attempt to threaten and coerce the Belize Government – telling politicians that if they wanted debt relief they would have to comply with the British Government's requests by tackling the two areas where Short wanted to harm me.

Belize had little choice but to go along with the requests of the British Government, and on 27 April 2000 Tim David wrote a letter to Ralph Fonseca outlining an unrealistically fast timetable for the process. David said that in June a team of tax consultants would arrive in Belize. This team was expected to prepare a draft report within a month and, following comments on it from the Belize Government and DFID, prepare a full report in August. In September, after studying the report, the British Government intended to review the issue of debt relief to Belize. The implication of the timetable was simple: if the Belize Government could, with the help of the tax consultants, find a way to get rid of my company's tax concessions, then Belize would get its debt relief.

As is often the case with such matters, the timetable could not be met. Four tax experts from KPMG, one of Britain's 'big four' firms of accountants, arrived in Belize on 19 July. I was told that, at the very first meeting with officials from the Belize Government, the KPMG consultants said that they thought they had found a way to revoke my company's tax concessions without the need for any compensation payments. This brought home to me the nature of the briefing that must have taken place in Britain. In other words, even before they had investigated the situation, KPMG was offering the solution that DFID wanted.

On 17 July, the Belize Government had written to Philip Johnson, the president of the Belize Bank, inviting him to meet the KPMG team. It was not difficult to decline their kind offer. I have never been one to play poker for high stakes with a loaded deck. I realised KPMG wanted to obtain information that it would twist and turn for its own purposes.

Philip Osborne, my senior lawyer in Belize and secretary of Carlisle Holdings, left KPMG in no doubt that it would face legal action if its team abused its position of influence. In a letter dated 10 August, Philip wrote:

> You should not underestimate either the gravity with which we view the current position, nor our determination to respond as is necessary. Over the last year or so, we have witnessed the extent to which the Labour Party, in its political pursuit of Sir Michael [this was before I had taken up my peerage], has been prepared, through the offices of Government, to damage Belize's reputation within Britain and within the international community. You will be unaware of most of this, and we have no wish to see KPMG used as an unwitting pawn in another's chess game.

In a further letter written eight days later, Philip made it clear that we considered the deal with the Belize Government to be binding. 'We have also been advised, in unequivocal terms, that any interference with Carlisle's rights under this contract would immediately allow us to pursue a claim for breach of contract should Carlisle suffer damage as a result of such interference.' Philip also pointed out that any third party – in this case KPMG – could also face legal action if it was responsible for 'interference with Carlisle's contractual rights'.

KPMG seemed unhappy to be caught in the crossfire between

the Labour Government and myself. Given the uncompromising nature of Philip's letters – he had at one stage asked the firm to alert its insurance company in case it was sued by us for a substantial sum – KPMG's tax experts were cautious and, to their credit, were not prepared to be bullied by Clare Short, Tim David and other government officials. So when the tax experts came to deliver their draft report on 18 September, they avoided confronting the issue of the PICs head on. Instead, they said it was beyond their remit because it was protected by the 1990 agreement.

I am told that Short was furious about the outcome, while David indicated that DFID would not be prepared to accept the report as it was. He insisted that KPMG should look again at the issue of PICs. In early December, the Belize Government quite reasonably asked the British Government to send its Commonwealth Debt Initiative review team to Belize because there was no longer any justification for delaying the process. However, the Belize Government again bowed to pressure from Short and her team: five days before Christmas the Government and DFID asked KPMG to address the lost revenues from the PICs once more and to report back by 31 January 2001.

Through Carlisle Holdings, I had a controlling stake in Belize Telecommunications (a stake that I have since sold). Under a licence agreement with the Belize Government, Belize Telecommunications was given a monopoly of the telecommunications system which began in 1988 and expired in 2001. Such an arrangement is not uncommon in small developing nations that need to build up their costly infrastructure. If a government allowed the telecommunications and other similar markets to open to competition too soon, the services would not get off the ground. No company would have been willing to make the initial investment – millions of pounds – knowing that modest profits would have to be fought over between several operators. Instead, it is sensible and logical to allow a monopoly operator a given period of time to get its operation up and running before throwing it open to competition at the end of a licence period.

The agreement meant that my company had to invest heavily in the infrastructure of Belize, including setting up a new mobile network, at substantial cost. The Belize Government also insisted that all local calls should be heavily subsidised, a cost that Belize Telecommunications had to bear. The profit for my company had to come, therefore, from international calls. With such inevitable cross-subsidisation, the international calls were not going to be cheap, by either local or international standards. These international calls were Belize Telecommunications' source of profit, and an important source of revenue – through a 19 per cent business tax on turnover and an 8 per cent sales tax – for the Belize Government. The Belize Government, therefore, under the terms of our deal, had banned any other operator from offering a service out of Belize.

At a time in 2000 when my company's monopoly licence was still valid, a rival company based offshore and called *gotalk!* was offering a service to Belizeans that enabled them to make a free telephone call to an exchange and then provide a number where they could be rung back. Moments later their phone would be rung by a computer and the caller given a dialling tone to make an international call. *gotalk!* claimed in its literature that it could save callers up to 90 per cent on international calls. Although this was not technically a call coming from Belize, it was quite clearly illegal under the terms of Belize Telecommunications' licence agreement with the Belize Government. I discovered that *gotalk!* was owned by a Swiss parent company – a family business – the ultimate ownership of which lay in a Caribbean tax haven, no less.

The British High Commission of all people not only started using this illegal service but actively encouraged others to do so by circulating *gotalk!*'s literature. Belize Telecommunications was in danger of being deprived of millions of pounds in lost revenues. Not only did my company suffer, but so did the Belize Government because it was deprived of its taxes. I had to protect my business and did so vigorously. After taking legal advice in both Britain and Belize, I wrote two strongly worded letters to Tim David in December 2000. In the second, I asked him for a commitment that neither the British High Commission nor any employee would take advantage of the service. In his reply in

January, David insisted the call-back service was not illegal, though he did agree to stop circulating literature about *gotalk!* in future.

As I tried to resolve this issue, David attended a Christmas party in December 2000 at the Radisson Fort George Hotel in Belize City. The party for some 400 guests is one of the social highlights of the Christmas season and is hosted by the Belize Bank, which I own. David was a third-rate diplomat, thoroughly pompous and devoid of charm, all too eager to be Short's poodle in Belize and heedless of his poor relationship with the local Government. He tried to pick a verbal fight with me moments after entering the party. Almost the first words he said to me were: 'I hear you are leaning on KPMG.' I told him I had noted his hypocrisy in arguing for pro-poor measures and then – by using an illegal outside call-back company – depriving the poor in Belize of millions of substantial tax revenues. The discussion became heated and eventually, after a frank and lengthy exchange of views, I told him to 'Fuck off out of here.' David finished his drink and left. Although I undoubtedly had the moral high ground, I reflected that perhaps neither of us – me as the host and David as a diplomat – had handled the situation well. I had also used inappropriate language and so I wrote him a short letter of apology the next day, 10 December.

This was plainly a private and confidential letter. I wrote in the top right-hand corner on three separate lines: 'Strictly private. Tim David. Sunday [the day after the party]'. The letter began: 'Dear Tim, To varying "degrees" I don't suppose our diplomatic skills yesterday evening would have obtained a first. For my part, I sincerely apologise where such skills would not have made a third.' As a gesture of my regret, I asked him to contact Philip Johnson, the head of the Belize Bank, with the name of a nominated charity so that I could make a donation to it.

This personal, handwritten and hand-delivered note should never have been seen by anyone other than David, and yet within ten days of its dispatch a photocopy of my private note had appeared in the *Guardian*. The newspaper ran the story on the front page under the headline 'Tory treasurer says sorry after blazing diplomatic row'. Ewen MacAskill, the newspaper's diplomatic editor, wrote:

> The controversy over Conservative treasurer, Lord Ashcroft, came back to haunt the party last night after leaked Foreign Office memos disclosed details of a blazing row with the British high commissioner in Belize.
>
> According to the memos, the billionaire peer told the commissioner, Tim David, during a Christmas drinks party that he was pompous, a liar and that he could 'fucking well get out now'.
>
> The row was so heated that the following day Lord Ashcroft sent a handwritten letter of apology and offered to make a donation to a charity of Mr David's choice … The diplomat described Lord Ashcroft's behaviour as shocking and deeply offensive.

I was distinctly unimpressed that the contents of a private letter had been leaked in an attempt to embarrass me and the Conservative Party. Given the speed and the motivation of the leak, it was impossible not to conclude that it had the fingerprints of Short and/or her department all over it. We discovered that Short had received a copy of my letter to David as part of his report on the party incident and its aftermath. It turned out that after the leak the Foreign and Commonwealth Office (FCO) had initially told DFID there would have to be a 'full inquiry' into the leak. Such an inquiry should have been relatively simple because, on the face of it, these documents were not widely circulated – and the trail was still warm. When my legal team asked about the progress of the leak inquiry – whether anyone had been identified and punished – the FCO and DFID admitted that 'some inquiries would have been made but there was no formal inquiry of any kind'. In other words, the 'inquiry' was effectively non-existent. Once again, it was hard not to come to the conclusion that Short did not order an inquiry because she knew the answer to it in advance and did not want the man – or indeed woman – to be exposed for his – or indeed her – misconduct.

With the benefit of hindsight, I have only one regret over the drinks-party incident: David is such an obnoxious character that I wish I had never apologised to him.

As the British Government realised that it was failing to achieve its aims in Belize, Tim David was not the only one to show the true – and unattractive – side of his character. Clare Short also betrayed her frustrations in a handwritten note to her staff in DFID. Some two years after it was written, I – as a result of legal action against the British Government – obtained a copy of a typed memo which Desmond Curran, then the head of DFID's Caribbean operations, had written to his then boss on 15 December 2000. Headed 'Belize; Commonwealth Debt Initiative [CDI]', it updated his Secretary of State on the situation in Belize relating to KPMG's report. Short was clearly frustrated by what she read and therefore scribbled a note at the top of it. Her instructions were short but to the point: 'I would like a meeting on this. I think we should simply cancell [sic] CDI mission and say messing about means they don't qualify for the initiative. CS.' Quite apart from revealing the Secretary of State's poor spelling, the note also disclosed just how willing she was to end the much needed and deserved support for the poor in Belize. The twenty-seven words had, however, provided a fascinating – though not surprising – insight into Short's twisted mindset.

Even New Labour's old friend, *The Times*, made no attempt to hide the true reasons for Short's interest in Belize. In an article published on 22 December 2000, and headlined '£10m relief for Belize suspended', Dominic Kennedy and Tom Baldwin reported: 'The confidential terms of reference given to KPMG by Ms Short's Department for International Development have been seen by *The Times*. They appear to target Lord Ashcroft's interests.' In the same article, the newspaper went on:

> Gian Gandhi, a Briton who served as Solicitor-General of Belize and now heads the country's International Financial Services Commission, said from his office in the National Assembly building: 'We have taken this point to the British Government. Debt relief to Belize should not be mixed up with the Ashcroft factor. It is very strange

that the Government of Britain should get involved in that kind of vendetta. Normally the British Government takes a very broad view, especially when dealing with a small country like Belize.'

As Short tried to step up her campaign against me in Belize, other Labour colleagues were doing their best to intimidate senior Belizean officials. I learned that on 16 December Assad Shoman, then the Belize High Commissioner to the United Kingdom, met in London with George Foulkes, the Parliamentary Under Secretary of State for International Development. Foulkes, who in a recent mini-profile in the *Daily Mail* was described with great accuracy as a 'bibulous crawler', told Assad that DFID was not prepared to move forward on the subject of debt relief unless the issue of Public Investment Companies had been resolved in conjunction with KPMG. It was now beyond doubt that the Government was linking the question of Belize's debt relief to my business interests in the country.

The British Government's attitude towards the poor of Belize was particularly callous given the timing of the refusal to grant debt relief, for these discussions were all taking place in the aftermath of the devastation caused by Hurricane Keith in October 2000. The hurricane had left an estimated 3,300 homeless in Belize and caused widespread and catastrophic damage totalling millions of pounds. Such was the desperation of the people of Belize that their Government had to negotiate a £13.6 million loan from the World Bank to tackle the problem.

By the end of December, the dispute over the call-back service was becoming tedious, so I decided to up the stakes a little. In a letter sent on the 29th of that month, I threatened to cut off the telephone service to the British Embassy unless it promised to stop using the call-back service. Unsurprisingly perhaps, this caused something of a furore. News of the dispute reached British newspapers, many of which carried stories about it. 'Crossed wires as Ashcroft takes on FO (again)' was the headline in the *Guardian* on 18 January 2001. The Foreign Office had responded by telling newspapers that my warning was unjustified and a breach of the Vienna convention on diplomatic rights. One High Commission official was quoted as telling the *Daily Telegraph*: 'Would you believe that a peer of the realm would threaten to cut off the telephones of a British diplomatic mission?' Eventually, the British High Commission quietly agreed to stop using the service and I, in turn, dropped my threat to cut them off.

The issues of my company Carlisle Holdings' tax relief and Belize's unresolved debt relief were rumbling on and on. On 29 December 2000, Philip Osborne, our company secretary, had written a letter to KPMG which left it in no doubt that we knew of the pressures that were being applied behind the scenes. Philip wrote:

> As you know, we are aware that you have completed your report, but that the British Government has, for its own political purposes, described your work as 'inadequate'. We understand that the High Commissioner has written to you requesting you to give more thought to the subject of Public Investment Companies, and that his letter has also been signed by a Minister of the Belize Government.
>
> We have learned that the second signature on that letter was applied with great reluctance, and only after threats of sanctions were made should Belize have refused … If there was any residual uncertainty as to the true objectives of this exercise, all doubt has now been removed. What has emerged in stark clarity is a co-ordinated attempt by various agencies, acting at the behest of the British Government, to attack and to damage the interests of their political opponent, Lord Ashcroft.

We again served notice – even more vigorously than before – that we intended to seek substantial damages from anyone unfairly targeting my commercial interests.

KPMG again appeared slightly unnerved by the firmness of our position and in February 2001 the tax experts suggested that counsel's opinion should be sought on the delicate issue of PICs. The following month the Belize Government, under pressure from the British Government, supported this view. However, when KPMG's supplementary report was published on 24 May 2001, it yet again sidestepped the issue of PICs.

After announcing that I was stepping down as Treasurer of the Conservative Party in June 2001 – following our election defeat – I felt able to write an article for the *Guardian*. This appeared on 21 June under the headline 'I'm ready for a fight'. It also led to a news story in the paper on the same date headlined 'Ashcroft claims Short is "out to get him"'. I was determined to expose Short's discreditable and hypocritical stance: far from seeking to help the poor people of Belize, as she claimed, she was using them as pawns in a strategy aimed at targeting me. I ended my article:

> If Clare Short was indeed concerned about the poor of Belize, then Britain would presumably have spared little effort or expense to help the poor of this hurricane-ravaged Commonwealth nation. So what precisely has Britain's preoccupation in Belize been during the last six months? Repairing broken buildings and roads? No. Mending drainage and sanitation? No.
>
> Britain barely lifted a finger to help – it sent a handful of extra troops and a cheque for about £100,000, which was handed straight to the Red Cross. To add insult to injury, Britain has reconfirmed its suspension of debt relief due to Belize under the Commonwealth debt initiative until – and unless – tax relief to the evil Lord Ashcroft is terminated.

I added that I had no doubt that Short would deny that her department had made 'unwarranted demands with menaces', and that she would probably accuse me of lying.

> But the facts speak for themselves. Instructions have gone out to 'Get Ashcroft!'
>
> All of this would count for little, if it were not for the very people who Ms Short says she is so keen to help. I am now unconstrained by political considerations and I

can look after myself. But the people of Belize do not have that choice. There is a saying in Belize that when the elephants fight, the grass gets trampled. The elephants have, in the minds of Belizeans, been squaring up for some time now. There is a popular view of the Caribbean nations that they are of little or no account – bankrupt, populated by the indolent and useful only for the acquisition of a suntan. That is not my view, neither is it my experience. Its people are on the whole proud and hard working, and they deserve all the assistance and support which the international community is able to give.

Keen to play their full part in the world, the people of Belize are currently stigmatised by the actions of the UK government, which the wider international community interprets as indicative of a wider malaise within the administration of the country. Nothing could be further from the truth. If the Labour party wants to pick a fight with me, it should do so at a time and in a place when poor and innocent people do not stand in the way. I will be ready.

In June, the British Government, still desperate to pursue its anti-Ashcroft agenda, instructed Michael Beloff QC to examine the issue. He, too, qualified his advice to such an extent that the British Government was unable to get what it wanted. Short, I am told, was left on the point of apoplexy with her latest plan to 'Get Ashcroft' in tatters. Eventually, too, Belize quietly received the debt relief to which it had always been entitled. (One of the most disgraceful aspects of this whole shoddy episode was the way in which the media was often informed of events before representatives of the Belizean Government had even been told what it was they had 'agreed to' jointly with the British Government.)

I must admit I felt a degree of satisfaction when I read a report in the *Financial Times* of 28 December 2001. The newspaper, which had always closely followed the twists and turns of my battle in Belize over financial regulations, ran a story under the headline 'Government backs down over ex-Tory treasurer's Belize links'. The report read:

> Lord Ashcroft, the controversial tycoon and former Conservative party treasurer, appears to have won two separate battles with the government over his business interests in Belize.
>
> The Foreign Office has backed down in its confrontation with Lord Ashcroft over telecommunications services in Belize.
>
> He also appears to have fought off an attempt by the Department for International Development to scrap the 30-year tax exemption enjoyed by Carlisle Holdings, his main company, in Belize.
>
> The British High Commission in Belize has resumed its use of Belize Telecommunications, which Carlisle has a majority stake in, for international telephone calls.
>
> Last January, Belize Telecommunications, the sole provider of telecommunications services in the country, threatened to cut off the telephone line to the high commission after it hired an unnamed company to provide cheap rate international calls.
>
> But the Foreign Office disclosed yesterday that the high commission had resumed its use of Belize Telecommunications for international telephone calls in May.

Meanwhile, the article continued, the Belize Government was 're-luctant to tackle Carlisle's tax exemption'.

> Michael Beloff, a leading QC, is believed to have warned that the Belize government might be vulnerable to legal action if it abolished the tax exemptions enjoyed by two so-called public investment companies in the country. They are Carlisle Holdings and Sonisa, a financial services group.
>
> Mr Beloff's legal opinion appears to have stalled the international development department's attempt to persuade Belize to take action against the public investment

companies as part of wider efforts to reform its offshore financial centre.

A person close to the Belize government said Britain had indicated it no longer wanted action against Carlisle. 'The Ashcroft matter has been put on one side,' he said. 'The British government is no longer pressing that' ...

If the much respected *Financial Times* could be regarded as the umpire in our dispute, I took that report as game, set and match to Ashcroft. Short, however, seemed dissatisfied with the umpire's ruling and wrote a letter to the newspaper which was published on 7 January 2002. It read:

Your article 'Government backs down over ex-Tory treasurer's Belize links' (December 28) was misinformed.

Despite Lord Ashcroft's repeated insinuations, I have no interest in him or his business affairs. My concern is with the poor of Belize and the encouragement of improvements in economic management to their benefit. The tax concessions Lord Ashcroft's companies have negotiated obviously reduce the revenue base and therefore the services the Belize government can provide for its people. But the management of the economy is causing concern to the International Monetary Fund as well as ourselves. The Commonwealth debt initiative is designed to encourage good pro-poor economic management. Belize did not qualify this year. We shall consider the case again after 12 months.

The letter was as disingenuous as Short herself and I dismissed it as the ramblings of a bad loser. Short also showed her lack of understanding of how tax concessions to companies work. She wrongly suggested that there are just two scenarios to compare: Carlisle in Belize doing business but not paying tax and, alternatively, Carlisle in Belize doing business and paying tax. The reality is that governments – including British ones – have discovered that trying to raise tax can be counter-productive: taxpayers and others who contribute to the economy sometimes disappear to other countries when tax regimes become less favourable. My companies would certainly not be operating in Belize on the same substantial scale as they are today – and stimulating the economy in the way they are – were it not for the binding agreement I reached with the Belize Government in 1990.

To this day my companies in Belize, under the umbrella of Carlisle Holdings, retain the tax-free status that they were guaranteed in 1990. We are now, in 2005, halfway through the agreed period of the tax exemption. I have kept my side of the bargain and I expect the Belize Government to continue to do likewise – with or without pressures from the Labour Government to renege on its deal. However, I think the Belize and British Governments are now aware that I will defend my position robustly and I do not envisage further problems on this front. I think it is fair to say, however, that it is unlikely that Short and I will be sitting down for a second friendly dinner together in the near future.

THE LABOUR Party – sometimes in conjunction with *The Times* and sometimes on its own – had done all it could to make life difficult for me from the summer of 1999 onwards. A number of backbench Labour MPs tried to get on my case in late July of that year and some asked parliamentary questions that were intended to embarrass and smear me.

I was particularly irritated when the Labour Party needlessly and vindictively dragged decent friends and well-meaning colleagues into the controversy solely because of their tenuous links to me. One of those to be targeted completely pointlessly was Bowen Wells, the Conservative MP for Hertford and Stortford and the third member of the dining team when I had met Clare Short in 1998. Bowen is as decent and honourable a man as it is possible to meet, yet some of the Labour boot-boys on the left of the party decided to try to make mischief.

Denis MacShane, the Labour MP for Rotherham, wrote on 20 July 1999 to Elizabeth Filkin, the Parliamentary Commissioner for Standards, asking her to investigate a tedious (and tautological) claim alleging 'the potential for a possible conflict of interest'. For a year, from 1997 to 1998, Bowen had been a remunerated non-executive director of my company Belize Holdings Incorporated (BHI), at a time when he was also chairman of the International Development Select Committee. He had not tried to hide anything and his directorship – as with some of his past links to my companies during the early 1990s – was listed in the Register of MPs' Interests. Bowen had also declared his role with BHI when he was elected chairman of the select committee. In short, he could not have been more cautious, straightforward and honest. However, MacShane asked Elizabeth Filkin for a ruling on 'whether there is a conflict of interest if the chair of a select committee a) sits on the board of a company controlled by someone who is a major donor to a political party b) sits on the board of a company whose direct financial interests are related to the work of the select committee'.

Elizabeth Filkin was forced to investigate this complaint and a similar one from Alan Whitehead, the Labour MP for Southampton Test. It was tiresome and time-consuming for Bowen, who had to write to the Parliamentary Commissioner for Standards listing everything that he had done to make sure his links with my company were appropriate and above board.

It was not until 25 November 1999 that Elizabeth Filkin made her findings public. She found that Bowen had not breached the strict rule relating to paid advocacy, but suggested that he 'would have been wise' to have mentioned once again in committee discussions that he was a £20,000-a-year director of BHI. This was only because the committee had twice examined the issue of banana growing and the Belize Bank, a subsidiary of my company BHI, might – just might – have had links with banana growers. If there has ever been a more tenuous reason for 'redeclaring' an interest that had already been declared, I have yet to see it. Since MacShane had failed to make the thrust of his allegations stick, he ought to have apologised to Bowen – but not a bit of it. Instead, he told journalists that the Tories had lost all sense of political judgement and 'were like rabbits in Ashcroft's headlights'.

It strikes me that MacShane might be better advised to put

his own house in order rather than make unfair trouble for other MPs. I was interested to read in Peter Oborne's splendid book *The Rise of Political Lying* how MacShane, as Minister of Europe, had been caught out as he went around making wild allegations against others. While being interviewed on BBC Radio 4's *Today* programme, he was asked by Ed Stourton, the presenter, to justify some remarks he had made in a newspaper interview in which he accused Euro-sceptics of 'xenophobia' and 'hatred'. MacShane said: 'Do you remember in the winter there was all this hysteria [about people] from Poland or Hungary coming into the country? They were described in one of our papers as a "murderous horde" – a "murderous horde". These are nannies and hospital workers from Poland, they're European citizens, they're paying taxes here. When is someone going to stand up to that kind of language?' However, Peter Oborne searched through computer records and rang the Foreign and Commonwealth Office to try to get to the bottom of the 'murderous horde' allegations, but without success. He was surprised when MacShane himself came on the line within minutes of his call to the FCO. Peter writes: 'When I asked about the "murderous horde", he became vague, and after wriggling for a while denied that he had ever used the phrase. "I never said it," he insisted. But he had.'

Two days after MacShane's letter of complaint had been lodged with Elizabeth Filkin, it was the turn of the egregious Peter Bradley, the Labour MP for The Wrekin, to try to put the parliamentary spotlight on my interests in Belize. Just twenty-four hours after he had joined forces with *The Times* and abused parliamentary privilege to try to link me to drug smuggling and money laundering, Bradley was trying to make further problems for me. He demanded to know why I had funded an all-expenses-paid, eight-day trip to the Caribbean for four Tory MPs. On his return, Sir Tom Arnold, one of the MPs, had tabled some parliamentary questions about Belize and offshore financial regulation.

Bradley had delved into the history books to make mischief. The trip five years earlier – in 1994 – had been declared by all the MPs in the Register of MPs' Interests. It was paid for by one of my companies, Deanland Ltd, because I thought it would be useful for MPs to see Belize for themselves. Furthermore, the invitation had been extended to Conservative and Labour MPs alike, but the two Labour MPs who had been invited both declined. As with the complaint by his Labour colleagues against Bowen Wells, Bradley was guilty of a risible attempt to make something out of nothing.

By the summer of 2001, and after a two-year campaign to discredit me, I was getting thoroughly fed up with the way that some people felt they could freely leak confidential information with the aim of damaging my personal reputation and my business interests. The most alarming aspect of this trend was that it was everyone from senior members of the Government to lowly civil servants who seemed to feel they were entitled to take whatever steps they liked to cause me trouble. The leaking of information about me had gone on ever since the Labour Government and *The Times* first launched their campaigns against me in the summer of 1999.

I knew Downing Street and Whitehall were morally wrong to do this, but I took legal advice to establish whether they had also acted illegally and whether I had any course of redress through the courts. The early indications were that I might indeed have a case against the Government, but that any legal action would be prolonged and complicated.

The first official leak inquiry relating to me was instigated by Michael Ancram, the Conservative Party Chairman, in a letter to Sir Richard Wilson, the Cabinet Secretary, on 13 July 1999. It followed an article in *The Times* by Tom Baldwin and two other journalists on that date headlined '"Shadow" over Tory treasurer'. The story was based on two leaked and old Foreign and Commonwealth Office documents: I have referred to both documents earlier in the book when I established that the claims in them were groundless. Michael pointed out to Sir Richard that both documents were classified and that passing them on appeared to be a breach of the Official Secrets Act as well as 'an organised political vendetta against the Treasurer of the principal opposition party'. He urged 'an immediate and full inquiry' into the leaks. A leak inquiry was ordered by the FCO and it duly reported back in

September that year, although I, the target of the leak, was never informed of its outcome. It was only after I had spent thousands of pounds on lawyers' fees, and in the face of fierce resistance, that I was able to force the disclosure of the findings of that inquiry. This is surely one of the greatest iniquities of New Labour's ways of doing business. They are able to abuse power by publishing the shameless tittle-tattle created by civil servants against members of the public. Yet they use public funds to resist any attempt by the same members of the public to get their hands on information which might serve to repair the damage which has been done by those leaks. Furthermore, there is clearly no hope whatsoever of a successful outcome of any leak inquiry which might end up exposing one of their friends. However, should a leak occur which has not been planned and which they perceive to be damaging, no stone is left unturned in relentlessly seeking out those responsible. I have little doubt that this will go down in history as one of the most corrupt administrations of the modern era.

The report confirmed the first document as written in October 1996 by Charles Drace-Francis, then head of the West Indian and Atlantic Department, to a colleague in the Economic Relations Department. It described a meeting with me over my plans to set up a bank in the Turks and Caicos Islands and contained the inexplicable claims from Drace-Francis that I had looked 'hungover' and that I now had 'about $1 billion in cash and would obviously like to have his own bank to put it in – but cannot use the Belize bank [that is, my own Belize Bank]'. The second document was a telegram to Drace-Francis sent in April 1997 by Gordon Baker, the British High Commissioner in Belize. Baker said that he was no nearer knowing the truth of 'the rumours about some of Mr Ashcroft's business dealings. But those rumours do cast a shadow over his reputation which ought not to be ignored.'

The leak inquiry noted, perfectly accurately, that 'by summer 1999 press activity largely consisted of recycling previously published material, much of which had been printed up to 10 years previously'. Drace-Francis had denied being responsible for the leak. He said that he believed it was politically motivated, and had been engineered either by Downing Street or by one of the special advisers.

The report concluded by pointing the finger of suspicion for the leak at Drace-Francis, who had a reputation for being unconventional, eccentric and indiscreet. 'There is evidence that documents, including those reproduced in *The Times*, were given in 1997 to a journalist [on a Caribbean magazine] by Mr Charles Drace-Francis, an official at the Foreign and Commonwealth Office. It is not certain that the journalist used them in any way, or that this is the source of the leak to *The Times* newspaper. During this investigation, no other officials in the Foreign and Commonwealth Office, or in other government departments, have come under suspicion of leaking the documents.' Drace-Francis was later – in December 1999 – disciplined and suspended for his admitted role in the earlier leak.

Although Drace-Francis had foolishly, and for no good reason, leaked documents to a journalist on a Caribbean magazine, I do not believe he had any role, directly or indirectly, in those documents reaching *The Times*. The leaked report, however, also published some other interesting information. It referred to Andrew Hood, a special adviser for the Government, and while it did not finger him for the leak, it recorded that he had known Tom Baldwin, *The Times*'s political journalist, since childhood. Hood said the two of them had 'a trusting relationship based on shared confidences from the past which had not been betrayed'. Hood, predictably enough, denied being the source of the leak of the FCO documents. Nevertheless, I found this piece of information about the relationship between Hood and Baldwin to be far more intriguing than the historic leaking of documents from Drace-Francis to the journalist in the Caribbean. I later learned categorically from an informed source that Hood, Baldwin's one-time schoolfriend and contemporary at Oxford University, had, indeed, been involved in the leaked FCO documents despite his denials.

Later, too, I was to obtain possession of a copy of a quirky, but perhaps rather telling, handwritten letter from Charles Drace-Francis to Sir John Kerr, the Permanent Under Secretary of State at the Foreign and Commonwealth Office. Dated 17 August 1999, and marked 'personal', it read: 'Dear Sir John, I would be very grateful if you could ask the special advisers to <u>stop</u> leaking classified documents to *The Times*. They do it so badly. No need for a reply. Yours ever, Charles.'

By 2001, however, I wanted to tackle bigger figures than the likes of Drace-Francis. I wanted to challenge the Government itself over its attempts to smear me. I repeatedly asked for access to information that the Government was holding on me, but I was turned down every time.

I particularly wanted to establish the origins of five substantive and potentially damaging leaks about me between the summer of 1999 and the end of 2000. The first leak aimed at discrediting me had come in June 1999 when it was disclosed that I had been rejected for a peerage by the Political Honours Scrutiny Committee. The following month came the leaks of the two internal Foreign Office memos to *The Times* that I have just detailed above. In the early spring of 2000, there was the leak of information that my second nomination for a peerage had run into difficulties. Then, even after these difficulties had been overcome, there were further leaks to Sunday newspapers about the phone call that William Hague had been forced to make to Tony Blair to obtain my peerage. Finally, in December 2000 came the leak of the handwritten letter than I had written to Tim David, the British High Commissioner to Belize, after our bust-up at the Christmas party.

I employed a team of specialist lawyers to come up with a game plan. They advised a series of ground-breaking legal actions whereby I sued the Government under the Human Rights Act of 1998 and the Data Protection Act of 1998. Initially, in June 2001, I served a writ against the Foreign and Commonwealth Office and the Department for International Development alleging that my human rights had been abused. It was also reported in the press that I was seeking damages of up to £50,000 but, of course, this was never about money. It was about a principle, and the intention was always to give any compensation that I received to charity.

I was determined to hire a formidable legal team to ensure that I had the best possible chance of winning my case. I instructed Clare Montgomery QC, a specialist in extradition, commercial fraud and human rights law and a member of the Matrix chambers that was co-founded with Cherie Booth, the wife of the Prime Minister. In fact, Clare was eventually unable to represent me because of her commitments to another lengthy legal hearing. As events turned out, this did not prove to be a serious handicap – not only did I have extremely able alternative legal representation, but the thrust of my action changed to being more about privacy and the Data Protection Act. I therefore instructed Michael Tugendhat QC, a formidable expert in privacy. It was at this point that my legal team started to make a series of requests for access to 'confidential' records under the Data Protection Act.

With limited degrees of success, my legal team continually tried to gain access to the confidential documents containing information about me. They discovered that there were many unpleasant internal memos circulating about me in government circles, some of which they were able to obtain. One of them, a handwritten note by Peter Westmacott, a diplomat and former deputy private secretary to Diana, Princess of Wales, bizarrely said of me: 'He was "in love" with Princess Diana a few years ago. Looks a bit dodgy.' Despite my fondness for the Princess, it was laughable to suggest that I was in love with her. It was equally ridiculous to suggest in a note that was kept on permanent file that I was dodgy when it appears to have been based on little more than my wealth and the location – Belize – in which I chose to do business.

As is normal in such matters, the legal process was slow, but by May 2002 I had amended my Particulars of Claim lodged in the High Court: a legal technicality meant that my action was now formally against DFID and the Attorney General, who was deemed to have overall responsibility for the FCO. In my claim, I said that the two government departments had misused confidential information they held about me and I was therefore seeking damages for the 'severe personal distress and embarrassment as a result of the various wrongful acts and/or omissions referred to above'. Most important of all I was seeking a ruling from the court that Jack Straw, the Secretary of State for Foreign and Commonwealth Affairs, and Clare Short, the Secretary of State for International Development, had breached their duties.

By the spring of 2003, I had three separate actions against the Government pending. The first and main action was a case against the Attorney General and DFID aimed at finding out who was responsible for the five leaks and gaining compensation for them. The second was against the same defendants aimed at establishing my right to obtain information that the Government held on me – parts of which had been leaked – particularly relating to a 'dirt file' that had been drawn up on me. The third action was against the Cabinet Office, the Transport Department and the Office of the Deputy Prime Minister and was aimed at obtaining the Cabinet Office file on my peerage nomination and also discovering what other government departments had said to the Political Honours Scrutiny Committee in relation to me. The Government, however, said in all three cases that it was within its rights to withhold the information that I was seeking. Its defence to the actions was that the part of the material it was holding back was 'unstructured' – informal paper records rather than computer data – and therefore not covered by the Data Protection Act, while it claimed that other material was restricted by an exemption which applied to information relating to the honours system.

The logic of some of the Government's arguments was extraordinary. As part of our action my legal team was provided with photographs of some of the so-called filing systems which the Foreign and Commonwealth Office had in the Caribbean. The chaotic scenes in the pictures had to be seen to be believed, and the word 'shambolic' does not do justice to some of the ways in which supposedly confidential data was being organised and stored. This meant, however, that when the Government argued that I was entitled under the Data Protection Act only to material from a 'relevant filing system', I was being denied material solely because its files were disorganised. It implied the worrying proposition that the more haphazard and chaotic a government filing system becomes, the more an individual's right of access is impeded. The Government also argued, in all seriousness, that even nominated files relating to an individual could fall outside the definition of 'relevant filing system'. This created the absurd possibility that officials might find files marked 'Michael Anthony

Ashcroft' but feel they did not have to hand them over to me because, once again, they considered they fell outside the strict definition of 'relevant filing system'. Yet I know from experience that when a government official wanted to leak material about me, he or she never seemed to have much difficulty finding the relevant document. If this whole episode over 'relevant filing system' had not been so ridiculous and frustrating, it would have been funny – and if they ever make another series of the BBC comedy *Yes, Minister*, such madness might provide some good material for the script writers.

A hearing date for the second legal challenge – the one relating to the 'dirt file' – was set at the High Court in the Strand for early June 2003. I hoped to win a ruling that would revolutionise freedom of information laws by forcing the Government to disclose all but the most secret information it holds on individuals. In written submissions to the judge, Mr Justice Gray, prepared by my legal team, we said:

> The essentials of the case are simple. They involve a clash between a citizen (MA) who happens to have held an important post in the Opposition party, and a government which has been willing to see him harmed, but most unwilling to let him have information it holds which would enable him to do something about that harm – to claim a remedy for what has happened in the past, and take steps to prevent future damage. The case demonstrates the tension that exists between the executive's reluctance to disclose personal information and the fundamental right of a citizen to access his personal data.
>
> Over an 18-month period when he was Treasurer of the Conservative Party, MA was repeatedly wronged by leaks of government information, quite clearly designed to damage him and undermine the Opposition. And he was the victim of deliberate and malign interference with his prospects of appointment to the House of Lords as a working peer – efforts which successfully kept him from that post for a year, and nearly succeeded a second time.

This, he is confident, was a political vendetta. His attempts to find out who was responsible, and how, have met with little success ...

This action is about access to information. From the information which he has got out of the government MA has discovered that it holds in its files a range of information about him, some of which is inaccurate, damaging, outdated or irrelevant, or a combination of these. He has also learned that there is a lot else on file about him. Yet the government refuses to reveal what is there. In particular, it refuses to reveal information which is on its files and which would show – or help to show – why MA was refused a working peerage in 1999, who was responsible, and how – or what – happened the second time he was nominated, when his nomination was obstructed. The FCO, Cabinet Office and other Government departments have all taken the same position: the information is secret and must remain so ...

In a civilised and democratic society a citizen must be allowed to access his personal data held by the Government ... The executive must grapple with these principles and must cast away the culture of secrecy to which it has hitherto become accustomed. It is this court's duty to ensure that this legislation is effective.

My written representation detailed the crazy and totally inadequate response from the Government when I had sought information about the leaks against me. 'MA's first request for information was responded to in an Alice in Wonderland fashion. For example, an entire page was disclosed with every word redacted save the word "Belize" ... Worse than that, it can be shown that information which could have helped MA bring claims for compensation was deliberately held back at that time, though it is now admitted that he was entitled to it.'

I was told by informed sources that as the date of the hearing loomed advisers to Lord Goldsmith, the Attorney General, told him that I would be unlikely to go through with my action because I would not want the matter heard in open court. I was told that Peter replied: 'I think you will find that he will.' The Attorney General is a talented lawyer, so good at his job, in fact, that I had instructed him, when he was still Peter Goldsmith QC, to represent my company, ADT, in a civil action against Binder Hamlyn, the audit firm. On that occasion, as Peter knew all too well, I was the first man into the witness box and spent more than half a day there being cross-examined by Jonathan Sumption QC, who is known at the Bar as 'the cleverest man in England' and who has a formidable reputation for grilling witnesses. The case in 1996 ended with ADT being awarded just over £100 million in damages and costs. Peter knew, therefore, that if I said I was willing to go into the witness box, I probably meant it; and that I was unlikely, once there, to be intimidated by the occasion.

In my battle against the Government, I was going to be represented in court by Michael Tugendhat QC, arguably the greatest legal expert in the country on privacy laws, particularly the Data Protection Act. Like Jonathan Sumption, Michael has a brilliant legal brain: he is the lead editor of *The Law of Privacy and the Media*, a 779-page tome published in 2002 and the major practitioners' text on the subject. Only a matter of weeks before the hearing was due to commence – and shortly after successfully concluding the month-long Michael Douglas and Catherine Zeta-Jones versus *Hello!* magazine trial – Michael was asked whether he was prepared to take on a judgeship. He was given only a weekend in which to make up his mind, but it was an offer he could not refuse and he duly accepted. It was announced on 17 April 2003 that Michael and three other QCs had been made High Court judges. The appointment had been made by Lord Falconer, the Lord Chancellor, the very man who had been given the role of trying to resolve my legal battle with the Government. Michael's well-deserved appointment meant that he was immediately off my case and could not represent me in the High Court. If I was a conspiracy theorist, it would be hard not to come to the conclusion that this was a deliberate attempt by the Government to weaken my attack. I had, however, also instructed Mark Warby QC to mastermind my legal argument. Mark was arguably the second greatest legal expert in the country on privacy law, which meant I was able to proceed without too much of a hiccup.

In late May 2003, less than a fortnight before the hearing was due to open at the High Court, my office in Belize City received a call from the British High Commission. They had a message: Lord Falconer, the Prime Minister's long-term friend and colleague, wanted to see me. I met Lord Falconer – for the first and last time – at his office in Victoria Street, London: he was reasonable, charming, full of bonhomie, and it was difficult not to like him. He began the meeting by saying that the Government was prepared to settle: it was prepared to apologise but it was not prepared to pay my costs, which it did not think were important to me. I, in turn, made it clear that I would abort the action provided the apology was worded as I required *and* legal costs of around £350,000 were paid. An apology is unusual in a claim for information, but my claim had uncovered a series of what Mark Warby QC was to call 'disobliging references' to me and I felt strongly that the Labour Government should accept publicly that it had behaved badly. The meeting had been dignified and professional, but stopped short of resolving the situation. I left the meeting thinking there was an opportunity to settle my legal action before it came to court, but that there were still hurdles to overcome. Despite getting on well with Lord Falconer, I felt he was capable of being a little slippery.

I thought I had been extremely reasonable but I heard no more until the day before the case was due to begin when the Government made a further proposal, offering exactly the sort of apology that I was looking for but still refusing to pay my costs. As the case was due to open in the morning, a settlement looked likely, so both sides asked the judge to adjourn while discussions took place. The stumbling block, however, continued to be the issue of my costs, even though the Government was now indicating that it was willing to make a contribution. I declined the offer, stating that I wanted my costs paid. With the Government unwilling to match the amount that I was looking for, I instructed Mark to open my case in the High Court after lunch. There was one major advantage to opening the case: it meant that all the documents given to me as part of the discovery process were now in the public domain, so I could, for ever more, distribute them freely.

'MY LORD, this is a claim for information, as you know,' began Mark as he opened my case. 'Lord Ashcroft wants to know what these two government departments have on file about him so that he can correct it or have it removed or, if appropriate, claim compensation for what has been done with it, and he is relying on rights under the Data Protection Act (the DPA), under the European Data Protection Directive and, if it is necessary, under the Human Rights Act.' He went on:

> The defendants have provided him with a limited amount of information but they are resisting his claims for more, maintaining that they are entitled to keep it to themselves, and legally the case raises issues about the interpretation of the DPA and statutory rights of that kind as well as other directives and as to the application of the European Convention and Human Rights Act. But I am going to start by just standing back and looking at the factual background because the claims are not made from idle curiosity but are brought against the particular background which we suggest raises important questions about democracy.
>
> In short, what Lord Ashcroft does know about the background is this. First of all, in the 1990s, and possibly before, civil servants in the Foreign Office (the FCO) were in the business of collecting a file of what they called 'dirt' about him, and the contents of that file are still held by the FCO. Secondly, FCO civil servants in the 1990s, and again possibly beforehand, circulated memoranda detailing rumour, innuendo and gossip about him, none of which they could substantiate. And thirdly, and perhaps most importantly, over an 18-month period in 1999 and 2000, there was a series of events which left Lord Ashcroft convinced that he was the victim of a political vendetta,

because the events I am about to describe very shortly occurred at a time when he was the treasurer of the Opposition party and at a time when he was providing that party with substantial funds.

Mark listed the five leaks before concluding that 'to use the usual metaphor that is used about leaks would be unfair to sieves'. He then posed some telling questions about the chain of events and suggested that they amounted to a vendetta against me:

> There are some important constitutional questions because if Lord Ashcroft's suspicions are right, it is a very grave matter indeed; Government and/or the Civil Service has been guilty of conduct which undermines democracy in two ways. First of all, these are attacks on someone funding the Opposition party and in a democracy which depends, as ours does, on parties being funded by private means and not by the State, that is a serious matter. For Government to use official records and power which it exercises to damage the funding of an Opposition party is, of course, an attack on democracy. And, secondly, if someone was kept out of Parliament in the form of the House of Lords for political reasons, that is itself an attack on the democratic system, and we ask if indeed that is what happened.

The court heard that the Government had repeatedly been asked since 1999 to give me access to information it held about me. 'But he has had few answers and very little help,' said Mark. 'Far from being forthcoming, the Government has been secretive and obstructive, and that has led to three claims being brought against Government departments by Lord Ashcroft.'

As Mark began our case and gave a two-hour address to the court, the Government was panicking as ministers and civil servants correctly anticipated a series of unwelcome headlines in the national press the next day (even *The Times* headlined its report 'Ashcroft seeks access to "dirt file" that blocked his peerage'). The court heard that I had wanted to use the Data Protection Act to gain full access to fifty-six FCO and DFID files in which I had been named. Mark told the court that, if successful, I would consider proceedings for compensation against those responsible for smearing me. 'So, my Lord, we say in summary that this is a case, when one looks at the background, [that] lends the words "open government" a very hollow ring,' said Mark. 'If your Lordship were to uphold the position adopted by the defendants in this case – it is not a party political point, I emphasise – it would lend encouragement to any government which was, or is, as Lord Ashcroft suggests this one has been, ready to leak and willing to knobble a political opponent and that, we suggest, is not only unacceptable in a democracy, it is simply wrong as a matter of law.'

The court was presented with evidence of just how unfairly I had been treated and just how careless the Government officials had been with their facts. It would be tedious to list the full catalogue of errors, but I am glad that the extent of the political vendetta against me was aired in public. I am grateful, too, that the Government's 'dirt file' was exposed for what it has always been: worthless and false innuendo and gossip. For example, Charles Drace-Francis, the British official in Belize who had leaked information against me to a Caribbean magazine, had once written by hand an internal note saying: 'I attach a memo which has some but not all of the dirt.' That memo claimed that I had run a wallpaper company that had collapsed and that my father had been made redundant from the Commonwealth Development Corporation (CDC). Both allegations were preposterous: I have never owned a wallpaper company and he had confused me with another businessman called John Ashcroft. Similarly, my late father had never worked for the CDC, let alone been laid off by them. In other words, the Labour Government and *The Times* had sought to damage my good name by, respectively, leaking and publishing the inane ramblings of a junior official who was as foolish as he was indiscreet and as incompetent as he was dishonourable.

During the day's hearing, I kept getting messages that the Government was prepared to pay *towards* my costs. It seemed that every couple of hours I spoke to someone from my legal team and the amount of money the FCO and DFID were prepared to pay had risen by a further £50,000. I stood firm: I wanted my costs. The talks extended into Wednesday evening, long after the court had adjourned for the day. Kevin Bays, my solicitor, was carrying out the discussions by phone at his third-floor offices in London's West End. When the Government eventually agreed to meet my costs of £350,000, Kevin also got officials to agree to the precise wording of an apology to me to be read out in open court.

It was appropriate that Mark Warby QC, who along with Kevin handled the case brilliantly on my behalf, should have the satisfaction of reading out in open court a statement agreed with the Government. Shortly after 10.30 a.m. on Thursday, 5 June 2003, Mark said:

> During the years 1999 and 2000 documents held by certain government departments, and which contained references relating to the affairs of Lord Ashcroft, were disclosed to the media. Despite investigation, the Government was not able to establish how the unauthorised disclosures to the media occurred. The Government has, however, recognised that various disobliging references relating to Lord Ashcroft, which were contained within documents held by government departments, were without foundation. Lord Ashcroft commenced litigation following the unauthorised disclosures. That litigation has today been settled with the Government departments with the defendants to those actions apologising to Lord Ashcroft.

So, in a matter of minutes on the second day of a hearing that had been due to last a week, my action was halted in what Mr Justice Gray described as a 'happy outcome'.

It was certainly a happy outcome for me – indeed it was a great victory. I felt justice had been done and some wrongs had been righted. I issued a statement to journalists saying: 'I am delighted that the Government has finally come clean. Those who know me have never gone along with the suggestions which appeared in print, but many people, understandably under the circumstances, have concluded that I was – in what it now seems is Foreign Office parlance – a "bit dodgy". I am glad that the truth is out.'

The settlement meant that I did not get to see all the documents that I wanted to examine. I also agreed to halt my other two actions against the Government, including my main damages action for compensation which had been scheduled to be heard five months later in October 2003. I was disappointed that my attempts to challenge the law had been thwarted. As Kevin Bays put it in a further statement to journalists: 'From a legal perspective, it is perhaps a shame that the High Court will not have the opportunity to clarify the Data Protection Act legislation which has been likened to a thicket or even treacle. But, from Lord Ashcroft's point of view, he has achieved his objectives and it is now clear to all what was at the root of that dreadful episode.' Indeed, my sense of disappointment was tempered by a famous legal victory which gave me access to official documents about me that I had never seen before.

The newspapers the next day were a deep embarrassment for the Government. Headlines varied from 'Spin win: Government has to pay Tory billionaire in peerage "stitch up"' in the *Daily Mirror* to 'Government pays for Ashcroft row' in the *Financial Times*. Perhaps understandably, *The Times* downplayed its own role in the sordid affair under the headline 'Whitehall issues apology over Ashcroft "dirt file"'. The newspaper, which by now was no longer edited by Sir Peter Stothard, had the good grace to ring me up and get some extra remarks from me on top of my statement. I was quoted as saying: 'I got smeared. It was a vicious campaign. The fact that I got through it, left the party in the black, resigned at the moment of my choosing having got the job done and was not forced out, from my point of view was very relevant.'

A leader article in the *Daily Telegraph* on 6 June 2003 was headlined 'The smearing of Ashcroft'. It was deeply critical of the Government's role and, in just four paragraphs, it neatly summed up some of my frustrations of the previous four years:

Yesterday, the Government admitted that it held documents on Lord Ashcroft, the former Conservative treasurer, containing 'disobliging references' that were 'without foundation'. Between 1999 and 2000, these found their way into the hands of two newspapers. This was an appalling breach of security and an abuse of privilege. But rather than investigating the matter further, the Government has contented itself with saying it was 'not able to establish how the unauthorised disclosures occurred'. That is not good enough.

The extent to which Lord Ashcroft was, as he believes, the victim of a sustained and politically motivated campaign to discredit him has not been established. As a result of yesterday's court agreement, there will be no legal ruling on the matter.

This case has offered an unsettling insight into the government departments responsible for compiling the documents. What business does the Civil Service have to record someone as 'hungover' for example? Almost none. Whether Lord Ashcroft is a 'morning person' has nothing to do with national security. Innuendo was consciously and maliciously used to damage Lord Ashcroft's reputation and his ability successfully to carry out his role in public life. Information held by the Government is, by its nature, privileged. That privilege was abused, and yet its abuse will remain unpunished.

In exchange for costs and an apology, Lord Ashcroft has dropped the action, due to come to court in October, which would have got to the source of the leak. As he left the High Court [in fact I was not present at the hearing], he told the press: 'I am glad the truth is out.' On the contrary, the truth will not be out until the identity of those responsible for his treatment has been established. Had Lord Ashcroft been a Labour grandee, treated in this way by a Conservative government, no stone would have been left unturned until his defamers had been uncovered.

At this point I had never met Stephen Glover, the journalist, but he is a columnist and commentator that I respect. He is a perceptive observer and has the ability to distinguish right from wrong. He wrote an article for the *Spectator* which was published on 10 June 2003 and headlined 'Why was *The Times* so eager to do the government's dirty work?' He said he had been surprised that newspapers had not made more of the collusion between the Government and *The Times* in an attempt to do down William Hague and myself. 'More questionable is the conduct of my old friend Peter Stothard, the then editor of *The Times*, who set out to bring down Lord Ashcroft and to damage Mr Hague with a ferocity that even now is baffling.' He added:

> *The Times* in its hundreds of thousands of words about Lord Ashcroft has produced no evidence that he was, or is, corrupt.
>
> What is so shaming is that, at least at the beginning of its long succession of stories, the newspaper should have worked hand-in-glove with government sources in a campaign which so manifestly served the government's interest. Sir Peter Stothard (for he was, in the end, rewarded) wrote a long and preposterously sententious piece on the eve of the 1999 Tory party conference in which he tried to justify the persecution of Lord Ashcroft and Mr Hague. He represented himself in virtuous terms, cleaning out the Augean stables. Now it emerges that *The Times*'s own stables were pretty mucky, and it recycled at least some of the government's lies.

Some of the documents that I was able to obtain as a result of my legal action provided interesting, if alarming, reading. For example, an internal 'teleletter' from an unidentified official at the British Embassy in Guatemala City and dated 17 May 1995 read like an excerpt from a Graham Greene novel:

> Subject: Michael Ashcroft. Summary: Michael Ashcroft spotted in Guatemala. Detail: On 16 May, I spotted Vice-Minister for Foreign Affairs Bernardo Arevale having breakfast in a local hotel with an English-accented

businessman. Arevale introduced his interlocutor as Michael Ashcroft. Ashcroft, looking slightly embarrassed, said that he had intended to touch base with the Embassy, and, producing a Belize Holdings visiting card, said he would be in touch ... Comment: ... Ashcroft is presumably up to something in Guatemala. He may be here simply to sound out the Government on what its attitude would be to investing in Guatemala, given continuing political sensitivities over Belize. Seen from here, any new Belizean investment in Guatemala would be a welcome development, and consistent with our aims of encouraging the normalisation of relations between the two countries. However we must hope that Ashcroft's dealings here are above board and respectable. If any hint of sleaze were to emerge from dealings between a Belizean investor (as he would be seen here) and any members of the Guatemalan Government the press here would have a field day ...

Similarly, I obtained an internal Foreign Office document dated 3 January 1996 relating to a visit of mine to the Falkland Islands. A memo written by an unidentified official was headed 'Visit of Mr Michael Ashcroft and party to the Falkland Islands: further information'. It stated:

(1) On arrival at Sea Lion Island Lodge Mr Ashcroft was disturbed that the telephone link was not adequate for him to carry out some of the commercial conversations during the evening. He therefore asked if a FIGAS plane could bring him back into Stanley with his party on that evening and, as this did not inconvenience FIGAS, this was accommodated.

(2) The same situation pertained at Port Howard where he did not stay the night, but returned to Stanley once again ...

(3) On the Wednesday he flew out he was proposing to do a flying tour of Antarctica before returning to Punta

Arenas to refuel and then spend Christmas touring the Chilean fjords from Porte [sic] Montt. His three-engined Falcon jet, of which he was justifiably proud, was most impressive on the inside and possessed the kind of ostentatious luxury which only few can attain.

(4) His final comments were that he would return to the Islands which rather contradicts my conclusions of 19 December. However, his comments were of a very general nature eg 'very interesting people', 'some useful opportunities' and 'an unusually friendly atmosphere'.

(5) I do not believe that he had any meetings with local businessmen and we await any further developments here with interest.

The existence and tone of these two documents and other similar ones made me feel uncomfortable and angry. I felt that I had been spied on wherever I went in the world and I was annoyed that any lowly Foreign Office official should have felt free to write sly smears about me without having to justify his or her claims. In fact, my visits to Guatemala City and the Falkland Islands could not have been more innocent. Guatemala borders Belize and I was there for a routine business visit, while I was on the Falkland Islands only because my interest in military history meant I wanted to see some of the battlefields of the Falklands War, including where two Victoria Crosses had been won.

MY SUCCESSFUL legal action against the Government eventually ended with the FCO paying two-thirds of my £350,000 legal bill and DFID paying one-third. I suspect that the Government, allowing for its own substantial costs, could not have seen much change from £1 million. The episode was totally unnecessary and an absolute waste of taxpayers' money. Clare Short in particular, given her role in the leaking which led to my action, owes the British taxpayer a great deal of money and a handsome apology.

By the time the case was settled, Tony Blair had, of course, realised that Short was more of a nuisance to her own side than she ever was to her political opponents. Her actions before, during and after the war to topple Saddam Hussein as President of Iraq confirmed her status as an embarrassment to her party. Immediately before the war with Iraq, she had described the Prime Minister as 'reckless' in a radio interview. She had also threatened that, like Robin Cook, she would resign if Britain went to war. She reneged on this pledge just days later.

In March 2003, after she had allowed Tony Blair to talk her into staying in the Government, William Hague enjoyed one of his finest hours when he made a short speech from the Tory backbenches. Even the Prime Minister could not conceal a smile as William said of Short: 'It was whispered in the corridors last week, when she said that the Prime Minister was reckless, that he would take his revenge in due course. I believe that by persuading her to stay in the Cabinet, even for this last 24 hours, he has now taken his revenge.'

Two months later, of course, Short jumped before she was pushed and resigned from the Cabinet. During her period in the Blair Government, her disloyalty and dishonourable behaviour were matched only by her lack of judgement and her ability to waste public money. There is one consolation to voters and taxpayers: Short's numerous failings are now common knowledge.

There is one character that I have mentioned only in passing up to now. He is Alastair Campbell, who as Tony Blair's chief spin doctor helped him to victory in three successive general elections. The fact that I have devoted so few words thus far to Campbell does not mean that he played no significant role in the campaign against me – far from it. However, in a book which criticises others for making unsubstantiated allegations against me, it would be wrong if I were to do the same – even if they are made against a bully and a bruiser who is more than capable of defending himself.

I will present the facts about Campbell as I know them and let the reader draw his or her own conclusions about the extent of the role that he played. He has repeatedly proved over the last decade that he is willing to resort to virtually any tactic – fair or foul – to promote his beloved New Labour and his friend Tony Blair.

I commend two books for anyone wanting to read in detail about the lengths to which Campbell has over the years been prepared to go for the 'cause'. The first is *Alastair Campbell* by Peter Oborne and Simon Walters; the second is *The Control Freaks: How New Labour Gets Its Own Way* by Nicholas Jones.

Over the past decade, Campbell has built up close working relationships with a number of senior journalists, but none more so than Tom Baldwin, who in 1999 was deputy political editor of *The Times* and was at the forefront of the campaign against me. One political journalist who knows both men well described Baldwin as 'fawning' and his demeanour as 'homoerotic' when the two are together. Although neither man is homosexual, Baldwin clearly gets a frisson of excitement when he is in Campbell's presence and is pleasing him – either because of a pro-Labour story that he has written or because Campbell is laughing at one of his jokes. When Campbell gives one of his rare on-the-record interviews, it is often to Baldwin, whom he knows will portray him sympathetically and will avoid uncomfortable and challenging questions. More often, however, Campbell has preferred to feed Baldwin information on an off-the-record basis, making it hard for anyone to detect his fingerprints. It has been a long and cosy relationship between two men who know better than almost anybody else how to spin a story.

I do not know exactly which stories about me Campbell gave to Baldwin or helped him with, and in all probability I will never know. The relationship between a journalist and his source is confidential – not dissimilar at times to that between a GP and his or her patient, or between a Catholic priest and the person who is giving confession. Unless the relationship between them breaks down, a journalist and his source will invariably keep to themselves exactly what is said between them. What is certain is that, year after year, the relationship between Campbell and Baldwin has been mutually beneficial. Campbell has had a useful and influential vehicle – the national newspaper Baldwin is working for at any given time – for pro-Labour stories, as well as for negative ones about political opponents. Baldwin, in turn, has had a well-informed source at the heart of New Labour who is willing to give him material that pleases his editor and scoops his rivals on other newspapers. Campbell undoubtedly provided Baldwin with stories about me and others that he thought would be damaging to the Conservative Party – and Baldwin readily ran them because they meant that his name would be prominently displayed in his newspaper and because the articles would cause mischief, something upon which Campbell and Baldwin thrive.

Even those at the heart of the Government have acknowledged that Campbell was happy to exploit the campaign to discredit me. When John Williams, Campbell's friend and former colleague on the *Daily Mirror*, was interviewed as part of an official inquiry into the leaking of government information about me in the summer of 1999, he came up with an interesting statement. A note of the interview with Williams, who at the time of the leak was Deputy Head of News in the press office of the Foreign and Commonwealth Office, conducted on 9 September 1999 reveals: 'He agreed that the press campaign against Ashcroft was helpful to Labour, and Alastair Campbell was trying to use it to most advantage. But he did not believe that AC was masterminding a spin operation. The FCO has been criticised by AC for not being aggressive enough in using its evidence to hand ...' In short, Campbell was unquestionably acquiescent in the campaign against me and he even wanted the FCO to raise its game and follow suit – a clear abuse of the department's role and that of civil servants.

Campbell and Baldwin have become embroiled in numerous scrapes down the years, but none more so than in the bitter battle between the Government and the BBC over whether Campbell had 'sexed up' the Weapons of Mass Destruction (WMD) dossier of September 2002 so that Iraq appeared to be a greater and more immediate danger to Britain than was the case. Initially Baldwin was trying to run with the fox and hunt with the hounds – having meetings and telephone calls with both BBC executives and government officials about what was going on and trying to appear sympathetic to both. Predictably enough, however, *The Times* quickly decided that its loyalties lay with New Labour, and there is ample evidence that Baldwin and Campbell traded information. As the row escalated in the summer of 2003, Campbell became anxious that the identity of the BBC source – the weapons expert Dr David Kelly – should be publicly disclosed and even wrote in his diary on 9 July 'that the biggest thing needed was the source out'. This wish came true the very next day when Dr Kelly was named for the first time as the source used by Andrew Gilligan, the BBC Radio 4's defence correspondent who had broken the WMD story the previous year. Three newspapers, including *The Times*, published Dr Kelly's name on 10 July. *The Times* was ahead of its rivals when it reported: 'No 10 is "99 per cent convinced" that Mr Gilligan's source was David Kelly.' Dr Kelly was found dead on 18 July 2003, having apparently committed suicide. An inquiry conducted by Lord Hutton looked into how and why the tragedy had happened. Although there were plenty of rumours and, it seems, circumstantial evidence that Campbell had given Dr Kelly's name to Baldwin on 9 July – the day of Campbell's diary entry and nine days before Dr Kelly's body was found – both men denied the suggestion under oath. I have no inside evidence into who leaked Dr Kelly's name to *The Times* and I am certainly not suggesting that the two old muckers were guilty of misleading Lord Hutton.

To conclude, the relationship between Alastair Campbell and *The Times* over the past six years – under two successive editors and both during and after he resigned as press secretary in August 2003 – could hardly have been much closer. Not only did Campbell have an incredibly close, indeed symbiotic, relationship with Baldwin, but, after Peter Stothard had decided to support New Labour rather than the Tories, he saw the Rupert Murdoch-owned newspaper as the perfect place for his stories. It was not only political stories about me and others that were leaked to *The Times*, but also details of royal appointments and even of honours lists. By a long-standing convention, such stories are *never* leaked in advance by Buckingham Palace or Downing Street. In May 1999 Buckingham Palace was, however, annoyed when the appointment of Andrew Motion as Poet Laureate was leaked to the newspaper. Writing about this episode in their book on Campbell, Peter Oborne and Simon Walters said: 'Number 10 seemed the only possible culprit. It [Buckingham Palace] could hardly fail to notice, either, the way that honours lists found their way into Labour-supporting newspapers with unfailing regularity.'

After Campbell stepped down as Blair's press secretary, he received his pay-back for all his help over the years, taking up a lucrative appointment as a sports writer for *The Times*. He also continued to feed them titbits of information about politics and other topics that he inevitably picked up. After the May 2005 election – for which he had returned to play a crucial advisory role for Tony Blair – he gave one major interview about his behind-the-scenes work. Sure enough, it was to *The Times*. Talking to the paper's Robert Crampton, Campbell was inclined to be smug about the role that he had played in bringing Tony Blair and Gordon Brown together for the election campaign and, as an aside, could not resist taking a swing at Clare Short. In the interview, which appeared on 14 May under the headline 'Live and explicit, the unexpurgated thoughts of one Alastair Campbell', he stressed that Short had received a 20 per cent swing against her. He told Crampton: 'I resent people like Clare Short who parades herself as though she's the only person in the world who's got principles.' Even New Labour and its master of spin – themselves ardent devotees of hypocrisy – have long tired of Short's brand of windy insincerity.

10 The Aftermath

ON ELECTION night in June 2001, I hosted a champagne reception at Conservative Central Office for party donors, board members and those who had done most to help me during my three years as Treasurer. The event was held in the gloomy boardroom, at Smith Square but someone with flair and imagination had put up flowers and decorations to make it appear more welcoming for the night. Among the guests were Stuart Wheeler, one of the two £5 million donors to the party during the election campaign, and Michael Portillo, who dropped in briefly before departing for a weekend break in Morocco, where he would ponder the question whether he should launch a leadership challenge. Ann Widdecombe, the former junior minister, was also present and in the early hours of the morning found a settee on which to grab a couple of hours' sleep. We had giant television screens up in the boardroom to watch the results coming in and, as the evening progressed, it was apparent that we were not winning our target seats. Indeed, by 1 a.m. it was clear that the Conservative Party did not have a hope in hell of winning the election and that the result was going to be a virtual re-run of 1997 in terms of the numbers of seats the Tories won.

In politics, as in business, I believe that it is vital to learn from mistakes. During the campaign, we had been over-ambitious and spread most of our resources into winning 180 target seats. This decision was taken out of a desperate, if understandable, desire to oust New Labour from office, but it had undoubtedly been foolish. As the results continued to come in after midnight – and I had to put on a forced smile for my many guests – I vowed to myself that in future we would be more pragmatic. It was easy for us to be full of bravado – to say that we were targeting every seat we needed to form a government – but more importantly we had to be realistic. I resolved that we should never again fight an election campaign in which we targeted an impossibly high number of seats from such a weak starting point. At the next election, we would have to be more focused, even if it meant a two-term recovery programme. As I said goodnight to the last of my guests in the early hours, I was becoming ever more convinced that we should concentrate on perhaps fifty – and at the very most eighty – target seats at the next election. We had to be sensible about what was achievable within four or five years – and what was not.

Once William Hague had stood down after the election, the party effectively had to choose between Iain Duncan Smith and Kenneth Clarke as its next leader. It was a strange leadership battle because the party members were not really basing their votes on their fondness for either of the characters or on their judgement about which of the two they considered would make the more able leader. Instead, most Tories were simply supporting one of the men on the basis of a single issue: whether to support or oppose Britain having closer links with the European Union and adopting the euro. Ken was pro-Europe, Iain was anti-, and there was no room for compromise. The majority of the party was against Britain developing greater ties with Europe, and therefore, almost automatically, Iain became leader. I do not think that the party got it wrong. For all of Ken's formidable political talents and his appetite for battle, it would have been a disaster to appoint a pro-European leader at this difficult time.

I was never particularly close to Iain, who became leader late in September 2001. In fact, I do not know many people who managed to become close to him during his tenure as leader. After William's defeat, I stepped into the political shadows because I needed to devote some time to my businesses. I was delighted, however, when I learned that Iain believed, like me, that we should target around sixty winnable seats at the next election, many of them seats that the Liberal Democrats had won over the past two elections. This was an uncomfortable period for the Tories but I admired Theresa May, the party Chairman, for her insight that there was a fundamental problem with the message being given out by the Conservative Party. She appreciated that, as Tories, we came across as too old, too white and too male.

Once Iain was elected leader, the party should have united behind him. Unfortunately, this never happened: in no time, the Conservative Party was up to its old tricks of disloyalty and sniping from the sidelines. Senior Conservative Central Office officials were even leaking confidential, embarrassing and damaging memos that undermined Iain's position. The media, God bless them, enjoy blood sports, and journalists revelled in the prospect of fresh meat being tossed to the pack. For those of us with the party's best interests at heart, it was not an attractive spectacle. It quickly became inevitable that a new leader would have to be appointed before the next general election if the Tories were to have any chance of doing well. Some in the party believed that Iain was to blame for its shambolic state because he was a weak leader, but my view was that, with the Conservatives determined to self-destruct, he never stood a chance. I was ashamed of the way the party conducted itself during those two years: if there was a loyal band of helpers doing their best for Iain, it was too small to make a difference. Although Iain will never go down in history as a great party leader, he did, in fact, launch a serious attempt to redefine Conservative policy and to bring the party into the twenty-first century. He put down foundations upon which his successor was able to build.

MICHAEL HOWARD, who succeeded Iain, is an experienced politician and a strong leader of extraordinary intellect. Following a call from his office, I went to see him two days before the vote-of-confidence ballot that saw Iain's defeat in October 2003. At the time of the meeting, it was fairly obvious that Iain would not survive and that the party increasingly wanted Michael to be its next leader. I walked into his office at the House of Commons and my first words to him were 'Last man standing, Michael.' The principal purpose of the meeting was to discuss party finances because Michael was clearly anticipating that he would be leading the party sooner rather than later. I still believed at that stage, however, that there would be a leadership election and I did not think this was good for the Conservatives because it would take time and create further divisions within the party. I doubt there were many people who, before Iain was defeated, envisaged that Michael would be handed the leadership in a 'coronation'.

I was delighted, however, with the way the party seemed to come to its senses almost overnight. It appreciated that Michael's time had finally come and, in a sudden and unexpected outbreak of party unity, chose him without the need for a bruising and damaging leadership battle. Fortunately, Michael's two most obvious competitors for the leadership chose not to stand, although for different reasons. I think Kenneth Clarke believed that nobody with his views on Europe would be elected party leader, while David Davis, though ambitious for the role and confident of winning among the wider party membership, did not want to inherit a ruin. Nevertheless, Michael's eventual coronation was a pleasant surprise: I did not think, at the time, that the Conservative Party was capable of doing anything to advance its own unity. Rather, over the years, I have become somewhat cynical about its ability to damage itself. Indeed, if someone were asked to design a party structure that was intended to lead to internal friction, turf wars and lack of discipline, I am sure they would be tempted to model it on today's Conservative Party.

I was confident that Michael Howard would be a force for good. He has a sharp mind and a steely determination to succeed. I hoped that he would become a strong, effective and successful leader. I believed, too, that I could work closely with him to the benefit of the party that we have both supported with a passion for decades. Three days after he became leader, I decided I wanted to give a clear indication of my support for him and I decided to donate £2 million to the party. I made it plain, however, that I wanted this money targeted directly at the marginal constituencies, the crucial battleground for the next election. It was during my time as party Treasurer that I noticed how the resources of the party were not always used in the most constructive way. Full-time agents are predominantly in the safe seats, while fewer than a tenth of marginal seats has one – even though it is the marginals which desperately need them. This had to be a mistake in terms of our priorities for the 2005 election. I suspected that there were those who would have preferred me to give the donation to Conservative Central Office so that my money could be distributed as they saw fit. My view, however, was that so long as the constituencies were independent, fundraising units any donor is free to give money as he or she chooses.

Those who know me well were not surprised when they learned that I had specific thoughts on how I wanted my political donation applied. As with my charitable donations, I am rarely willing to leave it to others to decide how my money should be spent. I have earned my money the hard way and I am not prepared to see it squandered – whether it is by a poorly managed charity or by an imprudently run political party that I felt was in danger of spreading my donation too thinly around the country.

THERE WERE some senior Tories, including Maurice (Lord) Saatchi, the Co-Chairman of the party, and Raymond Monbiot, the Deputy Chairman of the party, who were trying to persuade me that my £2 million should go to central coffers. I was even told I could have a place on a new committee which would decide how the money should be spent – an offer that I did not find difficult to decline.

Eventually, I was invited to see Michael Howard at his office in November 2003, and he too asked me to reconsider the way in which my £2 million donation was spent. I told him that I was not prepared to give the money to central coffers: Conservative Central Office had to be fair and objective in its distribution of funds to the marginal constituencies. In contrast, my programme could be subjective and unfair because I did not consider it appropriate to fund constituencies that did not need the money or where the candidate could not put together a business plan on how to win the seat. Michael said it was unacceptable for a donor to give money directly to the constituencies. I said that I did not agree with that assessment but that if he preferred I would withdraw it altogether in order not to rock the boat. Michael, however, who was aware of the party's perilous finances, made it clear that he did not want me to withdraw the donation. In reality, of course, the money was not Michael's to turn down – if it was offered to a constituency, only the constituency could decline it. This was the only meeting I have ever had with Michael Howard which I would describe as tense, although it ended with a pledge from me that I would continue to give him my full support.

The *Sunday Times* learned of my intentions and published a story on 9 November 2003 headlined 'Ashcroft fires up Tory cash drive with £2m gift'. Written by David Leppard, it began: 'The multi-millionaire businessman Lord Ashcroft is to donate £2m to the Tory party to bankroll its general election campaign and trigger its biggest-ever fundraising drive.' It went on to detail how I had met Michael Howard the previous week to tell him that I wanted the money directed at key marginal constituencies and that in a deal agreed on Thursday, 6 November – the day that Michael was officially declared as leader – I had appointed Stephen Gilbert, the party's former campaigns director, to run the fighting fund. I had been approached by the paper and I was quoted in the story as saying, 'We must take the fight to the only place we can win it – the marginal constituencies. Our collective energies and resources should be concentrated there.'

Despite the positive nature of the story, I discovered that Michael Howard and others were still strongly against my proposal: they were clearly worried that my ground-breaking move would create an unwanted precedent and lead to them losing control of funding to the constituencies. In short, some senior Tories wanted my money but did not want me with it. I saw it rather differently: it was my money and I would donate it as I wished. On 7 December 2003 the *Sunday Telegraph* ran a story by Francis Elliott, the paper's deputy political editor, headlined 'Howard rejects Ashcroft's £2m deal "with strings"'. The story began: 'Michael Howard is seeking to prevent Lord (Michael) Ashcroft from giving £2 million to grassroots Conservatives. The Conservative leader is furious that Lord Ashcroft, a former party treasurer, is determined to donate cash to his own preferred candidates fighting marginal seats rather than giving it directly to the party's headquarters.'

I did not believe that Michael himself was behind the article but I wanted to explain my motivation for keeping control of the £2 million. I therefore wrote an article for the *Financial Times* which was published on 10 December 2003. Headlined 'Time for Tory donors to empty their wallet', I spelt out my reason for wanting my donation to be used to fight marginal seats. 'This is the best way I can make a meaningful contribution, for winning large numbers of marginal seats is essential if we are to form the next government,' I wrote. 'Donations, though, are not the only answer. All of us in the party should challenge the culture of "fortress" constituencies – the constituency that is proudly, but misguidedly, independent. Within these constituencies, assets and talents are being wastefully applied to communicating with the faithful rather than winning back marginal seats.' I ended the article with a rallying call praising Michael Howard: 'I for one intend to roll up my sleeves and get down to work. I call on every donor and activist in the party to do the same.'

By Christmas of 2003, I had received about thirty applications for funding from Tory candidates in marginal seats. I did not need to advertise the scheme – eager candidates seeking funding had all heard of what I had to offer. The candidates who contacted my office were asked to provide a basic business plan, but I did not interview any of them. There were no political questions but I did want to know the financial circumstances of the candidate's constituency association. I was not prepared to fund a candidate from an association which was hoarding its money. Indeed, one extremely talented candidate, Nicholas Boles, who was fighting Hove, had a Conservative constituency association with £250,000 in its coffers but he was told he could not have the money for his campaign because it was being kept for a rainy day. Yet the association and its candidate were asking me for £25,000. Needless to say they did not receive a penny, which was terribly unfortunate for Nicholas. I hope, however, that it taught the over-cautious constituency association a harsh lesson, especially when the seat was won by Labour, whose candidate Celia Barlow polled just 420 votes more than Nicholas in the May 2005 general election. There is no doubt in my mind that Nicholas Boles could have been and should now be the Conservative MP for Hove.

There was a rigorous assessment of each candidate's business plan by Stephen Gilbert, my political consultant, who in turn passed on a recommendation to me. The recommendation I received was based – after taking into account the association's balance sheet – largely on the political and demographic make-up of the constituency. I asked for some basic information on the constituency, including the results at the last two general elections, and an indication of how a candidate intended to spend his or her funding up to the general election. I also asked how the candidate planned to spend any extra money that I was prepared to donate. This was not rocket science: I favoured giving money to a candidate who had a realistic chance of winning his or her seat and who I thought would spend his or her funding, including my potential donation, sensibly. Ultimately, I was looking to invest my money in seats where it would make a difference to the result.

As the applications came in, Conservative Central Office set up its own fund for candidates in its target seats, apparently confident that I would switch my resources to it at a later date. I felt rather sorry for those who opted for central funding because the candidates received only about £2,000 each. This was obviously not the fault of those helping to run the campaign, but was an unfortunate consequence of the ill-judged decision to target 180 seats. Those candidates who applied to me typically received between £20,000 and £40,000 – or nothing at all. By New Year 2004, I had approved half of the initial thirty applications. In addition, and as a goodwill gesture, I gave a smaller sum to a handful of quality candidates who had impressed me even though they did not have a realistic chance of winning their seat. I hoped this would encourage them to fight the seat again and win it at the second time of asking. I had noticed from observing the Liberal Democrats that some of their candidates had gradually built up local support over two or three elections before winning the seat.

By early in the New Year, Conservative Central Office realised that I was not going to give in on the issue of funding a maximum of eighty marginal seats. Senior officials therefore asked whether the candidates' applications could be sent to Central Office, who would in turn forward them to my office. At first, I resisted this offer because I thought Central Office would pressurise me to give money to the wrong candidates fighting the wrong seats. Eventually, however, in the interests of the party, I decided that up to twenty candidates could apply to Central Office for funding from me but they would be treated exactly the same as those who had applied directly to my office. I also agreed that, if any candidate was given funding, my office would inform Central Office of the size of the grant so that it could assess the overall picture. This would also prevent a constituency association independently going to Central Office in order to 'double dip' for money. There was still, however, an undercurrent of complaints against me from within the Tory Party.

I enjoyed the Conservative Party conference in October 2004, which was held in Bournemouth. It was a successful, well-managed affair and there seemed to be some fun people around. Indeed, after returning from the conference, I asked Conservative Central Office for another twenty applications from candidates for funding in marginal seats. This meant that by the New Year of 2005, the total number of applications had reached around 130, of which some sixty-five had been approved. By now, too, I had two important and generous allies who shared my desire to target marginal seats. They were Leonard (Lord) Steinberg, the chairman of Stanley Leisure and a long-established party donor who had been Deputy Treasurer while I was Treasurer under William Hague, and the Midlands Industrial Council, a group of Tory businessmen. Both wanted to join me in funding Tory candidates in marginal seats, and we decided that Leonard's donations should be concentrated in the north, where he was based, and that the Midlands Industrial Council's donations should be concentrated in the midlands, where it was based. This meant that I tended to fund candidates in marginal seats in Wales and the south of England, but between us we ensured that the maximum number of credible target seats received the maximum amount of money.

*

SOMETIME BEFORE that party conference, ICM, one of the most reputable polling companies in the country, decided to stop working for the Conservative Party. This was because ICM felt that it had been asked by Central Office to provide meaningless answers as well as loaded questions that did not produce accurate results. The pollsters felt that if they went along with this their professional integrity would be put at risk. ICM also felt that the results of its focus groups were being written up favourably, rather than realistically, by officials at Central Office who then presented them to Michael Howard in a way that did not give a true picture. Instead, the party started using the services of Opinion Research Business (ORB). The results of the latest Central Office polling were presented to the National Convention, the governing body of the voluntary party, at the Conservative Party conference in October 2004. Remarkably, given the findings of other polls before and after the conference, they were said to show that the Conservative Party was going to win at least 103 of its 130 'target seats'.

I thought that for the party to lose the services of ICM was madness: the company had devised the new polling methodology that the major polling firms were now using and had 'called' the result of the last general election to within 1 per cent. ORB, though highly reputable, did not have ICM's recent track record in political polling. A *Financial Times* article of 6 October 2004 written by Ben Hall revealed that the party's account of its research had raised eyebrows because it was out of line with other recent polls. Furthermore, the party had failed to publish the detail of its polling despite the well-established rule of practice that if poll results are announced all the underlying data should be put in the public domain. Nick Sparrow, the respected and experienced director of ICM, commented to the paper: 'If an organisation doing private polling is not prepared to release information to allow people to make up their own minds about the validity of the research, you should treat it with caution.' I certainly concluded that, for whatever reason, the results claimed were unreliable. The party was in danger of deluding itself.

I was curious enough about the results of the ORB poll to

conduct some polls of my own. I decided to use two polling companies: YouGov, which conducts on-line polling for the *Daily Telegraph*, and Populus, the official pollsters for *The Times*. Both polling companies use the most up-to-date methodology. The results from both pollsters revealed that far from being ahead in the target seats we were well behind: even more alarmingly, we were slightly more behind in the target seats than in the national poll. I wrote to Michael Howard on 15 November to give him the findings of the polls. A few days later, I met him at his office in the House of Commons to explain the findings, but he gave me a long list of reasons why he did not necessarily believe the polling results.

I looked into Michael's concerns about polling and wrote him a second letter on 22 November in which I rebutted all the criticism he had made. Not for the first time in my life, a brief flirtation with a subject led to a deep and prolonged interest in it. Almost overnight I became fascinated by polling and by what could and could not be achieved by the process. In no time at all, I was a polling bore. I decided to commission – in absolute secrecy – Britain's biggest ever programme of political polling. This started with an opinion poll of nine seats including those belonging to Michael Howard, David Davis, Oliver Letwin, Theresa May and Tim Collins. These were the so-called decapitation seats identified by the Liberal Democrats as ones which they hoped to win, thereby taking out the High Command of the Conservative Party. The polls showed that Michael was doing extremely well in his own seat after enjoying a boost from winning the party's leadership battle. However, eight other seats, including those belonging to his Shadow Cabinet colleagues, were seriously at risk.

I wrote to Michael Howard again on 14 December warning him that although he was safe his colleagues were in serious danger of losing their seats. Michael said he found the results 'very interesting' but did not appear to be convinced by them. Shortly before Christmas I passed on the poll's basic findings to David Davis, Theresa May, Oliver Letwin and Tim Collins. My polling uncovered many interesting facts, including that voters in the Liberal Democrats' decapitation seats were less inclined to vote against the sitting Conservative MP when they were told of the decapitation motivation. I told David, Theresa, Oliver and Tim that if they wanted to know more they should contact my office. In one way or another, they all received a briefing on my poll and, as a result, David and Theresa then asked me if I would help them with funding – a request to which I happily agreed. Oliver did not ask for funding but he clearly understood the importance of the message relating to the Liberal Democrat strategy because, when he was interviewed by Ann Treneman of *The Times* during the campaign, he asked her to use the word 'decapitation' a lot because he said it would help him get elected.

My fascination with polling continued and in the New Year I commissioned a vast poll by Populus of 10,000 voters across the country (the usual size of a poll is 1,500). The questionnaire was first rate and it looked at a whole range of issues, including tactical voting. Most importantly, however, it examined underlying attitudes to the party and society. It provided a vivid – and alarming – demonstration of how unrepresentative of Great Britain the Conservative Party had become and how far out of touch it was with the man in the street. My objective was to understand what the Conservative Party needed to do in the future to get more in touch with the voter.

I also began a daily American-style 'tracker' poll in which 250 voters were polled every day for four months between mid-January 2005 and the eve of polling on 5 May. I received a short report every morning, a detailed analysis every week and a 'big picture' analysis every month. This revealed the immediate effects of virtually every major policy announcement. For the first two months, the Conservative vote drifted between 31 and 34 per cent. It showed, for example, that people remembered the Conservative Party's policies on asylum seekers and law and order, but that they did not affect its share of the vote. Every time we talked about tax, our rating on the issue went down. I concluded from this that voters do not believe us on the economy and tax because we have let them down once too often in the past: the more we remind voters of this, the less inclined they are to vote for us.

I also commissioned another poll by YouGov in January of

the Conservative Party's target seats. Furthermore, I commissioned twelve individual constituency polls, six in constituencies where I was helping and six in constituencies where I was not. My team also carried out research with focus groups in the same constituencies. This enabled me to probe the effectiveness of my donation campaign and, more importantly, to get a real measure of the effect that the national campaign was having on the ground.

SEVERAL WEEKS after Michael Howard became leader I was approached for a £2 million loan to help finance the move of Conservative Central Office from Smith Square to Victoria Street. I agreed but I made it clear that I expected full and prompt repayment, and that if there was going to be any problem repaying the loan then it should not be taken out. A formal loan agreement was drawn up in July 2004 with a repayment date at the end of June 2005. Late in 2004 Jonathan Marland, the party Treasurer, a man I like and respect, said that as an act of good faith the party wanted to pay back £500,000 of the loan, but he also inquired whether some of the loan might be transferred into a donation or whether there was any chance of extending the loan. I told him that I felt I was already doing enough for the party through my support for candidates in marginal seats. Jonathan, however, stuck with his stated wish to repay the first instalment – a date which slipped first from the end of December to the end of January and eventually into February.

Jonathan came to see me in February and gave me a cheque for £500,000 but at the same time asked whether I might be in a position to give £2 million to the Conservative Party to help it fight the forthcoming general election. By now, most people were convinced that the election would be held in May. I said that I would think about it – even though I was amused that I was clearly being given my loan back early as a 'bribe' to encourage me to make a substantial donation to the election fighting fund. I was, therefore, less than delighted to find myself on the front page of the *Sunday Times* on 13 February 2005. A prominent story headlined 'Howard returns £500,000 to Tory billionaire' began:

'Michael Howard has handed back £500,000 to Lord Ashcroft, the Tories' biggest donor, after the peer claimed the party was heading for defeat in the forthcoming election. Ashcroft, who has made donations of at least £10 million to the Conservatives, last month pledged the six-figure sum to fight the election. However, 10 days ago the Tories repaid a similar sum to the peer, even though the party needs a further £5 million for its fighting fund, according to sources.'

The article, written by Robert Winnett and David Leppard, went on to say: 'Howard's decision to pay back the money at such a crucial time seems set to end Ashcroft's relationship with the Tories.'

I was furious about the article on a number of fronts. I was angry that someone within the Tory Party was briefing against me and trying to make a story out of nothing. Only a handful of people in the party knew that part of the loan had been repaid. I had hoped and believed that, after my time as Treasurer, I would never again be the victim of a smear campaign from within the Tory Party. However, I was wrong – and once again the claims against me were full of inaccuracies. The spin put on the story was preposterous – a decision by the party to pay back part of my loan early was portrayed as an attempt by the leader to distance himself from me. I believe I know the source of the leak but, since this is a book which criticises others for making unsubstantiated allegations, I will keep my suspicions to myself.

Shortly after the article appeared, I had a meeting with Michael Howard, who I am certain had nothing to do with the leak. I told him that because of the breach of confidence and the absurd spin on the story I was in no mood to help the party financially any further. In fact, I did later relent after the election date was announced. I rang Jonathan Marland and told him that I would lend the party a further £1 million and defer the June repayment of £1.5 million by seven months. This means that on or before 31 January 2006 the Conservative Party is due to repay me loans totalling £2.5 million.

*

BY EARLY January 2005, Stephen Gilbert, my political consultant, with a view to determining whom to support in the marginal seats, had seen 150 business plans. On his advice, I had selected forty-one core Labour–Conservative battleground seats where we – Leonard Steinberg, the Midlands Industrial Council and myself – gave the bulk of our funding. As I have indicated, these Tory candidates received between £20,000 and £40,000 each. We also selected nine Liberal Democrat–Conservative battleground seats (which were always going to be more difficult to win), six 'consolidation' seats where a sitting Conservative MP was under serious threat and a further twenty-five seats where the Conservative candidate had particular merit or where we hoped to win the seat over two general elections. Tory candidates in the Liberal Democrat–Conservative battleground seats received between £20,000 and £25,000 each, candidates in the 'consolidation' seats received between £10,000 and £35,000 each and the twenty-five 'hopefuls' received between £2,000 and £5,000 each.

By the time election day arrived, I thought that, overall, we fought a strong and disciplined campaign and that Lynton Crosby, our Australian campaign manager, as well as Michael Howard, deserved credit for the roles they played. However, as a party we also made mistakes. We were never able to convince enough voters that we knew how to manage the economy and we hammered away too heavily on immigration so that some voters concluded we had an unappealing, even racist, edge. Furthermore, the party's approach to targeting seats was misguided.

I spent election night at the new Conservative Central Office in Victoria Street at a convivial party for donors and other guests hosted by Jonathan Marland, the Treasurer. It was good to see some old friends, including Cecil (Lord) Parkinson. There were some memorable moments, notably early in the evening when Justine Greening, one of the candidates that I had supported financially, took Putney from Labour with a swing of more than 6 per cent. For much of the night, I had one eye open for the results in Labour MP Peter Bradley's constituency, The Wrekin. I had been intrigued to learn that Bradley, *The Times*'s great ally in its battle against me, had been behaving with mounting eccentricity in the days before he defended his seat. It seems that as election day approached he had developed reservations about an earlier article he had penned for the *Sunday Telegraph* on the subject of hunting. He had begun his article, published on 21 November 2004: 'Now that hunting has been banned, we ought at last to own up to it: the struggle over the Bill was not only about animal welfare and personal freedom, it was class war. But it was not class war as we know it. It was not launched by the tribunes against the toffs – it was the other way round.' Yet Bradley seemed to be ruing the fact that some of his comments might have alienated voters, including potential Labour voters, in his constituency – which has a large rural element. When the *Sunday Telegraph* and other papers tried to join him on the campaign trail, Bradley went to enormous lengths to try to throw reporters off the scent. Indeed, he was reduced to scuttling around his own constituency like a cornered fox being pursued by a pack of baying hounds. Apparently he repeatedly changed his itinerary at the last moment because he was worried about being 'stitched up' by the media. Another article that Bradley had written – this time on land reforms for the *Country Landowner* magazine – led to him being described as the 'Mugabe of the Midlands' by Dennis Allen, a local Conservative councillor. Unfortunately, Bradley did not relish comparisons with the dictatorial leader of Zimbabwe, nor, I suspect, did he enjoy the comments of Bill Tomlinson, the Liberal Democrat candidate, who summed him up perfectly when he told voters that it was possible to be both anti-hunting and anti-Bradley. 'Peter Bradley is clever – he comes over as friendly, understanding and warm,' he said. 'The more you get to know him, though, the less you like him.'

Bradley's seat was clearly winnable for the Conservatives – one that should be targeted. I was delighted that Leonard Steinberg and the Midlands Industrial Council, my partners in the project of giving money directly to target seats, agreed. Indeed, between them Leonard and the council gave donations totalling more than £50,000 to Mark Pritchard, the Conservative candidate. This proved to be money well spent. When the result came in at 3.40 a.m. on Friday morning, Mark had won, courtesy of a swing to the Tories of more than 5 per cent. I was still at the party at Central Office when the result was flashed up on the giant television screen. In a triumph for democracy and common sense, the voters of The Wrekin were free from their menace of an MP and the House of Commons was free from a member who had abused his privileged position. I could not have been happier with the result – especially as money from the marginal-seats campaign contributed by my two partners had played a significant role in it.

I left the party at 5 a.m. and reflected on a night of mixed fortunes. As I fleetingly looked back on the previous general election, I felt a mixture of pleasure and disappointment. I was glad that, by learning from the mistakes of 2001, I had played my part in helping to get more Tory candidates elected as MPs than four years earlier: we eventually won 197 seats in 2005, thirty-three more than the 164 seats we had won in 2001. As the results came in, however, I was disappointed that we did not make a bigger inroad into Labour's formidable majority. The Conservative Party had been given an opportunity to demonstrate that it was modern, relevant and in touch, but we had not seized the moment to change the public's perception of our 'brand' for the better.

On Friday, 6 May 2005, the day after the election, I was in my office in Westminster as Stephen Gilbert worked out how the candidates that we had supported financially compared with those who had not received our support. It soon became clear that we had been wasting neither our time nor our resources. Of the thirty-three candidates who won seats from Labour or the Liberal Democrats, no fewer than twenty-five had received support from the fund that I had set up with Leonard Steinberg and the Midlands Industrial Council. Of our forty-one seats, we had won twenty-four from Labour, and we had held five of the six 'consolidation' seats (those who significantly increased their majorities included David Davis and Theresa May, who had both received funding). In the seats where we were aiming to win in two elections, we also made important gains. We fared less well in the Liberal Democrat–Conservative battleground seats which we had always known were going to be harder to crack. We gained just one of our targeted nine seats, but we made real progress in other seats which I am hopeful will be winnable at the next election in 2009 or 2010. However, some of the sitting Liberal Democrat MPs who had won their seats in the 2001 election were actually able to build on their majorities because they had been good constituency MPs.

The Conservative Party did well in Wales, where we had won all our three target seats, and in each case I had supported the candidates financially. We did poorly, however, in the key battleground areas of Kent, Yorkshire and Hampshire, where the party's resources were clearly overstretched and where Central Office squandered money in a direct-mailing strategy which was never going to achieve its aim. I was particularly irritated by the party's ludicrous targeting strategy which meant that we failed to win Romsey in Hampshire by just 125 votes and made hardly any progress in neighbouring Winchester, which I had never thought was winnable. If we had poured all our resources from Winchester, which I did not back financially, into Romsey, which I did back financially, the party would undoubtedly have won the latter seat. The Liberal Democrats taught us a lesson in this respect when, after realising they were not going to oust Oliver Letwin in Dorset West, they diverted resources from their stronghold of Yeovil to Taunton where they took out Adrian Flook, our excellent Conservative MP, who was toppled by fewer than 600 votes.

It was, however, the detailed analysis of the various swings that told us just how important and rewarding our work had been. The national swing from Labour to Conservative was 3.2 per cent, yet the swing in the seats which we supported was 3.8 per cent. Our judgement had proved to be correct on other issues too. We had rejected applications from some Tory candidates on the ground that we thought they could win without us, and in several cases the candidates duly won. There was only one seat where we turned down an application for money because we did not think it could be won, only for it to be won anyway. In short, we spotted the likely winners and losers, and allocated our limited money wisely as a result.

I am glad to say that my polling was also a success. My tracker poll on the eve of election day had shown that Labour would get 36 per cent of the vote (precisely what they got), the Tories would get 32 per cent (1 per cent less than we got) and the Liberal Democrats 23 per cent (exactly what they got). By then Stephen Gilbert was so convinced of the accuracy of the polling that he won a bet with two friends for a fine lunch by correctly predicting we would win 198 seats (we won 197 on the night, followed a few weeks later by victory in a by-election, or rather re-run, in South Staffordshire). In the days running up to the election, it had been absolutely clear to me and to my political team that only fifty seats were in play on 5 May 2005. I am convinced that if the party had concentrated its resources late in the campaign on those seats we would have won up to ten more seats.

My polling also revealed, however, the failure of the party to get its message across to voters on the main issues. The tracker poll showed that we were only ever ahead of Labour at all times on one issue – immigration and asylum – and by polling day our lead even on this subject had dropped. For part of the time, we were ahead on the issue of law and order, but not by much and never consistently. However, for the key issues including education, the National Health Service, the economy and tax, we trailed Labour at all times and never made any significant inroads. From day one of the tracker poll until the eve of the election, more than 50 per cent of voters wanted Tony Blair as Prime Minister and no more than 35 per cent ever wanted Michael Howard to replace him. How could the Conservative Party hope to win an election when we were consistently trailing Labour on all the major issues of the day and when one of the most unpopular Prime Ministers of modern times was consistently preferred to our leader? In some ways, the Conservative Party went backwards during the 2005 election campaign. My polling showed that at the end of the campaign fewer voters than at the start of it agreed with the propositions that the Conservative Party 'shared their values', 'had plans to deal with the important problems', 'would do a good job in government' and 'stood for actions not words'.

This is not intended as a criticism of Michael Howard's leadership, but it is a criticism of the party's inability since 1997 to change with the times and to get across its message. I have remained a supporter of Michael and I have always encouraged any potential donors to support him financially. I think he will go down in the history books as a firm and principled leader. He was, at times, even too much of a disciplinarian and I felt his treatment of Howard Flight, a Deputy Chairman, in the run-up to the election was too drastic. It was one thing to sack him as a Deputy Chairman following his unfortunate comments about 'secret' Tory spending plans, but quite another to deselect him as our candidate for Arundel and South Downs at a time when Michael already had a reputation as a 'serial sacker'. The decision to deselect Howard Flight divided the party and caused a great deal of unease. Although I respected his decision not to stand as an independent candidate, there was also a mischievous part of me that would have liked him to do so because I felt his treatment had been unnecessarily harsh.

On Monday, 9 May, four days after election day, I was invited by Michael Howard to see him in his office. Michael had announced his decision to stand down as leader on the previous Friday, but I found him in good spirits. He thanked me for my support before and during the campaign and we discussed whether I would have an active role in the party once again. I told him that I wanted to play a part in the future of the party and we discussed the possibility of me rejoining the board for the first time in four years. Over the next few days, the details relating to my return to the board were finalised and it was formally announced in a press release on 17 May 2005. 'In view of his outstanding contribution to the party's progress in winning target seats Lord Ashcroft has been asked to join the board and he has accepted.' I was pleased to be back on the board, although I could not help reflecting on the irony of the tribute, bearing in mind that eighteen months earlier the party had been reluctant to accept my £2 million donation unless it went directly to Central Office.

On 30 June 2005, I published my own critical analysis of the Conservative Party's performance in the lead-up to the May election. This was based largely on the results of my extensive polling, including the biggest national political poll ever conducted in Britain. The 114-page study, *Smell the coffee: a wake-up call for the Conservative Party*, was well received by the party and the media alike, who I think recognised it as constructive criticism. Indeed, I praised Michael Howard for having fought 'a determined campaign and [having] restored discipline to the party'. I warned, however, that the Tories could not only lose a fourth successive general election but could come under increasing pressure from the Liberal Democrats if changes were not made and lessons were not learned. I noted that the Tories were perceived as less likely to care about 'ordinary people's problems' and I recognised that there were elements of the campaign that had gone badly wrong. 'We must realise that appealing to the conservative or even reactionary instincts of people who, in reality, are never going to support the Conservatives in large numbers, prevents us from connecting with our real core vote, and means that we will never attract the support of minority communities that we should seek to serve.'

The Conservative Party still faces enormous challenges at the 2009 or 2010 general election. Even now, it will still take one of the largest swings of modern political times to see us returned to power. That we did not get above the lowest number of Labour seats of recent times – Michael Foot's haul of just 209 in the 1983 election – in May 2005 was especially disappointing. The increased number of non-Conservative, non-Labour seats makes it more difficult to get a majority next time. I fear that, unless we learn the lessons of recent years then the best we can hope for at the next election is a hung Parliament and, if the Labour and Liberal Democrat parties form a pact, we could still find ourselves out of power for a further term. To win a general election with a bare overall majority, we probably need to win 42 per cent of the vote even after the marginally advantageous boundary changes that will soon come into effect. So we need to increase our vote share by around 9 per cent – about five times the increase we have achieved over the last two general elections.

As always, we must learn from our mistakes and failings. Over the coming months and years, the Tory Party has to restructure itself internally and it has to address such issues as the illogical autonomy of constituencies, improved selection of candidates, more effective use of its limited finances, better plans for the battle-field and, perhaps most important of all, how we can appeal to a broader church. My work on political polling and in the marginal constituencies has taught me lessons which must be acted upon. Polling is now so accurate that we have to use it professionally and – above all – honestly as a tool for better decision making rather than as a propaganda device. Furthermore, and however harsh it seems on Tory candidates in no-hope seats, we must concentrate our resources on areas where we can make a difference: we need one tactically astute person whose word is law on targeting seats for the next four or five years.

I have now given well in excess of £10 million to the Conservative Party. I will never know whether I am the largest political donor to the party of all time because, until recently, the size of political donations was never made public. What I do know is that I do not regret a single penny. Neither do I regret a minute of the immeasurable number of hours that I have given to the party's cause. I know, too, that I will always be a Tory and that I will always try to promote the party to which I have been loyal for forty years.

Epilogue

THERE WAS nearly no future for me to ponder. A mechanical fault on my plane in February 2004 almost achieved what the *The Times* and the Labour Party had tried to do but failed: to 'Get Ashcroft'. I had a scare in my Falcon 900EX jet when I was flying from Tanzania to Britain to attend the funeral of Peter Fox, the businessman friend whom I had known since my days with Pritchard Group Services more than thirty years before. When we were on the final approach to Stansted airport in Essex, the two pilots tried to put the undercarriage down. Three red alarm lights came on to indicate that the three wheels were not locked into position.

The pilots took the aircraft up higher and went through all the recommended procedures, including shaking the plane around in the air in an attempt to loosen the undercarriage. The three lights, however, remained on. So we ditched our excess fuel in mid-air to make the aircraft less likely to combust during a crash landing. We notified Stansted of our difficulties and the entire airport was closed down. As we approached, the emergency services were waiting for us on the edge of the runway. All those in the plane adopted the recommended crash position as we came in to land, expecting to hear a crunch on the runway as we did a belly-landing when the fuselage made contact with the tarmac.

There was a sigh of relief as we felt one wheel touch the runway. There was second sigh of relief as we felt the nose come down and we felt a second wheel touching too. However, as the right wing came down it hit the ground in a mass of sparks and we knew immediately that the right wheel was not down. It was impossible in the circumstances for the pilots to hold the aircraft in a straight line. The plane veered sharply off the runway to the right, bumped across the grass and, eventually, came to a halt. A

fire engine arrived and the fire fighters doused the aircraft in foam
to prevent it bursting into flames. An ambulance, too, arrived on
the scene and we were all given a check-up: I was told that my
pulse was beating at below its normal rate. As we stepped out of
the aircraft unscathed, I felt I had used up yet another of my nine
lives. Just a few hours later, I was at Peter's funeral with somewhat
confusing thoughts about life and death.

Incidentally, while on the subject of life and death, I have
prepared my will. I have never been a great believer in inherited
wealth. More than 80 per cent of my assets – and I never discuss
how much I am worth – will be left to a charitable foundation
in my name. My family will be trustees so that they can enjoy
spending money on worthy causes in my name. The balance of
my assets will be left to my family.

THE INFORMATION that I have gathered since I became a
peer five years ago has not come easily nor cheaply. I was determined to discover, however, how and why I was targeted and by
whom. I am fortunate that I have the means to carry out such
inquiries and acknowledge that such an opportunity might not be
available to others.

Over the past couple of years I have made efforts to rebuild
some bridges with both senior employees of *The Times* and the
Government, particularly those who are prepared to acknowledge
the error of their ways. I have already detailed how I have been
willing to improve relations with Michael Gove, the leader and
comment writer on *The Times*, and how I wish him well as the
Conservative MP for Surrey Heath. Early in 2004, I found myself
in Ankara and I asked Sir Peter Westmacott, who was by then the
British Ambassador to Turkey, if he would like breakfast. It was
Peter who had written one of the disobliging references about me
saying I was 'in love' with the late Diana, Princess of Wales and
that I looked 'a bit dodgy'. At the end of an enjoyable breakfast at
the British Embassy, I handed Peter one of my business cards and
told him that he would find something 'interesting' on the back:
it was a copy of his handwritten note with the famous disobliging

reference to me. I had reduced it in size on a photocopier and stapled it to the back of my card. I also gave him a copy of one of the Foreign and Commonwealth Office internal assessments of him, which I had obtained as a result of my actions against the Government. Fortunately, for Peter's sake, it was rather complimentary about his skills as a diplomat. We both enjoyed the humour of the occasion.

I have also settled my difference with Charles Drace-Francis, the former British diplomat who leaked his memo about me in 1996. He had already been punished by the Government and, after eighteen months of 'gardening leave' following the results of the Whitehall leak inquiry, he finally resigned his post in August 1991. He then swapped his £80,000-a-year job for an estimated £200-a-week job as a sales assistant in a Scottish kilt shop. His change of role attracted press attention, and a feature about him in the *Daily Record* of 31 January 2002 was headlined 'Our man in the Sporran Office: Incredible downfall of the £80k diplomat to humble assistant in Edinburgh kilt shop'. Yet, at the end of 2001, after a difficult and troubled year for him, Charles had even sent me a Christmas card offering his best wishes and adding: 'Good luck for 2002!'

On 9 September 2003, Charles wrote to me at length and apologised 'to you and especially your family for the embarrassment caused'. In a sincere and friendly letter, he described how he had obtained a 'satisfactory new position selling kilts and bagpipes'. He even cheekily said: 'I enclose a catalogue in case any of your American friends would like to place an order.' He signed off: 'Yours sincerely – and I hope you will be pleased to hear I am still contributing to Crimestoppers. Charles D. Francis'. I considered his generous letter had ended our short feud. How could I not forgive someone who was so apologetic despite losing his job over his error and who was still donating money to my main charity?

It has given me no pleasure to continue taking legal action. Such a process is time-consuming and expensive, not least because it diverts my attention away from my primary role as a businessman. However, since senior figures at *The Times* and within the

Labour Government chose to start the game, they will have to play on until I blow the final whistle.

I have, however, made my peace with most of the leading figures at News International and *The Times*. My limited dealings with Rupert Murdoch, the owner of News International, and Les Hinton, the company's executive chairman, have always been totally professional and entirely satisfactory. I have had lunch with Robert Thomson, the current editor of *The Times*. I like him and have no grievance against him. I have a good working relationship, too, with John Witherow, the intelligent and able editor of the *Sunday Times*. To be fair, *The Times* under Robert Thomson has also made an effort to rebuild bridges: in May 2002 it published an article of mine on party funding. In the article, I said that I favoured neither state funding of political parties nor a situation where parties relied on the generosity of a handful of substantial donors (like myself). I expressed the hope that in an ideal world the £15 million or so that it takes each year to run a national party effectively would come from 500,000 members each paying an annual subscription of £30. I wrote: 'And, however far removed we may be from that position at the moment, I believe it to be achievable.'

I am not yet ready, however, to make my peace with others. The likes of Sir Peter Stothard, the former editor of *The Times*, Tom Baldwin, the paper's senior political journalist, Alastair Brett, the paper's legal manager, and Toby Follett, their freelance contributor, have not heard the last of me. Jonathan Randel, their Drug Enforcement Administration mole, has now served his one-year jail sentence and is on probation. As a government employee in a responsible position, he was deservedly imprisoned for his actions. Yet why should he go to jail while those who also involved themselves in his illegal activities remain unpunished? And why should Gavin Singfield and the other members of the paper's grubby little team of private investigators remain free to carry out further illegal activities on unsuspecting and law-abiding individuals like myself? Follett, who encouraged Randel to break the law, through payments and other inducements, should be charged and, if found guilty, should be punished more severely than Randel, who simply did the dirty work he was asked to do. The conduct of those at *The Times* who were happy to reward Randel for his criminality, and to use the fruits of the poisoned tree, should also be investigated thoroughly, and censured. My enemies at *The Times* would have had no pity on me if they had discovered that I had done anything of this kind. I, in turn, am now returning the favour they did me by scrutinising their behaviour equally closely. I, likewise, will have no pity on them if it is proved that they broke the law.

I have obtained some enjoyment from observing just how rattled some of those at *The Times* have become by the prospect of seeing their actions subjected to further scrutiny. If they had played it by the book, of course, they would have no need for concern about the prospect of further legal action. Alastair Brett, in particular, appears to have been worried by the prospect of the behaviour of *The Times* and its staff coming under closer examination by the US authorities in the prosecution that was brought against Jonathan Randel. When US investigators wrote wanting to interview Peter Stothard and other senior executives, Brett told the *Daily Telegraph* that they were 'bemused' by the request. I rather doubt it. Meeting resistance, the investigators went on to seek information from *The Times* through legal routes, using the Criminal Justice (International Co-operation) Act of 1990 – a move which surely must have bothered Brett a good deal. It did result in the disclosure of details of payments made to Randel.

I know *The Times* has access to the best possible outside legal advice. This is fortunate for them – because they may need it. For future reference, if *The Times* is thinking of obtaining or using confidential computer files I would helpfully suggest that Brett might think about obtaining counsel's opinion on the Data Protection Act of 1998 in which section 55 is couched in wide terms, and offences extend to procuring the unauthorised disclosure of computer information.

I am currently considering various legal options. I was glad to see, however, that the activities of some private investigators have already come to the notice of Scotland Yard. Since early 2004, police officers have begun making arrests, laying charges and obtaining convictions as part of inquiries into the leaking of confidential information to the press via private-detective agencies. The action has been taken as part of Operation Glade, a wider investigation into links between the police and the press.

I am also taking legal action in America, where I have instructed lawyers to pursue the wretched Jonathan Randel through the courts in Atlanta, Georgia. In March 2004, while he was seeing out his jail sentence in a federal prison in Atlanta, he was served with a writ that I had brought against him for a $1 million-plus compensation claim. I have made two claims against him under American law. The first is under the Computer Fraud and Abuse Act which provides that any person who suffers damage or loss by reason of computer fraud is entitled to bring a civil action against the violator for compensation. Randel, after all, intentionally accessed a confidential computer database searching for restricted information on me and gave it to Toby Follett and *The Times* knowing that such information could, and would, be used to try to do me down.

My second claim is based on Randel's violation of my rights under the Fourth Amendment of the American Constitution. A case in the US in 1971 has established the right of an individual to bring a civil suit against a federal official for the violation of an individual's constitutional rights. There is no doubt that Randel, in his role as an intelligence research specialist for the DEA, exceeded his authorisation and, in doing so, abused my rights. In the case of *Ashcroft* v *Randel* I am seeking 'general and special damages ... in an amount to be determined at trial but not less than $1 million'.

In the summer of 2004, my lawyers in America made a special application to the US District Court, which will rule on my civil action for compensation. My legal team sought to obtain the sworn testimony of four people who were working for *The Times* at the time that Randel was illegally providing the newspaper with confidential DEA reports about me. The key individuals are Toby Follett, the freelance researcher who had been the original source and who brought the DEA material to the newspaper, and Alastair Brett, the legal manager for Times Newspapers.

I am delighted to say that on 27 July 2004 the court granted this request. Furthermore, it allowed the four representatives of *The Times* to give their sworn testimony under the 'special procedure' that we had requested: that each witness must give his or her testimony under oath or affirmation; that the testimony of the witnesses should be video- and audio-recorded, and then transcribed; and that my US lawyer (and if required Randel's representative) should be allowed to attend the examination of the witnesses and participate in obtaining the testimony.

I suspect that Brett was especially unhappy to learn that he was to be questioned under oath about his role. Indeed, on 4 August 2004, before he was aware of the court ruling relating to him, he wrote a long, rambling letter to the US District Court asking the judge to halt my legal action against Randel. 'I understand the Court has discretion to bring this matter to a quick and just end and I urge the Court to so exercise it. Mr Randel has already been punished to the full extent of the law. Neither he nor this American court should now be used as pawns in what appears to be a continuing vendetta against others well outside the jurisdiction.' It is just unfortunate for Brett that he is learning that the long arm of American law can stretch to the other side of the Atlantic.

Since then, *The Times* has tried to postpone – and ultimately defeat – my attempts to have Randel and his partners in crime questioned under oath. In turn, my lawyers in America have filed a detailed response to the delaying tactics of *The Times* and Randel. On 22 November 2004, my lawyers submitted what, in legal jargon, is called the 'Plaintiff's opposition to Defendant Randel's motion to dismiss'. It gives my answer to Brett's fulminations about a 'vendetta', explaining why my action should be allowed to go ahead: '[The] Plaintiff believes that Randel – aided by *The Times* and others – has consistently and methodically attempted to conceal the full extent and nature of his wrongdoing. Specifically, there is a strong reason to believe that Randel was not truthful to this court in his June 2002 guilty plea, in particular, that he was not candid about the full extent of his unauthorised access of NADDIS files, or about his motivation for doing so. Since his plea, Randel has engaged in a pattern of behaviour designed to continue to prevent [the] Plaintiff from finding out the truth regarding his improper actions.' Provided justice prevails and my lawyers are able to cross-examine them, I can guarantee that Follett and Brett will face some searching questions about their roles.

I am also pondering what to do next in my dealings with the Government after a deeply unsatisfactory exchange of letters with Sir Andrew Turnbull, the Cabinet Secretary. In a letter written in January 2004, I raised my continuing concerns over three leaks to the media: the two occasions when my peerage was turned down and the circumstances of William Hague's intervention when he was forced to telephone Tony Blair during an EU conference in order to get him to grant my peerage. I told Sir Andrew that I had been the victim of 'serial leaking' – which had caused me great harm – and that his predecessor, Sir Richard Wilson, had promised to hold inquiries into the leaks. When he failed to address these issues to my satisfaction, I wrote again on 8 June 2004. My letter ended:

> So far, you have admitted the following:
> Admission One. That, despite assurances given to me and to others at the time, no less than three of the four leak enquiries which were promised never took place, much less discovered anything.
> Admission Two. That personal, private and confidential correspondence between the Prime Minister and the Leader of Her Majesty's Opposition is unsafe from the moment of its creation by virtue of the everyday practice of wholesale circulation.
> Admission Three. That information about my consideration for a working peerage was deliberately withheld from me following my Data Access request, in wrongful reliance upon an exemption which you say applied to the conferral of a working peerage, but which in fact did not.
> I think you will agree this is a most unsatisfactory state of affairs. I am considering bringing these matters to the attention of the Commons Public Administration Committee.

After receiving a further decidedly unhelpful reply from Sir Andrew, I am still considering, together with my legal team, what to do next. I am examining a variety of options, but one thing is certain: I do not intend to let the matter rest. Another issue that I am looking into is why I was never given access to information about the reasons for the turning down of my first peerage nomination. The Government's lawyers continue to argue that there is an exemption under the Data Protection Act which applies to honours. My lawyers have, in turn, questioned whether a working peerage qualifies as an honour. It seems madness that the process of nominating, and then considering, someone for membership of the legislature should be shrouded in secrecy.

AS PART of a prolonged battle to defend my reputation, I have seen the man who tried to damage me jailed, I have seen a diplomat who leaked material against me disciplined, I have seen off Clare Short and her Labour Party cronies in Belize and I have successfully sued the Government over its disreputable behaviour in Britain. Now, through this book, I have exposed the sinister tactics of my enemies, particularly those on *The Times*. In short, as the truth has been revealed about those who sought to discredit me, they have instead been discredited themselves.

This has been an instructive exercise for me. It has raised important questions about the willingness of some people in Government and the media to exploit and abuse the privileged positions that they hold. The business world can, at times, be fairly ruthless. I have twice found bugging devices – presumably placed there by a business rival – in the offices of my companies. Nothing in my business life, however, prepared me for the behaviour of sections of Her Majesty's press. Until my dealings with *The Times*, I had no idea that some newspapers were prepared to resort routinely to breaking the law to obtain confidential information. Incredible as this may seem to the public, this is often done as a matter of course.

What of my future? I cannot imagine my life devoid of work, politics, travel or Belize. My staff know that there are certain words which I will not tolerate as an excuse for failure or an error. One of them is 'assume': I have lost too much money over the years by people wrongly assuming things. Similarly, I hate being told that something is not 'reasonable' because I find it such a subjective term. It annoys me, too, when someone says it is not 'normal' to do something in such a way or that something is a 'normal' term and condition. I am not interested in what is normal: if it can be done in a better, more efficient way then I want to do it that way. The expression I dislike above all others is 'can't'. My view is that there is no mountain too high to climb and no ocean that is too wide to cross. If there is the will, the determination and the clear thinking, just about anything in life *can* be achieved. Even now, at the age of fifty-nine and just six years away from drawing my pension, I do not consider retirement. There are still more companies to launch, more jobs to create and more money to make.

Similarly, politics has been a significant part of my life for so long that I cannot imagine wanting to turn my back on it. I intend, on my own terms, to continue supporting the Conservative Party financially. I am delighted to be back on the board of the Conservative Party and who knows, politically, what the future may hold? If any party leader wants me to play a more specific role, then I would naturally consider such a request. I think any leader could feel confident that any newspaper or political opponent would think twice before targeting me unfairly a second time.

Travel, too, has been a passion of mine for many years. I am curious to see new and exciting places, even if the countries that I go to are not always the safest places in the world. I have visited well over a hundred countries. In recent years, those countries have include post-war Afghanistan (twice including time in the capital city, Kabul); Herat (where I met the warlord Ismail Khan); post-war Iraq (I was in Baghdad the day after Saddam Hussein's two sons were killed in a gun battle); Zimbabwe (where I met Morgan Tsvangirai, the Opposition leader); behind rebel lines in southern Sudan (where I met with senior field commanders); and Sri Lanka (where I met and was photographed with leaders of the Tamil Tigers – I later found the photograph of us together on their website). I am always careful – on rare occasions employing private security guards – but if you are too cautious in life you end up not doing anything interesting. I want to continue to search for places that rival in beauty what I regard as the five most spectacular and wonderful places on earth: Alaska, New Zealand's South Island, the Rift Valley in Africa, the glaciers of Chile and the Kimberleys in north-west Australia. Indeed, if I had lived 500 years ago, I feel certain I would have been the perfect explorer.

I have learned to love Belize and its people for the second time in my life, and from now on the country will always be a part of my life. Since receiving my peerage, I am often affectionately known by locals in Belize as 'the Lord'. It is a bit disquieting to be walking down the street and hear a friend or acquaintance boom at the top of their voice: 'Here cometh the Lord.' My will states that I want to be cremated when I die and I want my ashes scattered in the sea from the end of the pier at the Radisson Fort George Hotel, close to my home in Belize. And what will be my epitaph? I hope it is nothing more and nothing less than: he was one of life's characters.

I trust that it will be many years before my ashes float away in the sea and others debate my epitaph. I hope to continue my existence on the edge of change for a long time to come. Today I remain as energetic, committed and inquisitive as ever. There are still objectives that I want to achieve, places that I wish to visit and people that I am eager to meet. I retain a desire for knowledge, fresh challenges and new experiences that I suspect will never be sated. I do not know where my life will take me next. However, if my past is any guide to my future, it would be surprising if the journey that lies ahead proved to be conventional, uncontroversial or, God forbid, dull.

Illustrations

The illustrations contained in this book are credited to:

Alpha
Dan Chung
Daily Mail
Alan Davidson
Financial Times
Tim Graham
Guardian
Mamta Kapool
John McLellan
Mail on Sunday
Press Association
Reuters
Solo
Keith Waldegrave
Les Wilson

Index